RESEARCH METHODS

*Palgrave Business Briefing*

*The Business Briefings series* consists of short and authoritative introductory text-books in core business topics. Written by leading academics, they take a no-nonsense, practical approach and provide students with a clear and succinct overview of the subject.

These textbooks put the needs of students first, presenting the topics in a meaning-ful way that will help students to gain an understanding of the subject area. Covering the basics and providing springboards to further study, these books are ideal as acces-sible introductions or as revision guides.

*Other books in the Business Briefings series:*

Quantitative Methods, by Les Oakshott

Marketing, by Jonathan Groucutt

Organisational Behaviour, by Mike Maughan

Human Resource Management, by Michael Nieto

Financial Accounting, by Jill Collis

Management Accounting, by Jill Collis

**The Business Briefings Series**
Series Standing Order ISBN 978-0-230-36385-4

You can receive future titles in this series as they are published by placing a standing order. Please contact your bookseller or, in the case of difficulty, write to us at the address below with your name and address, the title of the series and the ISBN quoted above.

Customer Services Department, Macmillan Distribution Ltd, Houndmills, Basingstoke, Hampshire, RG21 6XS, UK

# RESEARCH METHODS

## PETER STOKES
*UNIVERSITY OF CHESTER BUSINESS SCHOOL*

## TONY WALL
*UNIVERSITY OF CHESTER BUSINESS SCHOOL*

 macmillan education    palgrave

First published 2014 by
PALGRAVE

Palgrave in the UK is an imprint of Macmillan Publishers Limited,
registered in England, company number 785998, of 4 Crinan Street,
London N1 9XW

Palgrave Macmillan in the US is a division of St Martin's Press LLC,
175 Fifth Avenue, New York, NY 10010.

Palgrave is a global imprint of the above companies and is represented
throughout the world.

Palgrave® and Macmillan® are registered trademarks in the United States,
the United Kingdom, Europe and other countries.

ISBN 978–0–230–36203–1

This book is printed on paper suitable for recycling and made from fully
managed and sustained forest sources. Logging, pulping and manufacturing
processes are expected to conform to the environmental regulations of the
country of origin.

A catalogue record for this book is available from the British Library.

Library of Congress Cataloging-in-Publication Data

Stokes, Peter, 1959–
Research methods / Peter Stokes, Tony Wall.
pages cm.—(Palgrave business briefing)
Includes bibliographical references.
ISBN 978–0–230–36203–1
1. Management—Study and teaching (Higher)    2. Management—
Research—Methodology.    3. Business—Research—Methodology.
4. Dissertations, Academic.    5. Report writing.    I. Title.
HD30.4.S746 2014
001.4'2—dc23                                              2014038023

Typeset by MPS Limited, Chennai, India.

Printed in China

*I am a baby in your arms in the black and white photograph and I never had the chance to know you, to listen to you tell your own challenging story. But, as the years go by, I think I begin to appreciate more the drive, amongst enormous confusion and youthful strong-headed passion, to nevertheless stand up alongside your friends, against impossible odds for ideals of universal integrity, freedom and liberty.*

For Grandpa Andy and Great Uncle John Bermingham who heard and lived the moment of *Forógra na Poblachta h Éireann* (Pearse's declaration, GPO 1916).

"If I am not for myself, who will be for me? But if I am only for myself, who am I? [And,] If not now, when?"

*Hillel (Babylon, 10th Century commentary), Ethics of the Fathers, 1:14.*

Professor Peter Stokes

I am forever indebted to the humour of others, particularly the four Walls that propped up my childhood home: Vivien, Ronald, Suzanne and Debbie. Or may be that is five if you include Sally the Alsatian?

Dr Tony Wall

# CONTENTS

*List of Figures*                                                          viii

*List of Tables*                                                            ix

*Acknowledgements*                                                          x

*Introduction*                                                             xi

1   PROPOSALS, TITLES, AIMS, OBJECTIVES
    AND RESEARCH QUESTIONS                                                  1

2   LITERATURE REVIEW                                                      43

3   RESEARCH METHODOLOGIES                                                 86

4   RESEARCH METHODS AND DATA GATHERING                                   133

5   DATA ANALYSIS AND INTERPRETATION                                      174

6   ETHICS (GETTING APPROVAL AND DOING
    THE RIGHT THINGS)                                                     212

7   WRITING, PRESENTATION AND
    DISSEMINATION                                                         235

8   CONCLUDING THOUGHTS                                                   262

*Bibliography*                                                            264

*Index*                                                                   278

# LIST OF FIGURES

| | | |
|---|---|---|
| 1.1 | Research timeline | 3 |
| 1.2 | Folder or 'bucket' approach to collecting literature | 17 |
| 1.3 | A venn diagram of how fields can interrelate | 26 |
| 1.4 | The jigsaw concept of how all parts of research thinking should fit together | 37 |
| 2.1 | Key strategies for creating and writing a literature review | 64 |
| 2.2 | Literature review with different funnel shapes | 73 |
| 3.1 | An example of a realism–relativism spectrum | 111 |
| 5.1 | Types of quantitative data | 177 |
| 5.2 | Normal distribution of data (the bell curve) | 180 |
| 5.3 | Profit in millions of pounds (£) | 185 |
| 5.4 | Histogram | 186 |
| 5.5 | Relative size of employee type at ZXY organization | 187 |

# LIST OF TABLES

4.1   Diagrammatic illustration linking probable alignments of
      exemplar research methods and research methodologies        135
5.1   Frequency table for footfall in store 'X' 30th September–
      2nd October 2013                                            183
5.2   Profiles of organisations involved in the study             195

# ACKNOWLEDGEMENTS

This book came about because of the innovative thinking of, prompts from and discussions with, Martin Drewe and Ursula Gavin who are my Publishers at Palgrave Macmillan. We have now travelled a number of years and three books together. It has been a tremendous journey and I would like to thank both Martin and Ursula for the opportunities that they have provided me with and their ongoing insights, good humour and tremendous support. As academics, in the course of our work, we have many conversations and exchanges with publishers and editors, however, Martin and Ursula remain for me among the most focused, friendly and dependable co-producers of writing projects one could wish for. I would like to acknowledge and thank them for their contributions and long may it be so.

I also would like to offer a word of thanks to all my students, colleagues and friends in my professional life. There are many people to whom I would like to record gratitude but particularly worthy of note are Professor Caroline Rowland, Dr Neil Moore, Dr Simon Smith, Dr Tony Wall, Tim Brown, Peter Scott, Elsa Clare, Dr Shlomo Tarba, Professor Mark Saunders, Professor Peter Shaw, Professor David Cracknell and Professor Wes Harry. Thank you for keeping my humanity and professional mind and spirit alive in the face of challenging circumstances.

Above all, I would like to thank my wife, Emma, and our children, Joel and Ellie, for their love, patience, beauty, integrity and wickedly sharp ('plastic' Scouse Southport) humour. It keeps me grounded and going onwards.

Professor Peter Stokes
University of Chester Business School
May 2014


My thanks go to those people who make it their business to inspire and offer the gift of opportunity to others on a daily basis. This is the lifeblood of a beautiful society.

Dr Tony Wall
University of Chester Business School
May 2014

# INTRODUCTION

The subject of research methodology (i.e. the philosophies, approaches, methods and methodologies that enable you to undertake and write up a research investigation) is one that is rich and fascinating. On occasion, especially for the early researcher the subject can be difficult and challenging in certain regards. For many people, time is often at a premium with multiple demands being placed upon it and, therefore, books and sources that can assist you in a rapid manner to approach and understand a new area of learning are of great potential benefit. This book on research methods and methodology is an attempt to make a positive response to this sort of need.

The book is laid out in seven main chapters. Each chapter deals with key aspects of research methodological processes, methods and techniques providing insights into how to approach and tackle a range of questions and issues. The intent of the book (and indeed the kindred books of this series) is to provide a valuable handrail and overview text to a given sphere. Its purpose, in the concise space allocated to the volumes of the series, is not to provide comprehensive coverage on the subject but rather to provide an accessible, succinct yet rounded guide to the field. The various chapters direct readers to more comprehensive and pertinent readings on each of the key topics.

Working with research methods and research methodology is, and should be, much more than simply gleaning, appreciating and applying a range of techniques in a mechanical manner. It is also an opportunity to understand and appreciate the ways in which you approach and make sense of the world. In essence, an exploration of research methods and methodology can invite a process of self-discovery of your value and belief systems as well as those of others. This is, in part, because research methods and methodology should involve, both implicitly and explicitly, consideration of philosophical dimensions and these, in turn, provide spaces in which to explore and understand the ways you interact with the world around you. We hope you enjoy the book and the journey on which it may take you.

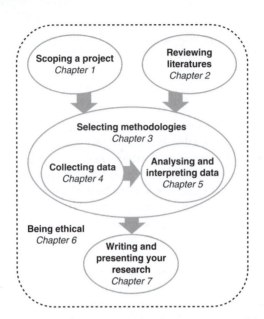

Diagram of the research process and chapters in this book

# 1

# PROPOSALS, TITLES, AIMS, OBJECTIVES AND RESEARCH QUESTIONS

## OBJECTIVES

*Successful completion of this chapter provides guidance on:*

- How to understand the various characteristics of the documents that are produced as a result of your research (including, for example, a dissertation or research project);
- How to format and develop a proposal;
- How to begin to develop a piece of research;
- How to develop an appropriate structure that will shape your study;
- How to develop, analyse and dissect titles in order to help you to develop your study;
- Understanding the differences between, and uses of, aims, objectives and research questions;
- Verifying that your work has developed appropriately and that the aims and objectives have been achieved.

## INTRODUCTION

Research is a process and set of actions undertaken with the goal of identifying and understanding something new or fresh about a given area, field, subject or discipline. Research takes place in many different ways and using many varying methods and methodological approaches. Within the subject areas of business, management and organisation, research traditions develop and use qualitative and/or quantitative data. Equally, different pieces of research work will elect to use different methodologies. Moreover, within particular subject areas within business, management and organisation, for

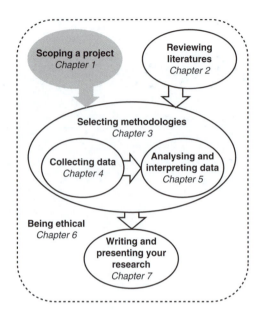

Current location within the research process

example, marketing, operations, supply chain management, accountancy, entrepreneurship and innovation – the potential list is extensive – different traditions and conventions of research methods and methodologies are likely to be employed.

When you are intending to undertake research (be it for a dissertation, project or other assignment), then it is a very good idea to develop a research proposal in order to plan out your ideas of what you intend to do and how you think you might go about it. A research proposal is a common way of tackling this and this is discussed below after an initial consideration of the differing nature of dissertations and projects. A typical research process is shown in Figure 1.1 below.

## TO WHAT EXTENT DOES THE STRUCTURE OF TITLES, TOPICS, AIMS AND OBJECTIVES DIFFER BETWEEN A DISSERTATION AND A PROJECT?

It will be useful and important to indicate at an early stage in the text some of the key similarities and differences between a dissertation and project.

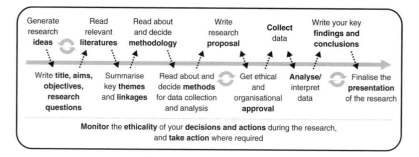

**Figure 1.1** Research timeline

## Dissertation

A dissertation is a substantial piece of research work that is usually the final module or section of an undergraduate degree such as BA (Hons) or BSc (Hons) or a Master's degree – MA or MSc. It is intended to be a very academic piece of writing and therefore should include a rigorous treatment of academic theory and literature and, moreover, have a theoretically underpinned methodology (Biggam, 2008; Greetham, 2009).

A dissertation is usually intended to comprise a substantial piece of work. The length of a dissertation can vary substantially ranging from 5,000–20,000 words; however, many institutions elect to make the document length approximately 10,000–15,000 words. This is laid out in the sections indicated below. Slight variations in structure may occur between universities and differing tutor approaches. Word counts signalled for the sections below are indicative and approximate – again various institutions, supervisors and commentators will have varying views and perspectives:

*(Abstract – optional) – outlines the entire work succinctly*
*(Approx. 100-500 words)*
*Introduction – opens the door on to the subsequent work*
*(Approx. 100-1000 words)*
*Research Aims and Objectives – is tightly focused on a question or issue*
*(Approx. 100 words)*
*Literature Review – analyses the academic writing connected with the objectives*
*(Approx. 2000-7000 words)*
*Research Methodology – shows the philosophical stance and methods adopted in order to accomplish the field study*

*(Approx. 1000-4000 words)*
*Findings – reports what was discovered through the execution of the methods*
*(Approx. 1000-5000 words)*
*Discussion – fuses the literature, methodological approach and data in order to respond to the aim(s), objective(s) and question(s)*
*(Approx. 1500-6000 words)*
*Conclusions – synthesises and pulls the overall impact of the work together*
*(Approx. 750-2000 words)*
*Bibliography – lists all the texts and sources used in an appropriate referencing format*
*Appendices (if required) – additional detailed materials referred to in the main sections of the work.*

You can also choose to structure your dissertation based on themes or issues stemming from the literature or from the data. For example, rather than have a conventional literature review section, you might choose to have two or three chapters that look at particular aspects of your work which are going to constitute the building blocks of your argument. For example, if you were looking at a study on psychological approaches to organisational training and development then you could, for instance, have chapters entitled:

- 'Historical perspectives on psychology in the context of training and development';
- 'Contemporary issues and approaches to training and development – the role of psychology'.

These could be either 'inside' an overall 'Literature Review' section header or alternatively simply independent and linked chapters.

## Thesis

As this book is aimed primarily at undergraduate- and postgraduate-taught programme students, it is not the intention to elaborate doctoral processes in detail. Nevertheless, it will be useful to understand the nature of a thesis in comparison with dissertations.

A thesis is the document that is written and submitted for consideration for a doctoral-level award. There are different types of doctoral award. A Doctor of Philosophy is a research degree that will take between approximately three to seven years to complete depending on the mode of study. In contrast, a Professional Doctorate could be a Doctor of Professional Studies (DProf) or a Doctor of Business

Administration (DBA) award. This type of programme often involves a combination of credits being allowed for advanced learning or experience and taught sessions on specific topics such as, for example, research methodology. Following these modules the delegate completes a thesis of between 40,000 to 60,000 words. The DProf programme involves the participant looking at some work-related issue and aiming to develop management practice and solutions against a backdrop of academic material and theoretical conceptual frameworks (Dunleavy, 2003; Murray, 2004).

The layout of the sections of a thesis is similar to the sections of a dissertation. However, the thesis must demonstrate depth, complexity and mastery of conceptual material and arguments at the highest standard. In addition, a doctoral thesis is generally expected to make contributions to knowledge whereas a dissertation is not. A dissertation is making a structured, in-depth study and commentary on an issue or issues.

## Project

The term 'project' is a generic term that can cover a wide range of investigations and studies. Projects can concern a range of purposes and objectives. For example, a project might involve developing or analysing a product or service brand; equally it could be about starting up a business, or, alternatively, it might focus on a product development idea. These are just illustrations, and the potential list of topics is almost inexhaustible.

A number of texts on research methods and research methodology use the term 'project' interchangeably with, and as a synonym for, the term 'dissertation'. While this usage is acceptable perhaps to some commentators, it equally risks causing confusion. A project is a piece of work following a particular set of aims and objectives. Varying formats are possible and these will quite often be indicated by the institution or organisation with which you are completing the assignment. An indicative and illustrative number of points concerning projects are outlined below (further insights are also available at www.pmadvice.co.uk (2013)).

- *Terms of Reference* at the beginning (these are akin to aims and objectives to be achieved). The Terms of Reference will often start 'To examine the effectiveness of … X.';
- An Executive Summary which will be positioned at the front of the document and serves a similar purpose as an abstract in a dissertation. The Executive Summary tells the person reading the report what the investigation involved and what it found out in a very concise manner;

- logically and incrementally *numbered sections* or blocks of text as it develops. Indeed, a dissertation will have numbered chapters and, on occasion, may also choose to have some form of notation or numbering within sections. More commonly, a dissertation will employ a series of sub-headings within the chapters. These may be notated or numbered but often are not;
- importantly, a project has a *focus on practitioner and practical means and ends*. This means that while it will engage with, and consult, a range of literature it will ultimately result in a set of explicit and clear recommendations to the reader regarding what actions should be taken in order to resolve or progress the issue examined. This is different to a dissertation which is primarily an academic-orientated, rather than practitioner-directed, document. A dissertation will offer insights and commentary on an issue or issues, and this may be intended to shape policy, guidelines and actions but it will not be overly directive.

## WHY IS IT USEFUL TO DEVELOP A RESEARCH PROPOSAL?

Before you start to work on your dissertation it is useful to work up a proposal. This is a much shorter document than a dissertation that maps out how you will approach and undertake your dissertation topic. The purpose of a proposal is to allow you to plan and think through the topic you want to study and what sorts of questions you want to ask about the area. Flowing on from this, it leads you to consider and write about what forms of methods and methodology you might employ; where you might conduct the research; with whom – which respondents or participants; and what sort of data are likely to be generated and how you will analyse it.

Generally, if you are undertaking a dissertation as part of a degree programme then a research proposal will be a prerequisite part of the process. A research proposal contains a number of typical sections. These together with a number of comments and points are detailed in Vignette 1.1 below.

### Writing a research proposal

A frequent and key action to take as you develop your research design is the drafting of a research proposal. This is a very useful thing to do as it consolidates and crystallises your ideas and approach. Many academic programmes (taught and research) or approval processes will require you to submit a proposal as a preparatory stage of your research.

VIGNETTE 1.1

A research proposal will typically comprise the following sections:

**Title**
(As discussed in Chapter 1 previously)
**Aims and Objectives**
(As discussed in Chapter 1 previously)
**Background Context and/or Problem Statement**
This generally provides a brief narrative about the subject to be considered by the research. In addition, it points at the relevance and the significance of the research and elaborates why it is timely and important.
**Literature Review**
(and Research questions)
**Methodology**
An outline of the approach to be adopted and the research design of the work.
**Approach to Analysis**
This section offers an outline of the method and techniques that will be used to examine the data that have been collected.
**Approach to Writing Up**
This section specifies how the write-up will take place. It indicates if the write-up will be in the form and style of, for example, a case study. Alternatively, will the write-up adopt a storytelling and narrative cameo approach or a critical incident report approach and so on and so forth?
**Research Schedule/Timetable**
This section provides a timeline that typically indicates sections such as:
• Initial meetings and discussion with supervisor
• Literature search/conducting review
• Developing research questions
• Design the research methodology
• Planning and securing access to the data
• Ensuring ethical approval for access and the overall study
• Data analysis phase
• Writing up
• Binding, final preparation and submission

### Bibliography/References

The final research proposal document can take a number of forms. If it is being produced within an undergraduate dissertation process, it is quite common for tutors to asks for an overview of what you intend to study and how you intend to approach and cover it. This form of condensed research proposal could occupy two sides of A4. Although disliked and criticised by some academics and observers, this brief form of proposal is not uncommon especially on undergraduate dissertation modules. The purpose of such short proposals is to prompt students into getting their ideas down on paper so that they can be shared and clarified with peers and tutors. Following feedback, and once set in the right direction, you can shape and modify the work and now dedicate time to expanding the proposal. On occasion, some tutors and institutions request a more extended proposal from the outset and the required output can run to several pages. More often than not, and certainly at Master's and doctoral levels, the expectation will be that you provide a developed presentation and argument of your intended work in the research proposal. In particular, supervisors will wish to see that you have conducted a detailed exploration of the relevant literature(s) and your approach and understanding of methodological and related philosophical considerations.

## WHY IS IT USEFUL TO HAVE SECTIONS SUCH AS AIMS AND OBJECTIVES AND RESEARCH QUESTIONS?

A piece of research or a dissertation will almost always include a title, aims and objectives, and research questions. This assists in shaping, structuring and directing the overall work. Working these out in a crystal-clear manner is imperative to the ultimate probable success of a piece of research.

Different pieces of research may need to adopt different approaches to laying out the work in relation to aims and objectives and various research traditions, and there are various ways of describing and categorising these (Chapters 2, 3 and 4 talk about these in an in-depth manner). To illustrate this at this preliminary stage of the discussion, one such possible dichotomy involves studies structured around using quantitative data and statistical analyses and approaches in some form as opposed to a study based uniquely on qualitative data.

A *quantitative statistical-style study/dissertation* is likely to follow the scientific experiment framework of:

- *Introduction* possibly with the statement of a research question(s); aims and objectives are likely to be stated before this section or as part of it.
- *literature review* – this will involve looking at the literature, and from each part of the argument that your work develops, writing in relation to the literature, the work develops hypotheses at various stages through the progression of the argument;
- a hypothesis is a supposition regarding what might be true or not. More colloquially expressed – it is a 'hunch' about what is found to be 'the truth' in relation to a particular question. Hypotheses (more than one hypothesis) are often considered a key part and building block of a quantitative approach.
- *Methodology*, detailing variables and measures to be applied to the data set;
- *Findings* – reporting the statistical findings on the data set;
- *Discussion* – analysing the significance and meaning of the work;
- *Conclusion* – reiterating argument and key findings.

Methodologically, or in terms of the overall underpinning, the work, together with its aims, objectives and research questions, will most likely be set in what is termed a positivistic framework or, in other words, it will be using positivism (this is explained at length, together with its aligned term of deductivism in Chapter 3).

*A qualitative piece of research or dissertation* may also employ similar headings to the quantitative approach outlined above for the sections of the research write-up; however, it is also possible that the discussion will have more extensive narrative and in-depth description. Furthermore, a qualitative approach could possibly use methods and methodological approaches such as focus groups, ethnography and discourse analysis (all of which are discussed in greater detail in subsequent chapters). In a qualitative piece of work it is quite common for research questions to be developed at the end of the literature review even though, in the case of a dissertation, the aims and objectives may well be stated at the beginning of the work or study in an initial section.

Moreover, this style of qualitative work can also employ hypotheses. However, whereas a quantitative piece of work will aim to prove, partially prove or disprove the validity of the hypotheses, a qualitative piece of work will aim to elaborate, explore and describe extensively the hypotheses. More is written on this later in the book.

In terms of underpinning philosophy, qualitative pieces of work tend to be based on inductivism and interpretivism which are discussed at length in

Chapter 3. As a note, qualitative studies may also employ a wide range of other philosophical-methodological approaches including, for example, Critical Realism and Postmodernism (which are also discussed in Chapter 3).

## CHOOSING YOUR WORDS CAREFULLY ...

It is important to remember that the words employed in a chosen title point to the key areas to be addressed in the research. Working to establish a clear title in conjunction with cogent aims, objectives and research questions helps to 'unpack', and understand, the title further. In particular, it is often the *nouns* in a title and other aspects that provide central clues as to the focal area or topic of the writing. An example of how to identify this is developed in the discussion below.

As mentioned, research questions are also important (White, 2008). Sometimes research questions will be explicitly stated in a paper or dissertation. However, on occasion, alternatively they may be implicitly stated through the argument built up in the literature. Again, more is explored in relation to this below. In essence, it is important to keep in mind, that matters such as title, aims, objectives and research questions constitute important structure for ensuring you are 'on the right track' and heading in the appropriate direction with your study and work.

On a final note to this particular section of the discussion, it is useful to note that a number of degree programmes, at both undergraduate and postgraduate level, now offer students the choice to undertake either a project or a dissertation in the final year of their programme rather than have to automatically do a dissertation. The rationale for this is to provide the student with a choice of approach to this section of their studies. Some students feel that the in-depth academic research approach and style of a dissertation is appropriate for them. Alternatively, other students feel that the greater practical emphasis and practitioner focus, combined with the highly structured format of a project, are more suitable to their learning style, needs and the task to be accomplished.

## IDENTIFICATION OF THE RESEARCH AREA

How will you decide and finalise what topic or area to research?

Identification of the research area that will be studied is a vital task for any student or researcher and it is intrinsically linked to thinking about the title, aims, objectives and research questions of a piece of work.

There are various ways in which you might identify the topic you will be investigating. You may have a relatively free choice of the area you wish to study. This is often the case when completing, for example, a dissertation within a broad business and management area. If the degree you are studying is, for instance, a BA (Hons) Business Studies or an MA/MSc in Management, then these encompass wide areas of potential topics and you will have an extensive range of choice. However, if you are studying a specific area or discipline, for example, HRM, accounting and finance or marketing either as a named pathway or award on your degree (e.g. MSc in Accounting and Finance or BA (Hons) in Marketing Management), then it is more likely to be the case that your course and dissertation handbook will indicate that your elected topic should focus on some aspect of the specialism of your degree. In relation to the two illustrations provided above, these might be by way of illustration only, accounting for brand value or using social media to develop brand awareness.

In other instances you may have the choice determined for you. If you are completing a piece of research as part of an assignment, you may, for example, be allocated the prescribed area by a tutor or research co-ordinator. Alternatively, the topic or research question may be pre-determined as part of a research funding bid or an independent sponsor's, or sponsoring employer's, brief. Here, the challenge is to ensure that you understand clearly what the area to be researched is and, moreover, what is likely to be involved. This will require you to conduct research into the terms and expressions being employed in relation to the research area.

## A cautionary note – How might you address potential supervisor difficulties in establishing the title?

If you are writing a dissertation or project you will usually be allocated a supervisor. He or she will generally be an invaluable aid in assisting you to shape your topic and you should engage with him or her as much as possible. However, here, a further issue on which to reflect (in relation to identification of a prospective research area) is the extent to which your supervisor should reasonably be able to exert influence over the choice of topic. In some cases, he or she may hold strong views concerning what would seem appropriate for you to study. Such situations may be entirely reasonable and be based on his or her in-depth experience, and overall, the advice is most likely to be invaluable. However, alternatively, on the rare occasion you may feel that you are being steered into a particular approach and feel uncomfortable with your supervisor's underlying rationale and reasoning. Such occasions can seem very challenging or even oppressive. You may feel restrained and unable to go against the wishes of your supervisor. The initial response here will be to try and discuss the matter and talk it through thoroughly. It will be vital to have researched your own view and suggested position fully and clearly so that you have a well-thought out rationale for your work and can argue it well (see Cryer, 2006: 44–54).

Similarly, on occasion there may be a tendency for a small number of supervisors to push students towards using a methodology to which the supervisor usually adheres. For example, if the supervisor typically uses a particular methodological approach, then this may be the approach he or she believes is the most valid way to develop data. These sorts of choices are often linked to issues of epistemology which is covered in depth in Chapter 3. Again, a supervisor may have useful and valid reasons for suggesting a particular approach. However, the preferred approach would usually be to identify the methodological angle that most appropriately suits the person conducting the study and the needs of the study itself. For example, if you want to examine trends in share data and company balance sheet values, then some form of positivistic and statistic-based approach supplemented with interviews from key figures and respondents may seem most suitable. However, if you are seeking to understand the thinking and decision processes of key figures in relation to company policies and strategies, then it is possible that a more interepretivistic style study would be more appropriate. Wilson (2010: 33) offers a useful list (echoing the SMART mnemonic of target setting) indicating that a 'good research topic [and approach] … is' 'achievable … specific … relevant … satisfies project guidelines and [perhaps most importantly] 'of interest to you'. The above noted challenges can occur at all levels – undergraduate through to doctoral-level study. Key factors that you need to keep in mind are:

- personality – who you are and what you would like to do in the research. In other words, the research approach needs to suit you and your work. The additional note on personality here is the need to develop yourself through your relationship with your supervisor. You will need to learn skills such as, for example, clarity, polite assertiveness, conviction of your beliefs, listening skills and social situation 'reading' skills. Linked to this it is possible to add political awareness – academic settings are known for often having politics with which you may need to occasionally contend. The potential list is extensive, and much of this wider development base can be undertaken only as a function of your progressive experiences.
- processes and procedures – ensure that you adhere to, and your supervisors follow, the appropriate procedures and processes for you research work and study. Generally, you will be happy with the way things are progressing; however, if you are not then the procedures in your student handbook or departmental and organisational guidelines will instruct you on what to do next.

### A supervisor-driven quantitative-based or qualitative-based approach? ... A case in point

A student was conducting Master's-level research into consumer perceptions of retail settings in relation to the sale of luxury clothing brands. The question considered was: when people purchase luxury brands in a market, online or in a high street luxury store in a major city what assumptions and sense-making are taking place in the decision-making process? The student was concerned with perception and how people form their opinions of place. After reading the literature on research methods and research methodology, the student decided to use focus groups as a research method and employ an overall methodology of interpretivism. The student used a range of images and photographs to prompt discussion in the groups and ask them questions in relation to how the focus group members perceived the retail environments. In addition, the student went into the field to make participant observations of retail consumer behaviours and these complemented the focus group work.

The above approach had been completely agreed among the supervisory team from the beginning of the study. Half-way through the study, due to staff changes a new supervisor joined the team. The newly arrived supervisor wrote a strongly worded email to the student (who had ambitions following completion of the degree to become a professional academic) indicating that it was imperative that a quantitative approach be used if a successful career were to be assured. This clearly unsettled the student and produced a sense of confusion. The principal supervisor was obliged to write to the newly arrived member of the supervisor and offer a gentle reminder that it is possible to build academic careers using a range of methodological approaches in the business and management arena and, moreover, in the marketing and retail area on which the study was centred (Cryer, 2006: 54). Equally, it was pointed out that the student had arrived, under supervision, at these choices and decisions in relation to methodology through a personal process of careful reading, deliberation and argument. The newly arrived supervisor reluctantly but gradually acquiesced to the student's and the overall supervisory team decisions.

### Reflective questions on the case situation

Question: If the supervisor had not intervened in this instance what might the student have done?

*Prompt*:

- Does the new proposal have validity – is it, in fact, worthy of consideration?
- Reflect on and become assured about the rationale and arguments on which your methodological choices are based;
- The ease, possibility of changing one or more the supervisors if a satisfactory resolution cannot be achieved.

The above type of situation, where a student is led unwillingly into conducting research in a particular way, whilst rare, may often be rooted in organisational politics or predilections in which the supervisor (rather than the student) is engaged. In nearly all instances, this unwarranted and unjustified steering of students and researchers should be considered unacceptable behaviour by the supervisor and, indeed, most supervisors will have the good judgement to allow students some latitude in developing their own ability to identify and develop a topic. If you are caught in this situation you should first discuss the situation with your supervisor. If this does not appear to resolve the matter then it may be appropriate to discuss it through relevant channels of appeal and representation (programme leader, year tutor or student's union representative).

## What issues arise when you are given a relatively free choice for your title?

If you have been granted the possibility of *choosing your own subject or topic and title*, then you should take considerable care in coming to a final decision. Some people believe it is best to think about the general domain or area of research. Others are keener to think of valuable and useful research questions and develop the title from those questions. In any event, in relation to having the choice of area for your work, some of the things you should consider include:

- Sustaining interest – you are probably going to be working on your research paper, dissertation or project for some time. It would be a good idea if it is something you find engaging;
- Is there an area you are already interesting in or have always wanted to study (Jankowicz, 2005: 28)?
- What might be useful for your future interests and/or career?

If you are responsible for thinking up and designing your own research title and questions, then this can sometimes be perplexing and seem hard to settle on one idea. One technique that can be of assistance here is the idea of using 'the relatively well-known technique of mind-mapping' (Collis and Hussey, 2009: 91–96). To start, just write down some of the words or nouns that you think you are interested in considering. You can write these all on a sheet of paper or alternatively write one idea/word per Post-it™ and stick it on a wall or flip chart board. You probably need only a few words to get going. To begin with write freely putting down anything that comes into your mind. Remember you can always discard and trim ideas later on. Then, in line with the other suggestions in this section, start moving the ideas on Post-its™ around the wall or board. This will help you to understand how they relate to each other and might fit together. When you think the ideas are beginning to fit together well you can then draw arrows and identify relationships between the words. This is a very powerful device for clarifying your thinking on a topic and it is sometimes much better than trying to hold all the ideas in your head. Get them on to paper and work them through.

## When establishing your title, aims and objectives for your work – what value and usefulness can be built in for your future career?

Linked to the issue of your interest in the chosen topic remember also that a piece of research – be it a paper, project or dissertation – can also be an excellent 'product' that can be used in discussions with existing and future colleagues, employers or clients. In other words, you can use the work in order to approach and position yourself for opportunities you wish to develop and exploit. For example, if you are interested in working in a business market research context then a decision to examine a leading-edge development in the field through a piece of research would be a potentially tremendous and useful talking point at a future interview or meeting. In addition, a paper, dissertation or project will act as a 'product' of your research output and as a concrete demonstration that you are an 'expert' or, at the very least, well-researched in the area. Cameron and Price (2009: 133) echo this approach by suggesting a range of forward-looking questions that you may wish to ask yourself at the same time as embarking on a piece of research, including, for example, 'where would you like to be in the next five years?' and 'what skills will you require?'. Your identification and choice of research topic can represent a significant way to develop your response and actions to these questions.

## THE MECHANICS AND TECHNIQUES FOR DEVELOPING TITLES, AIMS AND OBJECTIVES

### How do you avoid starting with a blank sheet?

When at the stage of developing ideas for your topic and research, a useful idea is to keep some means close by for jotting down thoughts and ideas on your intended research. Notes can be made anywhere including, for example, a note-pad, your phone or laptop. It does not really matter how these ideas are recorded; the essential point is that you are able to record them in a coherent manner (Saunders, Lewis and Thornhill, 2012: 26–67). A further potentially useful approach is to keep a word-processing document file on your desktop so that it is easily accessible. This means that while you are doing other activities and work, if an idea comes to you, you can rapidly open the file and jot it down. It is best not to postpone recording ideas in some way. You are more likely to make a better quality note of your thoughts if you write them down immediately. Do not think that you will necessarily remember it and record it later – you will no doubt know from experience how unreliable that approach can be.

In addition, and indeed aligned with the above approach, a 'bucket'-style technique can also be useful. To achieve this, simply have a box or a folder (i.e. the 'bucket') nearby in which you can put interesting articles, pieces of information and comment, notes and newspaper items, indeed anything that might seem potentially useful, into the container as they cross your desk or path during the course of your daily work and interaction. These items do not necessarily need to be ordered within the 'bucket', rather the receptacle acts simply as a collecting point. Then, when you are ready to write, you can return to the container and you will have lots of useful ideas that will act as a prompt for you. In this way you can avoid starting with a blank sheet which can be very daunting. You might even label the folder with your title (see Figure 1.2 below).

It is significant to remember that although such a collection process may appear 'ad hoc' you are unlikely to have collected these pieces of information in a random manner. They will have been selected by you, to use sociological terms: gaze, social construction of events and world view (Stokes, 2011). In other words, your unique set of interests and preoccupations will pre-determine what you notice, select and focus on in the world. Alternatively expressed, it is often no 'accident' that you cast your eyes and attention over particular things – there will be a range of reasons, stimuli and motivations.

### Why is it important to narrow down the research area topic and focus in a title?

When many researchers start to draft the title for their proposed research, a common pitfall is that of making the scope too broad. As you think about the dissertation you

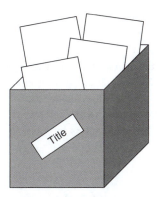

**Figure 1.2** Folder or 'bucket' approach to collecting literature

are undertaking, and you develop your proposal, it is a typical and normal process to move from a very general, broad and indicative title to a very specific, narrow and focused title.

The following is a real suggested early draft and version of a title from an undergraduate BA (Hons) proposal submission:

### Retail shopping parks – What is their future: A shoppers' perspective?

In some ways, this may seem a fairly clear and straightforward title. You might be interested in retail centres and enjoy large-scale retail and shopping outlets and want to see and understand more about what is going on in these establishments. You might also be curious to know how these centres will progress over time. However, such a broad title will present difficulties and challenges.

Such a title, as the one above, while being absolutely fine as a first working outline, presents a key difficulty in that it does not sufficiently focus on the work, and when you attempt to start the process of researching around the topic, many items in, for example, a library or on the internet are likely to seem to be relevant to some greater or lesser extent. In other words, a very broad title (or aims or objectives or research questions) tends to impede the progress of your study. In particular, during the information and literature search phases of your research, an overly broad title does not allow you to make clear and rapid decisions on whether or not a source such as a book or journal article is likely to be of potential value for your work. One possible metaphor here is the difference between a gun with a telescopic sight and a shotgun. The first focuses on a particular part of the target and concentrates its shot in a specific area. The latter commonly throws out a broad blast that scatters and hits a wide range of the target – even outside the target – in a largely uncontrolled and unfocused manner. Titles might be said to operate in a somewhat similar way – broad ones lead the researcher astray in a spread-out and wandering manner. However, tightly written and focused titles take the researcher logically to a specific meaningful destination or target (Dunleavy, 2003). It is therefore, always important to work and rework the title, aims and objectives, and research questions of your work, so that they will focus you in on a very narrow and precise area. Vignette 1.2 provides some ideas and an illustration of a process for working through the development and refinement of a title.

VIGNETTE 1.2

### An alternative approach to drawing up a title

One way to approach drawing up a title is to look at the *nouns* that have been employed in the title *Retail Shopping Parks – What Is Their Future: A Shoppers' Perspective?*

These are:

- *Retail Shopping Parks*
- *Future*
- *Shoppers' Perspective*

As they stand these are very general and broad nature terms to investigate. In order to be able to construct a research project that will be focused, make your task of conducting the research clear and provide meaningful results you need to define what is meant by the terms you are using and planning to examine. For example:

When the expression 'Retail Shopping Parks' is used you might ask:

- Are you looking at ALL retail shopping parks in the UK, in Europe … the world! Clearly, this is too much for a single piece of research and it needs to be dealt with in a more precise manner, so we need to narrow the area under consideration. Issues we might consider are, for example:
- Differentiating by **Scale or Sector**: What part or type of the business sector are we looking at – small-scale retail parks located outside of most towns, mega-shopping park complexes, such as, for example, in the UK, Brent Cross in West London, Meadowside in Sheffield or the Trafford

Centre near Manchester? Importantly, it might be that you wish to focus on a particular product or shop type, for example, fashion clothes, shoes, cosmetics, food produce, consumer white goods, etc.

- Differentiating by **Geography**: Where are we considering – All of the UK, an area of continental Europe, Shanghai, North-West England? Be very precise about the geographical area on which you intend to focus.

- Differentiating by **Time**: During which time period are you looking at your subject area? Will it be a long time-frame with a historical analysis as part of the work – the 20th Century and into the 21st and the 'Future'?; Will it be over recent decades in the 21st Century?, the last twenty years? If the title or aims and objectives use a broad term such as 'contemporary' then this too will need to be further defined at some early point in the study. The decision to use a given time-frame to look at a given phenomenon can help to limit and focus the study's concerns.

- Differentiating by **Sub-Area of the topic or subject**: In the example title above, it is not clear what exactly is being looked at. Are you looking at the issues surrounding their location strategy, environmental issues, sales performance, service cultures, organisational learning? The possible list is potentially lengthy. In thinking about this you need to be thinking about what aspect of a subject area you are interested in. More often than not this may well be linked to a particular literature base – all of the above have literature of more or less similar names that encompass very extensive writings by academic and practitioner authors.

Applying the same idea to the other terms, we could ask:

- What is intended by the term 'Future' in the suggested title? Are we thinking about short, medium or long term and how might you define these with regard to year time periods or, for example, phases of evolution of the business sector. Also you might ask 'the future' from which person or group's point of view? It will, for example, be useful to time-bound the idea of future – ten years, 15 years? Together with this you need to ask what will be feasible, reasonable and realistic to look at in terms of a time-frame. In a very different sense, you could think of 'future' in terms of scenarios or the idea of trying to predict what series of unfolding events might be proposed and what are the implications? Thus, we might think of 'future' in a very pragmatic literal way or alternatively in a more conceptual, abstract manner.

- When the term 'shoppers' is employed how is that to be defined. Indeed, is 'shoppers' the term that you wish to examine? Do you wish to consider shoppers as consumers, as customers, as a socio-economic group, as a generational (age/epoch-defined group)? For instance, are you actually wanting to focus on teenager behaviour in retail shopping parks? Could you narrow this down to a particular age-group, for example, 14- to 16-year-olds, or alternatively, 17- to 19-year-old groupings? Alternatively, are you actually interested in families shopping in retail parks rather than any other group? Importantly, as was pointed out above, remember also that certain terms will be associated with, and accompanied by, companion literatures. For example, the term 'consumers' is aligned with the vast writings on the fields of 'consumer behaviour' and 'buyer behaviour'. Looking at teenagers or families may well also invite you into sociological accounts on the academic fields of identity, sexuality and sexual behaviour, class, politics, aesthetics and many more.

- If you identify an area that does not seem to be aligned with a given literature, there are a couple of things to note. On the one hand, you may be making your life very difficult because when you go to write your literature review you are likely to find it very challenging to find books that relate directly to your chosen area. On the other hand, this is a potentially exciting moment and represents a new opportunity as you may well have stumbled on a 'gap' in the literature. You may well have identified an innovative and novel area for study. At undergraduate level, this is unlikely to be expected as a requirement. In some aspects of Master's study this may well be required and it is imperative at, for example, doctoral thesis level.

Taking account of the thoughts outlined above, we might be able to redraft the title as per the following illustrations:

Retail Shopping Parks in South Shanghai – What Are Their Medium-Term Future Prospects?: A Study of Late-Teens Shopper Consumer Behaviour.

The Consumer Dynamics of the Family whilst Shopping: An investigation into Families' Shopping Behaviour for White Goods in Retail Shopping Parks in the North of England in the Early 21st Century.

These constitute but two examples from the myriad possibilities and permutations. The key purpose is to make the question as narrow and as tightly focused as possible.

As a further point to note in relation to titles, it is important to remember that your first attempt to draft out a title will not necessarily resemble the final wording of the piece of research. The initial draft serves to provide a working guide of the area, terms and issues that the research seeks to address. As the research progresses there are a number of moments and stages in which you may come to the decision that some revision of the title (and perhaps consequently the aims, objectives and research questions) would be useful. These forms of revision are entirely normal, and you should not be overly concerned that they need to take place. As you write and research further, your understanding of the work should be naturally deepened and enhanced. It is therefore only to be expected that a fine-tuning and modification of the terms of the study might be felt to be necessary. On occasion, this might even happen towards the end of the study as the overall holistic picture of the research aim, journey and outcome becomes completely clear. It is often the possibility of being able to look back over the totality of a work that makes completely clear what was being sought in the first instance.

## How to develop research aims and objectives linked to your title?

Some researchers prefer to develop the aims and objectives first and then the title follows on from that. Others might see the development of the aims and objectives as an action that is useful to undertake in conjunction with the development of the title. The actions below are common to undergraduate and postgraduate dissertation work. For project work, it is more common to establish the aims and objectives stemming from the terms of reference prior to embarking on the overall work.

The research aim(s) seek(s) to point out the overall intent, scope and direction of a study. As was mentioned above, it needs to be refined and its focus narrowed to ensure that the study will have clear boundaries and limits (Wilson, 2010: 31–53). The objectives established for any study should flow from, and relate directly to, the aim(s).

As indicated above, the title *'Retail Shopping Parks – What is Their Future: A Shoppers' Perspective?'* was indicated as a suggested early draft version. It is important to refine and develop your title so as to focus your study to a greater extent. Vignette 1.2 above illustrates some ideas and techniques for thinking about and achieving this. Equally it is important to think about the technical aspects of terms and this too is discussed further below. At this point, the discussion is considering how you might develop aims and objectives from the title. Drawing on, and working with, the retail illustration above (and following the guidance on the development of a title in Vignette 1.2), it will be possible to make the terms of the title more precise and targeted. Leading on from this, it might, for example, be possible to develop a title:

*An Investigation into Consumer Behaviour in Retail Shopping Parks: A UK Perspective.*

Leading on from this, the aims of the study will break this down further and might be designated as:

A.   *To examine contemporary consumer behaviour in retail shopping park contexts with a particular focus on families as consumers;*
B.   *To examine retail shopping park behaviour in the context of the Manchester area, UK, with particular focus on white goods sales.*

It can be seen that each term in the title has been examined and made more exact in relation to what it encompasses and seeks to address. Again, it will be useful for you here to look closely at Vignette 1.2. Similarly, the two aims associated with this particular study break the title down further and target the efforts of the study to a greater extent.

Stemming from these aims it is possible to develop objectives that can be followed to achieve the aims. Some researchers might feel reasonably strongly that it is important for each aim to have a series of objectives. Alternatively, the objectives may align broadly but nevertheless clearly to the objectives. Even in this latter instance it is of course possible to indicate to which aim the objective is responding. Thus, in relation to the title and aims above, possible objectives might be:

1  To elaborate and define the key terms and concepts of 'family', 'consumer behaviour', 'retail shopping parks', 'Manchester area' and 'white goods'.
2  With reference to the literatures on consumer behaviour and retail shopping parks (with particular relevance to the definitions of white goods and family) consider the behaviour and dynamics of family units in these contexts.
3  Determine the issues, challenges and implications for the retail shopping park in the contemporary context of the terms as defined.

## How and why do you develop research questions?

It might seem reasonable to ask what is the purpose of research questions if we have already established aims and objectives together with a title that directs our work? Research questions point the research study very clearly towards answering a specifically stated problem. We know that by establishing a question we must ensure that, by the conclusion of the research, we have *answered it* as far as is possible. It is useful to recall Dunleavy's (2003: 20) succinct thoughts on the overall process: 'You define the question: you deliver the answer'.

In relation to research using and developing quantitative data and deductive, positivistic methodologies, it is common for this style of work to develop a hypothesis or hypotheses. This is elaborated further below.

If we take the example of the retail research discussed above, possible research questions might be:

1. What are the characteristics of contemporary family consumer behaviour in the area of Manchester, UK?
2. What are the issues and challenges surrounding retail parks in the Manchester area (with particular reference to family consumer group behaviour)?
3. What are the issues and challenges in relation to the consumption of white goods in retail park contexts (with particular reference to family consumer group behaviour in the Manchester area)?

You are not restricted to having a particular number of research questions. Usually often research projects will use two or three questions, sometimes more. Further examples of research questions which have been developed from titles and abstracts are provided in Vignette 1.3 below.

## An example of research questions

## Signs and Wonders: Exploring the Effects and Impact of the Investors in People Logo and Symbols

### Abstract

The paper examines and assesses the impact of the logos and symbols of the Investors in People (IIP) Standard which operates in the UK. It challenges the likely benefits of IIP to an organisation but considers the reputational consequences of the Standard's logos and semiotics on organisational member perceptions of issues such as signals to the labour market Smith and Stokes (2014) WIP. The argument considers the extant literature and identifies that a number of rhetorical and managerialist stances appear to be operating therein. In response to this situation, the paper constructs and invokes the possibility of surfacing an understanding of the perceptions of reputation and, in order to explore this, conducts field research employing 38 interviews. The field data indicate that among the managers and employees of the six IIP-accredited firms and one non-accredited firm studied, the logo, symbols and the Standard seemed to have very little impact on the development of the interviewees' everyday working lives and practices. However, there were some indications that the wider reputational benefits of carrying the logo may have some potentially beneficial effects. The paper concludes that this presents a potentially serious malaise for IIP and comparable initiatives, and that there is a powerful need to better understand the impacts, relevance and usefulness of the logos, symbols and indeed the overall Standard.

  **Keywords**: IIP; Logos; Symbols; Rhetoric; Realities

## Introduction

Investors in People (IIP) is a long-standing initiative and feature of the UK organisational workplace and purports wide-ranging impacts in terms of training and development outcomes. Furthermore, these impacts are also associated with reputational consequences as a result of attaining the award and the use of its badge and logo. This paper investigates and challenges the notion that IIP has significant staff skills developmental impacts in the workplace. In tandem with this, it also considers the extent to which reputational issues may play a role in areas such as organisational enhancement from the perspective of managers, employees, prospective employees in the labour market and customers.

(i) What are the reputational perceptions and effects of IIP in the internal and external organisational *labour market* – that is, with regard to existing employees and prospective employees' attitudes, respectively?
(ii) What are the wider reputational effects of IIP on the organisation in relation to benefits and effects on potential business development, for example, employee perceptions of consumer reactions?

## Why is it important to examine closely the terms employed in your title – further thoughts?

When working on the development of a title, an important point to remember is to exercise caution and to be wary of taking the words in your evolving research title too literally or *at face value*. The reason for this is because there are always likely to be a range of possible meanings and it is important to appreciate fully the possibilities. For example, imagine a title such as:

*An Investigation into the Extent to Which Organisational Learning and Management Learning Play a Role in Organisational Performance.*

This would, for example, be a typical area (although not exclusively) of topic for a Master's level study due to the managerial-level literatures and concerns to which it is directed. If this were a draft of a title you were attempting to develop for a piece of research, it would invite you to cover a very broad area indeed. As initial observations, there are two immediate general aspects to consider – the scope and the technical nature of the terms employed. Firstly, the title includes a number of nouns or terms that point at large areas or domains. Arguably, the scope of this draft of the title is too broad and will require narrowing down. This is discussed further below.

Secondly, terms used in a title, aims or objectives, or indeed research question, are very likely to have a particular *academic* or *technical* meaning and a significance that is linked to a certain topic area. It is important to identify and understand these specific linkages and meanings. This is usually achieved through identifying the *relevant bodies of literature* potentially associated with the given terms. When you have found these texts it is vital to establish an understanding and a 'feel' for the key concerns, issues and contributors to the body of literature. In the example above 'organisational learning', 'management learning' and 'organisational performance' are all specific academic terms and fields of research in the domain of organisation and management research and practice (Easterby-Smith and Lyles, 2011, and see also, for example, the journal *Management Learning*). Each term has prompted the production of a very substantial literature. It is not possible, for instance, to attempt to engage with, and understand, these terms necessarily in relation to simply their everyday or commonplace meanings. The words 'Learning', 'Organisational', 'Management' and 'Performance' all offer meaning to the public at large; however, when employed in an academic context a very different set of meanings, inferences and consequences may well emerge. The Venn diagram below illustrates this (Figure 1.3). Understanding these meanings will be an integral part of the study and will involve recognising various writers and how they have challenged and scrutinised what each term might encompass. This will assist you in developing academic and technical appreciations of the areas as opposed to simply engaging with the terms in an everyday sense. This part of the analysis will usually be conducted in the literature review (see Chapter 2).

## How does the process of choosing a title provide an opportunity to engage with methodological and philosophical issues and approaches?

As you develop the title, aims and objectives and research questions of your work you will start to think about what methodology and methodological approach(es) you will be adopting. The nature and question of research methodologies and

**Figure 1.3** A venn diagram of how fields can interrelate

philosophies are dealt with in considerable detail in the subsequent chapters (in particular Chapter 3). Here, suffice to say, philosophy in methodological terms means the overarching view and way of seeing the world or a given area that your work adopts. It is important to signal that various forms of these approaches are available to you and these choices are an integral stage in the development of your dissertation.

An in-depth discussion of the underlying philosophies of research is a requisite aspect of a dissertation at the Master's level. It is also important at undergraduate level, however, more often than not the learning outcomes of the undergraduate dissertation module require that these issues be reasonably and appropriately addressed rather than treated at length. In the case of project work, it is more likely that the study will contain comments on the general and overall methodological approach of the work, but it is highly unlikely to discuss the philosophical underpinning of the methodological approach in any depth.

To take a preliminary illustration of a discussion of the philosophical basis of a piece of work, for the purposes of illustration, if an interpretive or qualitative data-based approach is adopted then, within this, a wide range of philosophies and stances are available for your work, for example, Critical Theory, postmodernism, post-structuralism (Bronner, 2011; Linstead, Fulop and Lilley, 2009; Parkes, 2012) (as opposed to, although not exclusively, positivistic/modernistic approaches). Interpretivism, Critical Theory, postmodernism, post-structuralism and positivism/modernism are labels for systems of thought, beliefs and views of the way the world operates (i.e. philosophies). They are systems of thought that have been developed by different individuals and groups (or 'schools') of philosophers. Between the characteristics of these different philosophies, there are some similarities but quite often striking contrasts and differences. Depending on the background philosophy you adopt for your work, the various stages of your dissertation will reflect the characteristics and beliefs of that philosophy. While not wishing to over-simplify it is common to see most undergraduates adopting either an interpretivist or, in contrast, a positivistic approach. At Master's-level dissertations, this is still the frequent choice; however, other philosophical approaches are also in evidence.

The philosophical approach adopted is something that would potentially provide a particular angle of analysis in a literature review. Moreover, it is also the case that you might additionally choose to think about this at the time of establishing your title. Indeed, if the question were re-written to adopt this approach the question might, for example, be phrased as follows:

*Organisational Learning, Management Learning and Organisational Performance: Liberating Concepts or Old Wine in New Bottles? – A Discursive Analysis.*

In this instance, this title would be pointing at *Organisational Learning, Management Learning and Organisational Performance* as terms and associated literatures. The second half of the title *liberating concepts or old wine in new bottles* would be alluding to the idea that these ideas are arguably products of a particular (perhaps modernistic and rationalistic and objectified) philosophical way of thinking and that there is not really very much new that they have to offer business and management debate. As a consequence, there is scope to critique this and suggest alternative (more subjective-orientated postmodern or post-structural) approaches and solutions (these terms are explored more fully in Chapter 3). Within this particular title the research proposes to engage with a discourse analysis approach which will look at the myriad ways in which communication (through language, symbols, signs, expressions and human interaction and interpretation) and sense-making might be taking place in relation to the three named domains (Gee, 2011). This form of title and approach would, for example, be in contrast to dealing with the terms in a more positivistic and normative manner.

## A NUMBER OF FURTHER METHODOLOGICAL ISSUES AND CONSIDERATIONS

### The role of hypotheses in different types of research

A hypothesis is a proposition that a piece of research aims to prove or falsify in whole or in part. Hypotheses commonly form a part of positivistic research (see Chapter 3). This approach to research often collects and uses quantitative data to develop its arguments. The purpose of using hypotheses in research is to be able to say whether or not the hypothesis (or if there is more than one hypothesis, *hypotheses*) is proven or disproven in part or whole in connection with the aims, objectives and research questions set out at the beginning of the research.

For example, on completion of the research a paper may say that a hypothesis was proven. This means it is upheld as being true and valid, that is, to be fact and a case that exists and that has been, and can be, verified. Alternatively, the data, and analysis of the data, may be found not to be able to be proven and, therefore, cannot be said to be categorically true or upheld.

By way of a brief indicative and illustrative example, in a study entitled:

*Knowledge Transfer and Cross-Border Acquisition Performance: The Impact of Cultural Distance and Employee Retention.*

The authors developed a literature review and at the end of each sub-section of the literature review they developed the following hypotheses to be verified:

- *Hypothesis 1: Knowledge transfer has a positive impact on cross-border acquisition performance.*
- *Hypothesis 2: Organisational culture distance has a negative impact on cross-border acquisition performance.*
- *Hypothesis 3: National culture distance has a positive impact on cross-border acquisition performance.*

The paper employed a positivistic methodological approach and used extensive statistical techniques to analyse the data. The 'Findings' section of the paper reported the data, and the discussion interpreted the findings and confirmed whether or not the hypotheses had been fully, partially or not at all confirmed.

Vignette 1.4 provides a more in-depth illustration of a statistical and positivistic study that goes on to develop hypotheses.

---

### Illustration of an abstract from a positivistic-style study

VIGNETTE 1.4

*Extract taken from XiaoYan, Q., Yong, H., Qingli and Stokes, P (2012), Reverse Logistics Network Design Model Based on E-Commerce, *International Journal of Organisational Analysis*, 20 (2): 251–261

#### Development of a Reverse Logistics Network Design Model Based on E-commence

#### Abstract

**Purpose**
The aim of this paper is to study reverse logistics network design in order to better facilitate the location of factories, on-line retailers and the third-party logistics in the context of E-commerce.

**Design/methodology/approach**
Drawing on types of third-party collections of returned products, the paper proposes a 0–1 Mixed Integrate Linear Programming (0–1MILP)

mathematic model for reverse logistics networks in E-business and a further mathematical model in relation to determining the market demands and returns. Furthermore, a case study is developed and described with the intention of illustrating the value of this model and network.

### Findings

The paper identifies possibilities for the application of the reverse logistics network models to deal with returned products from customers in companies using E-business.

### Research limitations/implications

There is scope for future research to build on the present research and consider further factors in relation to the influences on return logistics.

### Originality/value

- This paper provides novel insights for E-companies for setting up and operating a reverse logistics network.
- The application of these models could decrease costs and allow optimal decisions on price and return price in order to increase efficiency and profit levels.

**Keywords**: E-commerce, return policy, reverse logistics, the third-party logistics

Hypotheses are also found in qualitative, interpretivistic-type research. However, here, rather than saying that a given hypothesis was definitively and categorically proven, the work tends to identify ways in which the hypothesis has been further elaborated and understanding of it deepened (see Silverman, 2010a: 109–111, and wider comments in his engaging and interesting text). Vignette 1.3 provides an illustration of an interpretivistic study and shows how it moves to build its research questions and quasi hypotheses.

# FEEDBACK LOOPS AND DOUBLE CHECKING THE DIRECTION OF YOUR WORK

As you progress through your work, it is vital to check that you are answering your research questions and responding to you research aims, objectives, title and research questions (Vignette 1.5).

VIGNETTE 1.5

**Exercise on studying and reviewing titles, aims, objectives and research questions**

Below you will find a series of titles and related aims, objectives and research questions. These are real titles from dissertations that have been completed at various points in the past. The purpose of the exercise is to provide you with an opportunity to look over actual titles that students and researchers decided to develop and work with.

You are invited to look over the examples below. Try to keep in mind the advice and comments provided in the discussion in the Chapter above. Reflect and, in relation to the titles, ask yourself the questions:

- How carefully has the given title been crafted?

- How might it be crafted differently?

- Are all the nouns and terms in the title necessary or do you think the title would benefit from additional terms?

- How is the title structured? Is it playful or matter of fact? Does it use semi-colons or other punctuation to achieve certain effects? How effective are these devices?

You will notice that not all the studies have used the same layout. For example, some have objectives and others do not. Some have modified the conventional terminology (note the use of 'purpose') and others are fairly traditional. In looking at the aims, objectives and research questions you might consider:

- To what extent does the stated aim add value to the study?

- How clearly and logically do the stated objectives 'unpack' or elaborate on the aims and the title?

- How do the research questions function in relation to the overall proposed framework of the study?
- What might you change in the aims, objectives and research questions for any given study?
- As you work your way through these questions and issues it will be useful to have a pen and paper to hand so that you can redraft and consider various ideas and options.

### *EXAMPLE TITLES, AIMS, OBJECTIVES AND RESEARCH QUESTIONS A–J*

#### EXAMPLE A
**Title:**
To What Extent do the Leadership Skills of Middle Management within the Technical Services Department (TSD) of Organisation 'X' Enable It to Successfully Deal with Change?
**Research question:**
To what extent do the leadership skills of middle management within the technical services department of organisation x enable it to successfully deal with change?
**Aims**
1. To understand contemporary thinking on leadership
2. To understand what is meant by the term 'middle management'
3. To understand any links between leadership styles and organisational change
4. To discover to what extent 'leaders' exist within the middle management later of the TSD
5. To investigate what impact types of leaders identified within TSD enable or hinder the department's ability to deal with change
6. To make recommendations on TSD's approach to leadership development

#### EXAMPLE B
**Title**
Technology Used as a Tool to Manage People
**Aims**
1. To present contemporary management tools
2. To present the 'new' model of HRM

3. To explore how this 'new' model which is related to technology
4. Based on aims 1, 2 and 3 above, show the advantages that this technology has brought to the human resources sector and how it has helped to become part of the company business and the organisational strategy

**Research question**

1. What are the barriers to using technology?
2. Which HR activities are usually integrated into an e-HR platform?

**EXAMPLE C**

**Title**

A Manager's View of Critical Success Factors Necessary for the successful Implementation of 'Economic Resource Planning' (ERP).

**Purpose of the study**

The purpose of this study is to examine prerequisites for successful implementation of an ERP system from the project management perspective.

**Research questions**

1. Did ERP implementation realise the intended benefits?
2. To what extent were critical success factors present or considered during ERP implementation?
3. Were project team and end users satisfied with ERP modules implemented?
4. What problems and concerns did staff have before, during and after implementation of ERP?

**EXAMPLE D**

**Title**

Would You Like Fries with That?: How Does Helpdesk Offshoring Impact on Employee Engagement.

**Research questions**

1. Does an off-shored helpdesk impact upon employee engagement?
2. What drives any impact upon employee engagement?
3. Is offshore call centre research applicable to corporate offshore help desks?
4. What recommendations can be made to 'Organisation X' on the off-shoring of the helpdesk?

**EXAMPLE F**
**Title**
Walking the Talk: Can Our Leaders Walk the Talk to an Engaged Workforce? – An Observational Qualitative Study of Engagement and Leadership Behaviour.
**Research problem statements**
**Purpose**
The purpose of this study was to answer the question: can leaders walk the talk to an engaged workforce? And evaluate the traits and behaviours of an effective engaging leader, one whose purpose is people-orientated.
**Aims**
The study aims were to explore leadership style and behaviour of first-line managers in relation to their trait and predisposition preference, evaluating the two key variables of first-line managers' self-perception of their team members.
**Objectives and justification for the research**
1. To identify the traits of engaging, people-oriented leaders as perceived by employees within the organisational study;
2. To critically evaluate research based on leadership styles and employee engagement;
3. To critically evaluate trait and motivational behaviour leadership in line with the Glowinkowski behavioural leadership models.


**EXAMPLE G**
**Title**
The Impacts of Different Cultures on Leadership Effectiveness
**Objectives**
1. To investigate the level of understanding of leadership and cross-cultural leadership within the organisation by leader-managers and employees
2. To understand what makes an effective cross-cultural leaders in different cultures (including characteristics, attitudes and working style)
3. To investigate the effect of cultural dimensions and leadership effectiveness
4. To make recommendations to improve leadership effectiveness in a different culture

The specific research questions are as follows:

1. What are the main characteristics of the leader in a cross-cultural environment?
2. How important do you think the role of the leader is of the leader who comes from a different culture to that of the organisation?
3. Which factors are important for leadership effectiveness in your culture?
4. What would need to happen in order to improve leadership abilities in a cross-cultural environment?

### EXAMPLE H
#### Title

The Effect of Service Quality on Customer Satisfaction within the Context of Retail Banking in Vietnam

The primary objectives of the current study are:

- Objective 1: To understand the contemporary thinking on service sector quality and customer satisfaction in the retail banking sector.
- Objective 2: To investigate the perceived quality and the level of customer satisfaction in the retail banking sector.
- Objective 3: To assess the effect of service quality on customer satisfaction in the retail banking sector.
- Objectives 4: To measure the effect of individual dimensions of service quality on customer satisfaction in the retail banking sector.

### EXAMPLE I
#### Title

Participatory Budgeting (PB): 'Is It 'Doorstep Democracy' and Does It Liberate Collective Wisdom?

The aim of this dissertation is to examine the role of PB within a local government context.

To achieve this aim the following objectives will be explored:

1. To understand contemporary thinking on PB and evaluate its impact as a mechanism for devolving public-sector financial management to the stakeholders they serve
2. To understand, analyse and critically examine the current approach to PB in local government in organisation X

3. To evaluate the impact of PB on the regional stakeholders
4. To draw conclusions and if appropriate make recommendations to mainstream PB not only as a core engagement tool within the organisation but also in the allocation of mainstream budgets

**EXAMPLE J**

**Title**

To What Extent Is E-mail Marketing a Factor in Relationship Marketing within SME IT Service Organisations?

**Research question**

To what extent are e-mail marketing tools a factor in relationship marketing within UK-based SE IT retailers?

**Aims of the investigation**

To understand contemporary thinking around relationship marketing and how best-practice e-mail marketing can be used by SME IT organisations to develop long-term relationships with their customers.

**Objectives**

1. Understand contemporary thinking on relationship marketing
2. Understand current best practice in e-mail marketing and how it can be used effectively to build relationships with customers
3. Investigate how SME IT organisations view their relationships with their customers and how they are using e-mail marketing within those relationships
4. Develop a framework to assist SME IT organisations to enhance the relationships with their end users

One method for doing this is to employ a metaphor to think about your work (Grant and Oswick, 1996). For example, your work might be like a wall or a jigsaw that is made up of bricks or pieces with each brick or piece linking into the one above and the one below it. Each one has to fit smoothly with the one that precedes it. This is reflected in the idea of 'new information follows old information' which is discussed at some length in the Chapter 2 on literature reviews. Imagine that each part or section of your research (or each part of your thinking) should be closely connected. Or in terms of a jigsaw, each piece should fit together (see Figure 1.4 below). This will help you keep a flow and consistency within your research, or a certain type of validity (this will be discussed in more detail in later Chapters).

**Figure 1.4** The jigsaw concept of how all parts of research thinking should fit together

One way that this can be achieved is by reading your work in a number of different ways. Again, this particular idea is discussed at length in the subsequent chapter on writing and dissemination. When you have written a piece of text and feel reasonably happy with it, it is a good idea to plan to re-read it in a number of ways and directions. For example, a key approach is to read the text for *sense-making*. To do this, read back over the work carefully sentence by sentence. Ask yourself the question, 'Does each sentence logically and reasonably add to, or progress from, the preceding sentence?' Then when you have done that, equally, ask yourself, 'Does each paragraph containing those sentences logically and reasonably flow into the next paragraph and so on and so forth?' In addition, and in conjunction with this, also look 'backwards' at your work from the last sentence towards the first sentence of a given paragraph and decide if you ended up where you wanted to arrive when you started writing.

## MANAGING THE RESEARCH PROCESS

The stages that you would be expected to engage in are shown in the research timeline shown earlier in the chapter. At the outset of your work, draw up a timetable for achieving the various stages and parts of the research project. For example, in the most straightforward of ways, this will plan and lay out what you intend to do and when. For instance, you might dedicate a number of weeks to identifying your topic and carry out the initial research on the literature(s). Equally, you may envisage that planning the methodology you are to adopt for your dissertation or research and, then, subsequently conducting the fieldwork will require certain periods or blocks of time.

Many researchers and students do this only to then see the inevitable slippage enter their neatly laid-out schedule. The point to take from this is that schedules need to be realistic. There is no point setting yourself aims, objectives and tasks that you will have difficulty achieving. Some people like to use various diagrams or charts to illustrate how each phase occupies a given time period. Experience tends to show that these are useful for showing intended general periods of activity and the overall length of the work schedule but lack detailed action plans. In this way, they do not help the researcher know what tasks to do day-by-day or week by week, but they can be modified to accommodate this.

Making lists is a classic and useful idea. Remarkably, this simple 'technology' is often overlooked. It is a good idea to have the big overall list and then, during each day or week, to write a list of tasks taken from the major list. This allows a 'chunk and chip' approach to moving through all that has to be done. In other words, you have an overall list and then a sub-list drawn from the overall task list.

Time is a precious and pressured commodity and, as is all too commonly the case, the swathes of time and space you set aside to achieve tasks seem to evaporate imperceptibly. One technique you can use is that of 'carving space' out of your diary or (as this was once explained to the author by a business community manager and leader with whom he was in discussion at an event) the 'red line' technique. It goes as follows. The community manager and leader in question was an extremely busy person. He had several hundred families to look after, seminars to organise and run social and other calendar events to conduct. In addition to this, with his wife he had a family with four children, was a prolific book and article writer on his specialist area, regularly appeared on radio and television and also led various initiatives. In essence, he was about as busy as anyone could be. He was asked 'How on earth do you manage to do all that and find time for contemplative activities like writing?' His answer was swift and clear:

> I use a red pen. I take my diary, I find a day or half-day at some point in the near future and I write a red line through that part of the diary. That is writing time. Nothing interferes with that time at all. The only thing that will cause it to be interrupted is a death in the community or a serious or tragic incident.

The lessons of the conversation were clear:

- Be focused.
- Be disciplined.
- Mark out time.
- Protect and use time fully and properly.
- Use the red-line technique to help you achieve this.

There are many approaches and aides to help you to understand and plan time. Perhaps one of the most well known is the SMART mnemonic which says that objectives and targets should be:

- *Specific* – they should be very focused and narrowly defined – not broad and general.
- *Measured* – There should be some way of assessing and gauging progress – this might be by using numbers in terms of proportions of research budgets spent, people interviewed, company case study visits accomplished, interviews tran-scribed, etc.
- *Attainable* – whatever goals are mapped out should be realistic and achievable.
- *Relevant/Realistic* – are the goals pertinent and useful for the research aims and what is sought to be achieved or are they too imprecise and actually dealing with areas and topics which are not strictly in line with the subject/topic being examined?
- *Time-framed* – map out the envisaged achievement of the goal or target in terms of time – hours, days, months, etc. How long will each section take? Remember the earlier point of being realistic.

For example, part of the planning of your research or dissertation might include interviewing managers at a range of companies. The objective, for instance, might be: to interview five managers in five different firms. An objective like that is likely to take a lot of time to plan and execute as managers are busy and may not readily accept to be interviewed. Developing a plan by using SMART principles could take the suggested form:

Overall, allow 15 weeks (approx. 3 months) to:

- Identify firms – this will take the first two weeks.
- (but opportunities and information may come to light through chance and network recommendations and referrals)

- Possible manager interviewees within the firms – allow a further six weeks.
- Be specific and focused about what types of manager you are looking for – level in the organisation, role, department type, gender, career profile, etc.
- Ensure the firms are within easily reachable distance from your home or base. What will be the costs involved in travelling to the interviews?

In terms of interim and mid-points targets, aim to secure agreement from:

- 3 managers by 8 weeks into the search for interviews;
- 4 managers by 10 weeks;
- 6 managers by 12 weeks (plan an extra manager in to allow contingency for cancellations and dropouts).

In principle, the above approach applying SMART thinking starts to make you be precise, detailed and, above all, realistic about how you approach planning your research.


## CONCLUSION

This chapter has sought to provide guidance in relation to the early stage of approaching and beginning to develop a piece of research. Things that you need to pay close attention to are:

- Developing clear and focuses aims, objectives and research questions;
- Developing a dissertation or research title that reflects yours aims, etc.;
- Do a research proposal before your start the main study;
- How a piece of research or dissertation can be tailored to, or play a role in, supporting your later career moves;
- Develop an awareness of the role of methodology and philosophy in your work and how this will shape your approach to literature, analysis, etc;
- Think about what role hypotheses might play in your work;
- How you will plan and manage time.

Paying sufficient attention to the above is vitally important and will assist you in ensuring that your dissertation or research project will start off on the right footing.

## GLOSSARY OF TERMS

**Aim** In relation to a dissertation or research project, an aim is an overall outcome or purpose that you are trying to achieve. An aim is usually accompanied by, for example, three to four objectives. These are practical steps that, when moved through, will enable you to achieve the aim.

**Objectives** An objective is a point you want to arrive at and accomplish. Objectives tend to be expressed in clear, practical language that will tell the reader what action and work is being done to achieve that step. A collection of objectives go to make up one or more aims. Sometimes it is useful to use the SMART device to make sure your objectives are well thought through – Specific, Measured, Attainable, Relevant and Time-framed.

**Hypothesis** A hypothesis is a proposed explanation of why something is the case. Colloquially expressed, it might be termed 'a hunch', a guess or supposition about a likelihood of something being possible. The plural of hypothesis is hypotheses. Hypotheses can be employed in research using qualitative or quantitative data.

**Title** A title is the overall label of a piece of research. A title is very important because it will aim to encapsulate the spirit and essence of the research focus and domain. The title is closely linked to the aims and objectives. It is useful to pay particular attention to nouns and terms that are employed in a title as they will often indicate areas of literature at which you are directing your study.

## KEY POINTS

1. Make sure your title is very focused and narrow in scope.
2. Make sure your research questions respond to, and develop, your title.
3. Look at past dissertations and papers in order to get ideas on topics and how the documents are laid out.
4. Make sure your research questions are realistic and achievable (i.e. SMART).
5. If possible, study something that you are really interested in.
6. Work to make your title as tightly drafted and honed as possible.
7. Remember the red-line technique – create space to achieve work and protect it.
8. Plan the next steps for the study from the outset – for example, dissemination.

## REVISION QUESTIONS

1. Examine the nouns you use in your title and/or research questions:
   • To what extent could you rationalise or economise these terms?

- To what extent might you be able to use alternative nouns that would serve your study in a more suitable manner? (A thesaurus might be useful for generating ideas).

2. Look over the SMART list (Specific, Measured, Attainable, Relevant and Time-framed.) In relation to aims and objectives, which aspect(s) of SMART are you generally good at assessing and which aspect do you often have to revisit and adjust? (Try to use the answer to this to decide where you need to improve your performance).

3. In addition to the strategies provided above, what strategies do you use or could you devise, in order to manage the work process of producing a piece of research?

## FURTHER STUDY

1. Go to a university/college library and see if you can access previous examples of dissertations and research projects that have already been accomplished. These can provide an excellent template on which you can model your work.

2. Ensure that you access a journals database in order to look at a range and variety of academic articles that have been written. Study how the articles have employed particular titles and how the research questions for the articles are developed.

3. O'Brien, M and DeSisto, M. (2013) Every Study Begins With a Query: How to Present a Clear *Research* Question, *NASN School Nurse*, March, 28 (2): 83–85.

   *Quite often it is useful to look across discipline boundaries in order to learn from various disciplines and fields. The above reference is a case in point. This article from nursing studies provides a helpful insight developing questions.*

4. Sandberg, J and Alvesson, M. (2011) 'Ways of Constructing *Research Questions*: Gap-Spotting or Problematization?' *Organisation*, January, 18 (1): 23–44.

   *This is a helpful article in the field of organisation and management from well-known Scandinavian commentators writing in the critical management domain and tradition.*

5. Williams, K. (2013) *Planning Your Dissertation*, Series: Pocket Study Skills, Basingstoke, Palgrave-Macmillan.

# 2

# LITERATURE REVIEW

## OBJECTIVES

*This chapter aims to assist you in writing a good literature review by helping you to develop and demonstrate an understanding of:*
- What is the nature and structure of a literature review;
- Why literature reviews are important in research;
- How to work with articles, books and materials in order to develop a literature review;
- Ordering your literature review;
- Acquiring writing techniques for your literature review;
- Avoiding common pitfalls that may occur when writing a literature review;
- How to link your literature review to other sections of your research.

## INTRODUCTION

A literature review is an essential and central component of research dissertations and theses at undergraduate and postgraduate level. By researching and writing a literature review, the writer seeks to become familiar, and connect, with the work that has been written and produced by other authors in relation to a specific field or topic. For many researchers, producing a review of the literature relating to your topic of interest seems to be a major and, at times almost insurmountable, task and it is approached with a range of concerns and on occasion trepidation. The points mapped out below are intended to ease and facilitate the process of writing a literature review.

Generally, in the case of projects there will be some allusion or reference to background models or sources; however, this is unlikely to be in such great depth as the dissertation. For example, if the audience is largely practitioner, or quasi-practitioner orientated, then a substantial literature base will generally not be a requirement. The

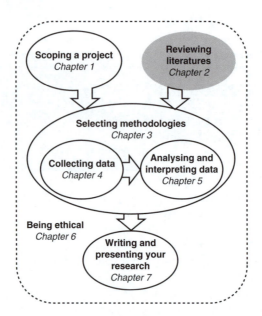

Current location within the research process

use of literature may still be important; however, this will depend on the prerequisites stipulated in module handbooks, other guideline documents and the end user and reader audience.

## UNDERSTANDING THE NATURE OF A LITERATURE REVIEW AND HOW TO APPROACH IT

### What is literature and what does it encompass?

The purpose of a literature review is to explore, summarise, compare and critically analyse what has been written by other researchers about the topic of your research. (Eriksson and Kovalainen, 2008: 44).

In general, in an academic piece of work, or in academic environments, the term 'literature' usually refers to a range of outputs and published materials – for example, scholarly books, journal articles, websites, newspapers, practitioner magazines, government reports and non-governmental organisational (NGO) reports.

Equally, a literature review can also legitimately draw on wider sources such as television and radio programmes, films, novels and paintings (see illustrative use and discussion of these in, for example, Corbett (1995); Knights and Willmott (1999); Dereli and Stokes (2008) and Panayiotou (2010)). While sources such as film, novels and television can provide useful, stimulating and up-to-date data and information, it is important to make a cautionary about bias and integrity of information also. These forms of source may not be necessarily based on generally accepted or accredited facts, nor have they been through an accepted form of academic review process. This means that the data and information from such sources, depending on the use being made of them, is likely to need cross-referencing and verification by other more academically accredited sources.

## What are primary and secondary sources and primary and secondary data in relation to a literature review?

The various articles, books, documents, outputs and artefacts used in a literature review are often referred to 'sources'. Most of these will be secondary in nature; in other words they were originally written or generated by someone else; however, in the odd case they may be primary, that is, they are outputs that you are involved in generating. This latter case is much rarer. In various ways, both primary and secondary sources may involve or refer to primary and/or secondary data.

### Primary sources linked to primary and secondary data

Primary sources are those sources which you as the researcher have identified and accessed in order to develop the data. These sources might be managers or employers who are respondents and participants in your study.

You are the key agent as the researcher in dealing with primary sources. The data generated are primary data – your primary data – and take the form of, for example, interview recordings and transcripts, focus-group films and recordings, and various forms of questionnaire.

Primary sources may also reveal or draw on secondary sources. For example, a manager in an interview or a questionnaire might refer to a company report. Because the company report was not created by you, unlike the interview in which you learn about it, it constitutes secondary data.

## Secondary sources linked to primary and secondary data

Secondary sources are those sources of data and information which you did not originally create or write. They are sources which were created by a third party. For the most part, the main secondary sources you will be using will be academic articles from journals and academic books and texts. A point to observe here is that these texts have been double-blind reviewed. This means that work will be sent off by an editor to other experts in the field to act as reviewers. These reviewers read the article or text closely and recommend changes and modifications which will improve the text. Other examples of secondary sources include, by way of example only, company reports, a research report from a research agency, a newspaper article, a non-academic book and interview transcripts that another person created from interviews he or she, as the researcher, conducted previously. In the contemporary era, many of these sources will be drawn through internet or other related e-resources.

As far as you are concerned as a researcher, secondary sources will generally contain and offer secondary data. Again, to reiterate, this is because they have been produced and/or authored by somebody else. However, as a small point, from another perspective they do of course contain the original researcher's primary data.

## A summary on sources and data

Primary data are those data which have been collected by the authors of the sources and written up by them. By way of illustration, a qualitative set of primary data could comprise interview transcripts and quotes from interviews conducted by you as part of a research investigation. Alternatively, a quantitative data set could be a statistical correlation analysis you had conducted of employee sickness in relation to the manufacturing production for a given company or overall industrial sector. As indicated, if these data were parts of research you had personally been involved with organising and conducting, then these would be *your* primary data. You would most likely go on to write these data up into a dissertation, project or article which would effectively 'publish' your work in the broadest sense of the word. Once written up your documents, and the data they contain, might then be available as *secondary data* for other people to read and consult (Bryman and Bell, 2007).

Secondary data are those data which have been collected by a third party and/or other authors (as opposed to you) of other works. These data are frequently drawn on, and used, by students and researchers in dissertations, theses, reports, books or articles. A literature review is an examination and critical synthesis of articles, books, internet-based and e-resources and other relevant materials which are secondary sources in relation to your study (Hart, 2001). Every academic paper or book will aim to build its arguments by reference to previous studies and academic writings carried out by other academics, scholars and commentators on the given topic under examination

## What should you make sure you cover in the literature review?

When you are researching a given topic remember that it is highly likely that in some shape or form, somebody somewhere will have considered and examined it previously. The authors of the already published and extant articles and books that you are reading in order to secure information will have already accessed, as part of their own study, many of the publications already in existence. As you are doing, they too will have been obliged to look over literature in relation to the questions they are seeking to answer. This means that other writers are likely to have already done a significant amount of the hard work of pulling information for a literature review together. This is not to say that earlier writers will have accomplished the task for you. Rather, the work they have accomplished may show you their view on, among other things:

i)   The seminal writings in the area;
ii)  The historical narrative and evolution of the writing in a given area;
iii) The different (and often competing) schools of thought in a given area;
iv) The key issues and themes that are being explored currently in the field.

It will be useful to consider these in a little more detail.

### i) Seminal writings in the area

When the term 'seminal' is used in relation to published work it means that the work is considered very significant or important in relation to the evolution and development of the given field. These seminal works will be widely cited or mentioned in other articles and texts on the subject or a given area.

If these works were not to be mentioned in a published account, be it a paper, book or other source, then this may act be considered a serious oversight or missing element of the research being undertaken. Equally, in relation to writing your literature review omitting key books and articles will be considered an oversight. While a literature review is not about trying to write a globally encompassing or exhaustive account of a particular literature (this would be a near impossible task anyway since literature in many areas continues to grow endlessly at a faster and faster rate) there is likely to be an anticipation of the inclusion of certain well-known works from a given subject area or field. This is not to say that your literature review will agree with or subscribe to the ideas and opinions of these key writers and their work. Indeed you may categorically disagree with some writers' views (Cottrell, 2011). It is more a case of showing the various sides of the argument. It will be useful to take a few examples of works likely to appear at some point in relation to particular topics. Of course, the possibilities are many and varied and will change depending on different commentators' views.

If, for example, you were writing on the historical evolution of the following fields then it might be anticipated by your tutor or reader that you will, at some point, refer to the following seminal works:

- *Motivation* - early work referred to in the field is likely to allude to writings by Taylor (1911/1967), Maslow (1970), Herzberg (1966).
- *French management culture* (from an Anglo-Saxon perspective) – this would potentially see reference to base-line work accomplished by Lawrence and Barsoux (1997)
- *Cross Cultural Consequences* (Hofstede, 1980)
- *Marketing* – Kotler (many and various references)

The above examples are by no means givens and absolutes for inclusion in a literature review on the above topics but they might very well be strong contenders for appearing at some point in the historical narrative (discussed below) however briefly. In addition, the undergraduate or postgraduate level of the work is likely to play a role. Whereas the above exemplar articles and books would be most likely to receive a mention, passing or otherwise, at undergraduate level in the case of postgraduate work, generally, the literature review would be anticipated to be more focused on a specific strand or stream of literature and be more in-depth and specific as a consequence (Greenfield, 2000). However, in relation to postgraduate dissertations it is important to note that where a Master's degree is effectively a conversion degree (i.e. the student is coming to a Master's degree in business and management from another discipline, for example Psychology, English, Modern Languages, and Accountancy etc.) then the dissertation will necessarily need to cover the early and basic-level sources. An example of this might be, for example the use and citation of Mullins' excellent and multiple-edition introductory text of Organisational Behaviour.

As a final and further point of complexity, it should be noted (and especially at Master's specialist programme level) that beyond the seminal writers there will also be various perspectives, standpoints, schools of thought which, depending on your research topic and focus, may be considered equally important for reference and inclusion in your dissertation. For example, particular traditions may require you to write in a particular way. Examples of this might include a dissertation couched in the traditions of Critical Management Studies (CMS) or, alternatively and quite differently, Work Psychology. In the case of CMS it would be expected that, for example, postmodern or poststructural philosophical and epistemological approaches (dealing with, for illustration, shifting sensemaking, fragmented realities and identities and discourses) would be expected to inform the methodology and general writing of the dissertation. On the other hand, work psychology might be anticipated to use a range of science-informed and statistical approaches. Echoing this and the overall discussion on seminal sources, Berman-Brown (2006:73) makes the valid point that the act of drawing up a literature review is also an act of legitimising oneself in the eyes of others in relation to the field:

> … the hidden agenda requires you also to establish that you are able to use literature appropriately in evaluating and synthesising the views of others to support your own investigation.

## ii) The historical narrative and evolution of the writing in a given area

When writing a literature review of a given field or topic, it is important to provide some indication of your view of the development of ideas in that area. This often, although not in any mandatory way, follows the approach of providing the older background and then laying out the contemporary situation in relation to this. The older background will indicate the origins of the domain and an outline of early approaches and schools of thought (Ridley, 2012: 25–28). It is important to note that this older background to a given field is most likely to be specific to the particular field. For example, if your dissertation is addressing a question about buyer behaviour within the subject of marketing you will need to access and analyse the very extensive literature on buyer behaviour going back over a number of decades. Equally, to take a different example, if you are writing a dissertation that deals with employee motivation, then there is a considerable historical and contemporary collection of work on this area which will need to be synthesised for, and related to, your argument. It is also important to underline some of the key critical incidents and moments that have brought about changes in thinking and direction of travel in the field leading up to the modern era. None of this needs to be necessarily exhaustive or overly comprehensive within the scope of a dissertation. In some instances it can be succinct and simply map out a number of broad historical lines of development in the field. The precise approach you adopt in relation to the background study will really depend on the title, aims and objectives, and requirements of your work.

Following this overall approach, the literature review then moves on to look at the focal issue of your research. This builds on the above preparatory work and allows you to set and situate your topic and the questions you are investigating about it in relation to a wider context. What emerges from such an analysis is an understanding of the development of strands of ideas. It becomes possible to see the impact of waves, patterns or cycles of thinking, approach and practice in a field. This is significant because it is important to recall that a key role of academic literature is to examine and develop theory in relation to a topic. The act of constructing a sense of this in your work allows you to see how your ideas and research fit into the on-going and overall evolution of the domain you are considering.

The example on 'sustainable and responsible change – cultural and behavioural dimensions' in Vignette 2.1 provides an overview of the points discussed above.

VIGNETTE 2.1

## A case study of a literature review and preceding sections

## Micro-Moments, Choice and Responsibility in Sustainable Organisational Change and Transformation – The Janus Dialectic

Peter Stokes, Chester Business School, University of Chester
Phil Harris, Chester Business School, University of Chester

### Abstract

#### Purpose
To examine the catalytic and pivotal role of micro-moments in organisations and their role in producing the possibility of sustainable or unsustainable change and transformation.

#### Design/Methodology/Approach
The paper employs participant observation within an interpretivistic methodological approach. This provides critical incident vignettes with which to explore issues.

#### Findings
The argument contends that macro-events in relation to either (un)sustainable and (ir)responsible events are rooted in 'micro-moments' centred on behaviour and choices. These myriad choices

occur repeatedly – a dilemma captured by the metaphor of Janus. Underpinned by templates of Aristotelian virtue ethics and Kantian Deontology, the paper argues that consistent 'good' character' and 'good behaviour' are central to ensuring sustainable change. Alternatively, 'bad' character and behaviours have a propensity to engender ambivalent unsustainable and irresponsible environments.

**Social Implications**

The work heightens awareness of seemingly 'insignificant' micro-behaviour in organisations undergoing processes of change. If allowed to occur without redress, negative micro-moments lead to negative impacts on the macro-aspects of the organisation whereas positive moments tend to engender more sustainable and responsible environments.

**Originality/Value**

The paper builds an amalgam of extant literatures on business ethics, organisational behaviour, corporate culture, organisational change management and sustainability and focuses attention on the under-developed phenomenon of the micro-moment.

**Type of Paper**

Conceptual/Empirical

**Keywords:** Micro-moments, virtue ethics, choice, responsible change management.

## Introduction

In the contemporary era, the concept of 'sustainability' has become well established (see Milne, Kearins and Walton (2006); Sharma, Starik and Husted (2007); Banerjee and Shastri (2010); Tams and Marshall (2011); PRME (2011)). Indeed, it would seem that sustainability and its kindred corporate social responsibility (CSR) have come of age but have yet to fully mature.

Indeed, in spite of these laudable developments, reports in the media of corporate scandals, dilemmas and disingenuous organisational behaviour remain commonplace. These macro-level misdemeanours are remotely witnessed by a public who, themselves, regularly experience difficult situations in *everyday* work, or 'micro'-domains/lives. Conversely, it is important to say that people also, of course, engage in positive relations grounded in what might be viewed as 'responsible' or 'good' ethical behaviour (McEwan, 2001; Crane and Matten, 2010). There is, therefore, potential to note a complex dialectic between competing micro- and macro-spheres. This dialectic is echoed in sustainable-unsustainable and responsible-irresponsible behaviour, cohabiting in a conjoined spatial and temporal manner that is not always *prima facie* apparent. The paper, through the application of the metaphor of the twin-headed Janus, explores these dialectics in change management contexts and focuses attention on micro-moments of choice and action and their implications for macro-situations.

## Sustainable and Responsible Change – Cultural and Behavioural Dimensions

In the late twentieth and early twenty-first centuries, 'sustainability' and 'responsibility' have emerged as independent domains underpinned by bodies of academic and practitioner commentary. Sustainability has infused many public areas, including economics and consumption, tourism, public affairs, architecture and higher education (Bell and Morse, 2008; Black, 2010; Harris, 2010; Stibbe, 2009; Wright 2003). Sustainability unavoidably informs the epochal *zeitgeist*. Elkington (1997) introduced the notion of the 'triple bottom line' (TBL) of *profit, people, planet* asserting that a business that does not develop a TBL approach is not properly mindful of its full impacts. Thus, good corporate citizenship embraces, *inter alia,* green, environmental, self-sufficiency, eco-preneurship, energy-efficiency, carbon footprint policies, and values and beliefs (Dixon and Clifford, 2007; Berners-Lee, 2010; Strawbridge and Strawbridge, 2010). However, in spite of the appeals of Elkington and others, much of the debate on sustainably changing organisations has been couched in terms of corporate *ends*: competitive advantage, cost savings or enhanced reputation and profits rather than altruistic or idealistic purposes (see EFMD, 2010).

## Rephrasing Normative Characterisations of Sustainable Change.

The juncture of the individual and the organisational collective (i.e. the micro and the macro) allows our gaze to turn to the micro-level. Central to ideas of sustainable and responsible behaviour at the micro-level are the *attitudes*, *values and mindsets* (Kira, Van Eijnatten and Balkin, 2010; Marcum, 2009). However, discussions in relation to these are often rooted in a performativity-oriented normative frames of reference (here, 'normative' can be characterised as generally espousing rationalistic, objectified, quasi-scientific approaches rather than subjectivised, 'lived experience' and rich appreciations of organisation and management (Knights and Willmott, 1999; Stokes, 2011). This mode exudes a *modernistic and managerialist* tone, whereby it is primarily management rather than other employees who are viewed as having the function and authority to bring to fruition agendas on sustainability (Stokes, 2011). Of course, managers *are* invested with authority to direct change in organisational affairs, but we should acknowledge that, on occasion, they may conduct their responsibilities in an unethical or irresponsible manner. Moreover, to privilege the role of management ignores the crucial contribution of a majority of other organisational employees. Thus, there is scope to reconsider sustainable and responsible approaches to change and process in a manner that moves beyond its current macro-discursive, rhetorical and normative representations. Development of a deeper understanding of micro-level sustainable and responsible behaviour and micro-moments will provide foundations for more effective change and transformatory processes in organisations.

## Introducing the Micro-Moment: Good, Bad, Grey-Zones and Choice

'Micro-moment' is a term that has received attention in populist media. For example, typical of this reportage is *The Los Angeles Times* (Roan, 2009) heading: 'The key to happiness is living in the micro-moment'. The subsequent article evokes the spirit of much of this genre of commentary emphasising *carpe diem* (seize the day) and the importance of the 'now' rather than postponing action.

Within management writing, it is interesting to consider the concept of 'Moments of Truth' as associated with Jan Carlzon, the former CEO of SAS Airlines (Carlzon and Peters, 1989). Carlzon underscores the crucial nature of every moment of customer interaction and, reflecting The Ten Commandments, he proposes examples of 'Moments of Truth':

When a customer walks through the door
When a customer asks a question
When a customer returns a product

Carlzon states that when a passenger boards a plane and notices litter and coffee stains on the seat and table, this represents a moment of truth. The customer might rightly ask that 'if this is the state of the cabin, is the same level of attention being accorded to more critical, technical aspects of the flight such as engine?' While there is a managerialistic tone common to Carlzon-style management edicts, that is, 'people are our most important resource', they are nevertheless valuable in drawing attention to the criticality and widespread nature of the 'moment'. Allusions to 'moments' are present in additional management writing including, for example, leadership and coaching literatures. Shaw (2010) presents 'Defining Moments' in peoples' lives.

In the present paper the term 'micro-moments' is employed to mean the many and varied interactions and minute events of the everyday life. These crystallise into the macro-situations that go towards forming ideas of culture, situations and atmospheres. Micro-moments consist of the dialectics and dualities of individual dubious and honourable conduct embracing a potent cocktail of *inter alia* Machiavellian-style gossip, lies, naivety, deceit, political manoeuvring jostling with aspirations of hope integrity, honesty, directness, reputation and wisdom – often simultaneously in any given moment or incident (Machiavelli, 1532/2008; Harris, Lock and Rees, 2000; Kessler, 2007). Within these often fleeting incidental moments, how managers and employees respond to issues of choice and responsibility is paramount. This is not simply a base question of organisational politics or micro-political survival in the organisational 'jungle' or what Stokes and Gabriel (2011 drawing on its originator Levi 1986/1988: 25–26) remind us is the 'Grey Zone' of ambivalent human behaviour. Rather it is driven by a desire for notions of satisfaction, happiness – the Aristotelian *eudemonia* – well-being and to live and co-habit in an environment that exudes a sense, albeit often highly subjective, of being decent, honourable, meaningful and worthwhile. This then would constitute an approach towards a notional *ideal* of a responsible and sustainable organisation. In their analysis of Levi's work, Stokes and Gabriel (2010) do not endorse the inevitability of 'Grey Zone' behaviour, rather, citing Frankl, they underscore the severe challenges that the choices within and at the margins of the Grey Zone can present:

> We who lived in the concentration camps can remember the men
> who walked through the huts comforting others, giving away their

last piece of bread. They may have been few in number, but they offer sufficient proof that everything can be taken from a man but one thing: the last of the human freedoms – to choose one's attitude in any given set of circumstances, to choose one's own way.

And there were always choices to make. Every day, every hour, offered the opportunity to make a decision, a decision which determined whether or not you would become the plaything of circumstance, renouncing freedom and dignity to become moulded *into the form of the typical inmate*. (Frankl, 1946) [Emphasis added].

Therefore, sustainable organisational life is accomplished through the building of responsible values and principles in myriad micro-situations. Vitally, this is not something that can be adhered to in one moment and allowed to become lax in the next. Rather, sustainable 'good' behaviour must be adhered to assiduously through multifarious choices and situations of everyday 'lived experience'. People *remember* and in particular experience the notion of 'remembered pain' from negative micro-moments which makes people wary of future interactions. As such, individuals' experiences accumulate and negative or positive reputation, made or lost in micro-moments, is accorded. The work environment does not unfortunately present 'clean' and clear-cut situations and choices, and there is constant invitation and temptation to enter 'Grey Zone' situations and behaviour and become, as Frankl expresses, a 'typical inmate'. In this way, a Janus-like Dialectic of sustainable/responsible and unsustainable/irresponsible actions and behaviours emerges at the heart of the organisation. They live potentially side-by-side and it is the choice by the individual towards the responsible (as opposed to irresponsible) actions and postures that will determine the success of the micro-moment of lived experience. On this depends the sustainability of the processes of organisational change at macro-levels – the micro-moment becomes the 'thin end of the wedge' for the macro-moment.

## Change, Behaviour and Ethical Frameworks – the Janus Dialectic of Sustainable Behaviour

Both macro-, but especially micro-behaviour, are potentially informed by a range of ethical frameworks. Within business ethics, 'good' and 'bad' behaviour – pertaining to responsible and sustainable conduct in

organisations – illustrates the manners in which individuals continue
to behave in ways that might be judged by others as 'bad' or 'good'. In
considering ethical behaviour in the micro-moment, the work on 'virtue
ethics' conducted by the ancient Greek philosopher Aristotle (384–322 BC)
is helpful and in his exploration of desirable human and ethical conduct in
the challenges of life, he stated that the development of 'character' was key.
This contrasted with, for example, attempts to develop prescriptive bodies of
rules and codes on behaviour.

   In other words, by developing personality and character of the individual
Aristotle contended that he or she would innately *be*, or have a nature
of a certain *positive* manner. This, in turn, is conducive to an individual,
conducting him or herself in an appropriate manner in the situations and
contexts that arise. Therefore, Aristotle appeals for the 'ethical individual'
rather than aiming to control behaviour through a set of rules or codes,
externally developed and imposed (MacIntyre, 1981; Fisher and Lovell,
2008).

   Aristotle's postulation contrasts with the deontological position
developed by Immanuel Kant (1724–1804). Kant argued that the path
towards 'good' ethical behaviour was through the progressive development
of the notion of the categorical imperative (Chryssides and Kaler, 1999;
Hartman and DesJardins, 2007). This imperative would build rules for
appropriate conduct that could be accepted and constituted a canon of
ethical behaviour. Rules, so devised, could be proposed as universally
applicable principles. Kant's position is commonly summarised as 'do unto
others as you would have done unto yourself' and exemplified by generic
codes such as The Ten Commandments. Thus, deontology offers rules to
guide behaviour and steer choice – *what we should do*, whereas pursuit of
virtue ethics tells us *how we should be* – and this good *being* will engender
the 'good' behaviour. It can be argued that both have a role to play in
personal and professional organisational life. On the one hand, we hope
for people to have a disposition that is inherently 'good', and yet at the
same time we may acknowledge that we need rules to guide people to
behave well or appropriately. Therefore, the crux for the present argument
is that the micro-moment is *the* instant of choice – a choice between
dialectics of good and bad positions, rights and wrongs, greater and lesser
evils – which have ultimate implications for responsible and sustainable

action and atmospheres in a given corporate culture. Corporate culture has been extensively commented in the wider literature, and it is not the intention within the space of the present argument to overly rehearse that literature here. Nevertheless, culture is highlighted as a crucial aspect of change management situations and is extensively commented in general management and change the literature (Mayo, 1946; Deal and Kennedy, 1982; Schein, 1990; Johnson and Duberley, 2011).

More importantly for the purposes of the present discussion, choices, values and beliefs of the individual at the micro-level go to produce the amalgam of group atmospheres and cultures. Cultures, therefore, are the sum of the micro-moments that make and remake those particular cultures in an on-going basis. In this way, the corporate sustainability-corporate unsustainability dialectic presents itself in something of a Janus-like manner.

In Roman mythology, Janus was the two-headed god who symbolised gateways, doorways, beginnings and endings in relation to time – in other words, the portals of choice of direction, action or movement. Metaphorically, therefore, as sustainable and unsustainable behaviour might seem to point in contrasting trajectories, so too do Janus' two heads look in opposite directions. Yet, paradoxically, akin to the heads of Janus that reside on a single body, so too sustainability and unsustainability, along with responsibility and irresponsibility, spatially co-habit side-by-side in the *same organisation*. Equally, choices and consequences within organisational change contexts align with the Janus notion of choices to move through alternative possible portals and gateways leading to potentially very distinct and contrasting destinations and outcomes. Through this analogy, the overall inference is that the proximity of good–bad, responsible–irresponsible and sustainable–unsustainable in the moment of choice in change and transformation settings is more apparent and centrally located in the micro-moment than might *prima facie* be apparent. Crucially, however, herein there is no intention to cast the issue of individual choice in any given micro-moment into a relativistic and inconclusive morass. Rather, the purpose is to explore positions between Aristotelian *being* and Kantian *adhering* behaviours in relation to which organisational actors, and hence organisations, can develop sustainable and responsible organisational atmospheres and cultures. The argument now turns towards a field illustration of these phenomena.

*[n.b. The paper then moves into the Methodology Section of the article. Please also note that this text was provided here for the purposes of writing approach and therefore the references employed have not been provided in order to economise space.]*

Source: Stokes, P. and Harris, P. (2012) Micro-moments, choice and responsibility in sustainable organisational change and transformation: The Janus Dialectic *Journal of Organisational Change Management*, 25 (4): 595–611 (Emerald Publishing).

The example, specifically relating to the 'Sustainable and Responsible Change' sub section, illustrates that the argument is addressing a particular period in the first sentence. This is the topic sentence and it sets the over-riding theme and tone for the rest of the paragraph. The follow on sentence 'Sustainability has infused…' serves the purpose of illustrating the extent to which the phenomena of sustainable and responsible change have entered different spheres of life and activity. As is common practice for a broad statement and the opening general part of the discussion, this is supported by a range of indicative and pertinent references. The introduction of the reference to Elkington effectively 'plants a marker' for the argument and indicates that Elkington laid down the idea of 'profit' as being an important idea alongside people and planet. The final stage of the paragraph starts to turn and introduce the central argument of the paper taking issue with rhetoric of many companies in relation to their sincerity towards sustainable and responsible management. Thus, this above passage illustrates the way in which an argument is introduced and positioned in relation to the historical and the contemporary aspects of a given topic, sphere and literature.

## iii) The different (and often competing) schools of thought in a given area

The issue of different schools of thought was introduced and briefly elaborated in points (i) and (ii) above. The creation of knowledge is not necessarily a neutral, unbiased or apolitical act. People develop ideas, theories and approaches for a range of reasons and motives. This work is underpinned by beliefs and values to which they are likely to adhere very strongly. Equally, other writers may have alternative views and challenge the views of differing and contrasting approaches. Sometimes these exchanges can be quite intense.

By way of example it will be useful to provide an illustration of a real example of such an exchange. Quite often an academic will develop an assertion and an argument on a particular matter or topic. This will cause other academics, with competing views, to challenge the argument and make a counter assertion. This happens quite regularly between the adherents in a given school or approach. It can also occur between commentators aligned to different, contrasting and opposing schools.

A useful illustration of this can be seen in the argument between Wray-Bliss and Collinson involving Wray-Bliss' (2002) paper and Collinson's (2002) response to it, in the journal *Organisation*. Wray Bliss' paper 'Abstract Ethics, Embodied Ethics: The Strange Marriage of Foucault and Positivism in Labour Process Theory' levels a number of criticisms at the apparently conflicting philosophical and methodological stances adopted by writers operating within the approach (school) known as Labour Process Theory (LPT). Typically, LPT has traditionally focused its attention, although latterly not exclusively, on the experiences, alienation, conditions and situation of rank and file employees rather than management. Broadly stated LPT engages with Marxist theoretical and socialist-inspired ideas in order to comment on the working conditions of organisations. Wray-Bliss is writing the paper from a Critical Management Studies (CMS) perspective. The principles and characteristics of CMS ideas, which extensively employ poststructuralist and postmodernist ideas, are often seen to conflict with LPT. In his paper, Wray-Bliss takes strong issue with the use of the French philosopher Michel Foucault's postmodernist work by some writers within the LPT School claiming that they misuse and misinterpret Foucault's ideas and writings. In a later issue of the journal, Collinson is provided with an opportunity to respond and produces an incisive attack on Wray-Bliss' arguments.

These tensions between differing perspectives and arguments are common to all fields and differing schools of thought. You are likely to encounter them on a regular basis. It is important to be able to demonstrate some awareness of these types of arguments and positions. Further and more in-depth discussion is conducted in Chapter 3 which deals with research methodologies.

### iv) The key issues and themes that are being explored currently in the field

In a literature review it is important to demonstrate that you understand what are the key issues and debates taking place in the field. Expressed more colloquially these would represent the 'hot topics' of the day. It may well be the case that your chosen subject and research focus is one of these areas. If it is a topic that has recently garnered interest from writers, then there may be a relatively small literature on it as not enough time will have passed to allow the writing and publishing to take place.

Alternatively, if it is a topic that has been more or less under discussion for a number of years, then the body and variety of literature will be greater. Again, do remember that many writers will already have conducted literature reviews within their own publications and these will be of great assistance to you in facilitating your summary of the salient themes and issues under debate in a given area.

On occasion, the purpose of some articles is to set out to be a literature review *per se*. This means that the whole paper is dedicated to being a review and summary of the writings on a given area rather than conducting fresh primary research. These are a great help to anyone trying to gain a rapid sense of the scope and range of a given field. To find these sorts of article the first point of call should be your college, institute or university library facilities. Alternatively, consult a journals database, Google Scholar or a less commercial search engine (e.g. Tahoma) and type in your subject area or topic + literature review, as in the example, 'Organisational Learning Literature review' or 'Corporate Culture Literature Review'.

There are also some journals or other publications which expressly focus on and produce reviews. An illustration of this type of publication would be the *International Journal of Management Reviews*, sister journal of the British Journal of Management and the flagship publications of the British Academy of Management. With a view to portraying the sorts of title and area that are addressed in the Journal, it will be useful to cite a range of illustrative work that has been published in recent years:

- Role of Cognitive Styles in Business and Management: Reviewing 40 Years of Research (Armstrong, Cools and Sadler-Smith, 2012).
- A Review of Theory in Family Business Research: The Implications for Corporate Governance (Siebels and Knyphausen-Aufseß, 2012).
- The Internationalization of Chinese Firms: A Critical Review and Suggestions for Future Research (Deng, 2012).

There is therefore a considerable amount of work that has already been accomplished and is already in existence in relation to a wide range of fields. When you are undertaking your dissertation and research, time will seem like a precious commodity and you will want to use it as economically and efficiently as possible. Literature reviews that have already been conducted in journals can be of great assistance in summarising and understanding an area rapidly and effectively.

### Where to start on the literature review and how to identify and avoid common pitfalls?

As indicated above, many early researchers writing articles, or students doing a research dissertation or thesis, are daunted by the prospect of completing a literature review. Common situations and pitfalls are:

- You will see a world of possible materials all around you – books, journals, libraries, internet, television, radio, lectures and presentations. You may immediately feel overwhelmed by this and remain in limbo, feeling somewhat powerless. As a consequence your actions may seem disorganised and fragmented;

- You might turn up to your first supervisory meeting with a particular book, article, newspaper column, website that has caught your imagination and interest and generally this is to be commended. However, sometimes it can also be a misguided first step because it can be a fixation to the exclusion of other things;
- You simply feel lost about how to start ... and so you vacillate and achieve little or nothing.

In response to these common dilemmas you can:

- Spend time becoming clearer about your title by following the advice and guidelines in the previous chapter. Once you have a reasonably clear idea of the title, aims and objectives, and also the research questions you intend to follow, this will provide direction on how to approach the literature;
- You should develop search or key-terms. A good starting point here is to look over your draft title, aims and objectives, and your proposed research questions (if you have these already formulated) and identify the nouns or terms employed within them. Alternatively, you might look over the terms used in the probable and intended disciplinary subject areas on which you are thinking of basing your study. These actions are almost certainly likely to produce your initial key search terms. The same can be done for the research questions, aims and objectives.

As you start to search library catalogues and electronic databases with your identified search terms remember to keep a brief note and list of:

- the word you searched with;
- the number of articles it returned;
- the date you typed in the search term;
- which database/library catalogue you typed it into ;
- any new search terms and key words revealed to you
  (www.library.manchester.ac.uk, 2013).

Following this simple but effective procedure will enable you to see which terms generate the most information. Some key words will not generate many articles or sources at all. Others will be very fruitful providing many interesting articles and documents for you to follow up in more detail. If you do not keep a list you will almost certainly forget when and where you searched and you risk repeating previous searches and wasting time. However, do remember that databases get updated and therefore it is important to date your searches so you can consider whether it would be timely to re-conduct a search on a particular database you looked at earlier in order to see if new information has been added. In conducting your dissertation or research work/project you will usually be part of, and connected to, a particular faculty or department. Therefore, universities and colleges usually have a liaison librarian who is familiar with the collection in a particular subject area. In the case of, for example, Business, Management and Organisation, there will probably be librarian staff who will be able to advise and direct you. Liaison librarians will be aware of the most up-to-date resources and it is important to develop a constructive and fruitful relationship with these people.

The above issue raises a further point concerning literature bases. Your key words or your search terms will direct you towards particular areas of literature. For example, if you were studying corporate culture you might think of looking through some of the following indicative literatures:

- *Human Resource Management;*
- *Organisational Behaviour;*
- *Strategy;*
- *Change Management;*
- *Work Psychology.*

Alternatively, if you are looking at, for instance, a title such as *The Creation of Meaning and Identity in Interactions between Employees and Customers*, then, depending on the angle of your analytical interest and your attempt to find out more about 'meaning', such a study might possibly lead you towards a number of areas of, for example, Critical Management Studies literature areas including topics such as:

- *(Organisational) Discourse Analysis;*
- *Identity;*
- *Employee Relations*

Equally, topics from the literature of Marketing may provide valuable materials, for example:

- *Consumer and Buyer Behaviour;*
- *Neuro-Marketing.*

All of these are well-formed topic areas within the overall sphere of the Business and Management Organisational disciplines.

The direction you actually take in relation to grounding your work in a particular literature base will be entirely dependent on your beliefs and the arguments you wish to make. In the case study literature review illustrated in Vignette 2.1 above, it can be seen that the paper draws on a number of literature bases. These include ethics, sustainability, organisational behaviour and change management. The ethics and the organisational behaviour literatures are addressed reasonably extensively and constantly throughout the discussion of the paper.

You will notice in the above example that the discussion of the literature tends to move from a discussion of general aspects of the subject in the initial or early part of the dissertation to more specific dimensions of the topic in the latter sections of the dissertation. In this way, the discussion should move from a broad and wide-ranging opening presentation of the topic and then move on to funnel down and focus in on the specific arguments with which you wish to deal. Alternatively expressed, these form what Philips and Pugh (2010) have respectively termed the *'background'* and the *'focal'* literature of the literature review. In the vignette example above, the sections on sustainability and change management tend to form a *background literature* or canvas against which to form the argument while the organisational behaviour aspects on micro-moments work to develop the focal literature. Overall, the literature development in the paper illustrated in the case study Vignette 2.1 above has the ambition of developing a rich context against which to explore the idea of 'choice' in organisational situations and, in order to achieve this, builds a title and approach, and draws on these particular literatures.

## RECAP AND FINAL THOUGHTS ON 'DOING' A LITERATURE REVIEW

### What does the act of 'doing' a literature review involve?

A summary of key strategies to create a strong literature review are shown in Figure 2.1 below. Each strategy will be discussed in more detail in this section. When you embark on a piece of research, be it a dissertation or paper, as discussed above, you are often told that you need to look at and *review* the literature that has been written in the area. As discussed in Chapter 1, your title, aims and objectives will be very important in guiding you towards which areas of writing and literature you should be accessing and reading. Simply stated, this means you have to look at what

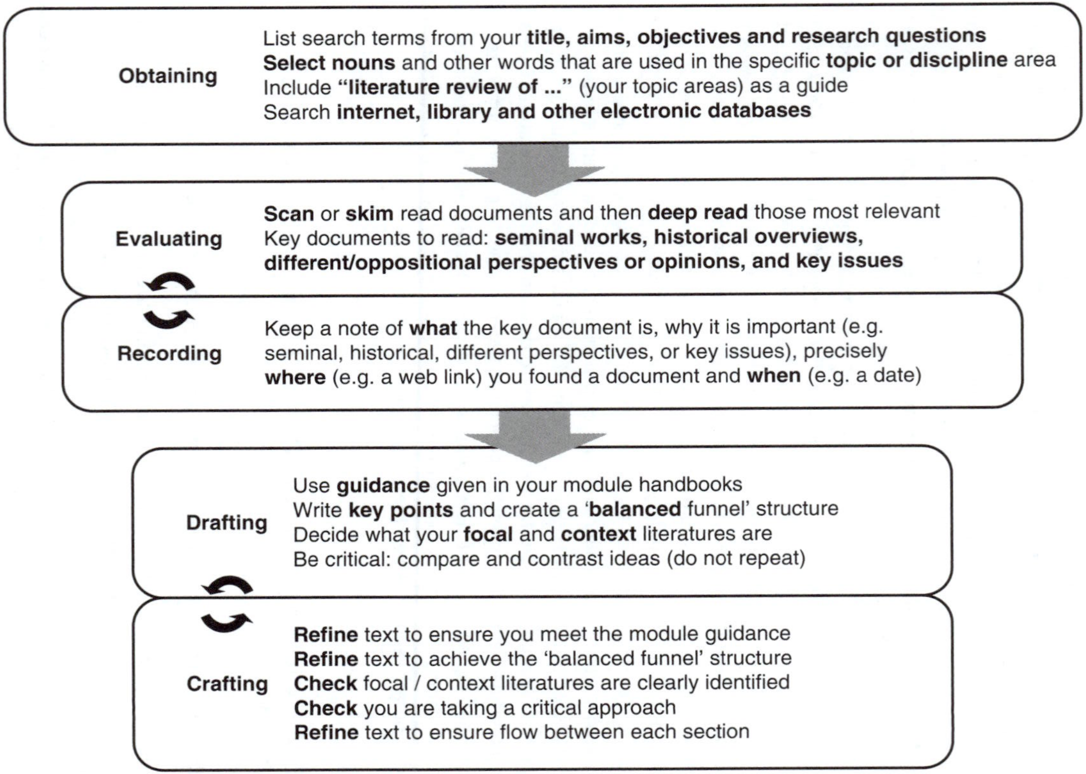

**Obtaining**

List search terms from your **title, aims, objectives and research questions**
**Select nouns** and other words that are used in the specific **topic or discipline** area
Include **"literature review of …"** (your topic areas) as a guide
Search **internet, library and other electronic databases**

**Evaluating**

**Scan** or **skim** read documents and then **deep read** those most relevant
Key documents to read: **seminal works, historical overviews, different/oppositional perspectives or opinions, and key issues**

**Recording**

Keep a note of **what** the key document is, why it is important (e.g. seminal, historical, different perspectives, or key issues), precisely **where** (e.g. a web link) you found a document and **when** (e.g. a date)

**Drafting**

Use **guidance** given in your module handbooks
Write **key points** and create a **'balanced** funnel' structure
Decide what your **focal** and **context** literatures are
Be critical: compare and contrast ideas (do not repeat)

**Crafting**

**Refine** text to ensure you meet the module guidance
**Refine** text to achieve the 'balanced funnel' structure
**Check** focal / context literatures are clearly identified
**Check** you are taking a critical approach
**Refine** text to ensure flow between each section

**Figure 2.1** Key strategies for creating and writing a literature review

people have already said about the subject and identify the recurrent and key themes and issues. It also means seeing who are considered to be the major commentators in the area and the various positions and arguments they adopt. This usually involves starting with a broad coverage and review of a general domain and then focussing in on the areas particularly relevant to your identified topic.

Writings and literature in any given area have usually been taking place for some time. Obviously, in relation to very newly emerging phenomena and topics the writing will have started later and there will usually be less written and produced on it. However, that having been said, it should be noted that even newly emergent areas and topics can be related and contextualised, in some way or other, in relation to some fields or events that have preceded it chronologically. An example here might be the relatively new areas of *coaching* or *talent management* (Stewart and Rigg, 2011). If you were writing on these areas then you might possibly use the backdrop of the very extensive *management training and development* literature, or, alternatively, the *organisational development* or *organisational learning* writings may be of value.

Once you have established your key words or search terms based on your title and research questions, most researchers will generally go to two places in order to secure information: a library and electronic databases. Remember that journals are often published in paper and electronic format. It is possible, although costs may prevent it, that your library or information source will store both forms. In the case of looking through the library catalogue, it may be that your search terms produce a list of books and materials that contain directly comparable terms in the title of the books and other items. However, it is often necessary to look through books in order to identify specific chapters as the main title may allude only generally to your topic. In these instances, the rest of the book may not be useful; however, a particular chapter within the text may be.

On the other hand, electronic resources, especially in relation to journals, are a central aspect of research in general and a literature review in particular. There are a range of electronic databases available, and often it will be a question of which databases your institution or organisation subscribes to or are generally available to you. Google Scholar™ is also a useful resource; however, in general, it is important to be careful with internet sources because their accuracy cannot always be relied on (see Vignette 2.2 for a word on Wikipedia™).

The key *caveat* here is to make sure that you subsequently *cross-check* the information from a more reliable source such as a research journal article or a reputable book. In addition, sometimes literature and secondary information may come from specific places, such as a corporate report or a company document. It is important not to ignore such possibilities in favour of books and journals, as they may reveal up-to-date and revealing insights (Lee (2012: 389–407) in Symon and Cassel (2012)).

## A word on Wikipedia™

Wikipedia™ is a well-known website that contains entries and information on a vast range of topics. The key feature, of course, is that the entries are written and updated by members of the public.

The fact that anybody can place or amend an entry has brought many people to challenge and question the usefulness, authority and validity of using Wikipedia™ as a reliable source of information. Many, indeed perhaps even a majority of academics, condemn and ridicule the website and its page contents. They point out that it has not been subjected to the usual academic rigorous double-blind review process that works to ensure high-quality and verified articles and outputs. All of these cautionary notes and tones are of course pertinent, valuable and important. However, it may be worthwhile to take a step back.

In their response to Wikipedia™ it may also be possible to detect a slightly reactionary and elitist tone from some critiques. This has been the case up to the point that the outcome, ironically, has been a surprisingly populist, almost unthinking, adoption of negative postures towards accessing material and ideas from this online site. Even people who do not generally use the site might trot out a clichéd and rhetorical repetition of this general denigration of the site's worth. This is unfortunate. It is time to take a fresh look at how we engage with Wikipedia™.

Nobody is saying that we have to automatically and unquestioningly believe what is on Wikipedia™. Indeed, surely, as researchers we should have this questioning and analytical posture in relation to all and any sources. Wikipedia™ can be excellent in order to get a first idea on the central thrust and the general scope of an area or topic. This provides you with a rough set of clues that you may or may not decide to pursue. In a world with an almost endless and inexhaustible flow of information and documents, Wikipedia™ provides an anti-elitist, generally liberal-style entry point in order to gain an overview of a field.

What you should always do is go to a more academic source to cross-reference, authentic and validate what you have found of interest in Wikipedia™. You can gain a first impression from the website if you need to get a rapid grasp on an area and then go more deeply into the information in other sources. Obviously, you should never use information from Wikipedia™, or many internet sources, without cross-checking with other written sources.

As a final note, in spite of the comments above, while you may access Wikipedia™ as part of facilitating your search, given the attitudes of many people as outlined above, it would not be a good idea to cite it in your references for your research piece or document.

Wilson (2010: 59–61) outlines some basic and useful phases of the typical literature review – 'obtain literature, evaluate, recording the literature, start drafting review'. This basic but useful outline can be employed in order to introduce some original and fresh ideas into the process:

- *Obtain literature* – This stage really encompasses much of what has been said above. In addition, remember to use the contents pages and the index of a text in order to assess in a rapid manner the value and usefulness of the book or part of the text.
- *Evaluate* – Make judgements regarding the quality of the material.
- *Review* – Reading academic articles can be very stimulating; however, it can also be hard work and challenging. This is particularly the case when the paper is using highly technical or sociological sources. This can make working your way through materials very difficult indeed. In an attempt to be able to address these specific issues, texts such as Stokes (2011) *Critical Concepts in Management and Organisation Studies*, Palgrave Macmillan, have been produced with the aim of providing rapid and easy insights into the terminology and language used in academic papers. There are a few additional strategies that can be used here. Firstly, take an initial look at the abstract of the piece. If it is reasonably well written this will provide you with an overview of the focus, scope, methodology employed, and findings and assertions of the work. Based on this it should be possible to decide whether it is of interest and whether it is worth looking at further. Equally, it is possible to skim and scan the article. Broadly, this means looking at the key headings, the initial paragraphs, taking in the abstract and conclusion of the article, chapter or piece. Doing this will enable you to get a very quick but reliable feel for the nature and potential contribution of the source. As you become aware and more expert in the literature in your field you will also be able to look at the references and bibliographies and very quickly establish the sources and debates that an article, for example, is employing to build its arguments.

It is important to remember that something of a hierarchy of validity of sources operates in academia: the *most highly valued sources* tend to be the *highly ranked journals*. This is because the articles they contain will have been subjected to a series of reviews and revisions before they are accepted for publication. Many articles will be rejected during the course of these processes. Next in the order of value and validity come the lesser ranked journals. There are a number of journal-ranking guides. While it is not at all anticipated that students will necessarily look up the ranking of journals when conducting their literature review, it will nevertheless be useful to signal the existence of, and examine, two such examples: the Association of Business Schools (ABS) Guide (UK) (www.associationbusinessschools.org (2013)) and the Guide assembled by Anna Wil-Harzing (www.harzing.com (2013)). Both of these particular guides provide extensive materials in relation to the perceived quality and ranking of journals. These forms of tables can play a useful role in allowing you to become familiar with the available journals and make judgements in relation to them for your research and writing. Books and book chapters tend to be valued next. Following this, outputs like corporate reports, newspapers, etc. internet websites come at the end of most commentators' lists in terms of value. While you may rarely consult the above ranking tables, nevertheless, at undergraduate level your work should demonstrate a competency in handling the range of sources. At postgraduate level you will be expected to handle the sources in your argument with greater fluency and eloquence.

## Recording

Always make sure you record or note down, electronically or otherwise, the reference or source fully and correctly at the time of first finding it and keep all of them in the same place, so that they are easily findable when you are writing up. References can of course be laid out in a range of different systems including, most typically, for example Harvard, and alternatively APA style. Detailed and up-to-date guidance on these systems is widely available on the internet and within your college or university teaching and learning and also library facilities.

It is also important to note that your University, College or Business School is likely to have its own stipulations regarding which referencing system should be followed. It is vital that you identify this either in your dissertation handbook or some other relevant and available guidelines supplied in your institution.

Using referencing software such as End Note™ can help with the sorting and retrieval of references. Software of this type is widely available and, if used from the outset of your research and study, can play an important role in easing and facilitating handling references in your work. Bibliographic software such as End Note™ allows you to collect and collate the references of articles, chapters and books that you consult for your dissertation. As you come across and use a particular set of ideas and information from a source, you enter the details into the data entry panels of the software package. This then allows you to subsequently retrieve and automatically insert, at will, any reference you wish into the text and as a component of you bibliography and reference list at the end of the dissertation. Equally, a further feature of these forms of software is that if you ever need to change the references in your work from one referencing system to another, for example, from Harvard referencing system to APA-style referencing, then the software can accomplish this in a couple of easy touch-button steps.

Accurate referencing is imperative. It is also all too common to spend wasted hours chasing round for the missing reference as you are trying to complete your literature review. The reference you happen to have overlooked and are missing will inevitably be a vital one for part of your material and will take an inordinate amount of time to identify later on! Best to note it fully and properly first time round.

## Drafting review

It is often a good idea (especially in this age of information technology) to write your notes straight into sections of your work and begin to form the chapters and sections of your literature review. This will save duplication and will enable you to see your ideas forming and taking shape as your write. Many metaphors and illustrations are possible here. Firstly, there is the possibility of seeing the chapters, and the sections within the chapters, as 'buckets' in which you straightforwardly dump and craft ideas. This is often a very easy, useful and rapid method for moving through complex and diverse materials. It provides a way of deciding on whether information is useful or not. The second analogy is to use the metaphor of sculpting an object, say a lion, out of a solid block of stone. 'How does one do this?' – 'You chip off all the bits that continue to not look like a lion!' This seemingly simple statement belies a serious point. Producing your literature review, or indeed any part of your work, is a gradual and progressive exercise in building and shaping. Judgement will be required for this and this is something you progressively develop. It is only through practising your writing sections in various drafts, and having something in relation to which you can compare new material with, that you will be able to hone your skills. Clearly, the opposite of this might be to keep thinking about your work and to carry it endlessly around in your mind, rarely committing things to working notes. This latter approach generally leads to confusion, procrastination and the problems and pitfalls described at the start of this Chapter.

The above points lead on to an objective all writers should seek – to write with confidence and purpose. This means that you develop a balanced argument but, equally, when you have marshalled enough evidence you are not afraid or reluctant to state a view on the material. This is important, since all too often developing writers of literature reviews and other texts tend to write too descriptively and hesitantly. This should be avoided wherever possible. In the Vignette 2.1 case study above it is possible to see an illustration of these forms of assertion emerging in the discussion. The authors are discussing the thoughts of Frankl (1946) and Levi's (1986/1988) notion of the 'Grey Zone'. At this point the argument makes some strong assertions which declare the authors' beliefs, but this is based on the argument that had been developed up to that point in the paper. A key guide here is the notion of *information*, *implication* and *inference*. First you state the information or point. Then you tell the reader what it means (implication) and what you would like him or her to understand in relation to your argument from the ideas you have introduced. Then, subsequently and based on all this, you make an assertion based on the first two steps and you try to convince the reader about this assertion (inferences(s)).

You also need to recognise that a literature review will take time; therefore, make sure that you start working on it a number of months ahead of the submission or delivery date for the completed assignment, work or output. Remember also that doing a literature review can, at times, seem like a laborious and challenging task because there is so much material to move through. If you feel like this you will not be the first person to think so – drive on and be tenacious. The next section will demonstrate what a literature review might look like and an approach to begin developing it. This will hopefully assist in overcoming feelings of anxiety about starting the review. Also, it is worth keeping in mind that these feelings and emotions quite often continue right up to the end of the literature review writing process.

A common error when starting out on a literature review is to commence by deciding to make an enormous amount of notes on sources. If this is the approach adopted, it often means that you are no closer to actually writing the review. You will have simply translated the complexity of the literature into a fresh body of notes and observations that you will have to analyse and reinterpret all over again later on.

### Re-reading and re-crafting your literature review

When you sense that your literature review is nearing completion of a first draft, it is a useful practice to plan to read over it in a range of different ways. These ways are:

- to read it for chronological and thematic flow;
- to check that the argument of your work is 'funnel' shaped;

- to ensure that you have written it so that new information follows old information;
- to check the language in your work – using a thesaurus and verifying register (*register* refers to choice and use of the appropriate 'level' of language employed. If, for example, in your dissertation you are discussing a 'major' change in the economy then the use of the word 'major' is formal, appropriate and fitting to the level and tone of a formal academic text. However, if a more simple, or even childish, word such as 'huge', 'big' – as was once witnessed in an early draft of a dissertation 'whopper' – these would be very inappropriate to the level and register of the text. The topic and issue of register is discussed further below.)
- to check that you have been critically analytical.

### *Chronological and thematic flow of the literature review*

Firstly, it is important to read over the overall literature review starting at the beginning and moving through to the end. The purpose of this first re-reading is to check that each paragraph logically follows on from the preceding one(s). In essence, this is a check that the narrative of your literature review flows and is coherent. Structure and fluidity of the narrative in a literature review is of enormous importance. Wilson (2010: 69–71) rightly points out that a literature review will have an introduction, a main body of the review and a conclusion. This is of course akin to the well-known observation that all stories and narratives should have a 'beginning, middle and an end'. Although this is commonly cited it is often surprisingly overlooked, and consequently, many literature reviews are hard to follow because they are disjointed. In order to address this potential issue there are a number of conventional ways to think about structuring your literature review:

- to structure the review chronologically – herein the historical material precedes the contemporary. In other words, the 'story' or narrative of the literature review is related by starting with the historical background and arriving at the current issue and current day situation (Philips and Pugh, 2010: 63–69);
- Thematic structure – you identify the key issues and topics and then present them as chapters. In this approach the themes might be apparent from your title. Equally, they may be particular issues or concepts around which you wish to structure your work;
- Use of tabular presentation and/or systematic reviews. A systematic review is a method for, and process of, conducting an in-depth and all-encompassing survey of all the literature relating to a particular field or topic. A systematic review will have clearly defined and stated inclusion and exclusion criteria in terms of its

search terms for the given body of literature. An example of these terms might be to consider, for example, only English language articles or, alternatively, only papers using a particular sample size of study or only a particular methodology or indeed a combination of these factors. This method attempts to draft a literature review in a highly transparent and reproducible manner. In a systematic review it is not uncommon to use a tabular form and to list the authors on the left-hand side and then in a range of columns to the right lay out the various comparative and contrasting characteristics of the papers including, for example: main research focus, methodology employed, key findings. A truly systematic review will also show the date of the search, the search terms used, which electronic databases were consulted, and the number of articles identified in each search. Systematic reviews are increasingly prevalent and, even essential, in some subject areas (Gough, Oliver and Thomas, 2012). For instance, systematic reviews are frequently called for in writing in the natural and applied sciences (i.e. biology, chemistry). In business, organisation and management research systematic reviews are less prevalent but this approach is nevertheless required in some North American journals.

Within either chronological or thematic structure it is common to use sub-headings. Sub-headings can be very helpful in presenting your argument and guiding the reader. Nevertheless, it is important to use good judgement in deciding when and where to employ sub-headings. For example, it is a common error to use sub-headings too frequently in your writing. Over-usage of sub-headings tends to interrupt the build-up and the flow of the argument. It can make the text composed of too many short sections.

### Thinking about the 'funnel' shape of your literature review and overall work

A typical model for the 'shape' or development of a literature review is the form of a funnel. The 'funnel' shape essentially starts broad and wide at the top and becomes narrower towards the bottom or the end. The literature review follows the funnel shape form and, in turn, the funnel shape of the literature review is set within a shape of the overall funnel-shaped study.

The literature review starts with a relatively general and broad opening section that follows the introduction. Then as the argument and discussion of the material progress, it begins to narrow down and focus on the key issues and turning points of arguments you wish to make. This leads up to the narrower and concluding sections which are tightly focused on summarising and reiterating the key findings and

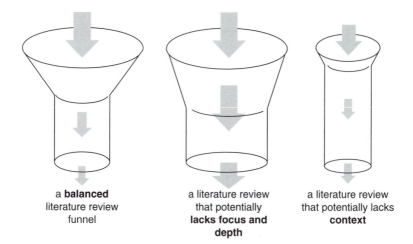

**Figure 2.2** Literature review with different funnel shapes

points of the discussion. The funnel model of the work then begins to open out again in these very final stages and the conclusion of the work in order to point at future directions and possibilities for further research. Figure 2.2 above illustrates this concept.

The funnel metaphor also helps you think about the shape of the funnel; ideally, you want a balanced shape where a broad context moves to a more in-depth discussion of particular theoretical ideas and issues (the funnel on the left in the figure). The funnel in the middle is an example where the literature review is not focused enough, so discussion remains within the general context or broad discussion in a field. This shape lacks focus and depth. The funnel on the right is one which lacks a context, which can make it difficult for the reader to understand why you are looking at such a specific area given the possible alternative strands you might have chosen. Always aim for a balanced shape to your literature review.

In this vein, Dunleavy (2003) makes a wide range of illuminating and engaging remarks about structuring and shaping writing and arguments and is worth reading in greater detail if you wish to read further about this way of modelling your writing. In contrast to this suggested form, some literature reviews (and indeed, overall dissertation shapes) fail to focus gradually on key argument points and instead just describe material. The temptation simply to relate and describe materials is an over-sight because it means that you are not conducting critical analysis on your literature review (and overall work).

## *Ordering new information after old information within the literature review*

The notion of writing the historical before the contemporary, in terms of eras or time periods, can also be rolled out in relation to the way you construct every aspect of your argument. Try to remember the principle of logic that *'new information should always follow old information'*. This idea is drawn from the field of pragmastylis-tics which is concerned with developing a deeper understanding of structure and meaning in language (Hickey, 1993; Hickey and Stewart, 2005). In the case of new information follows old information, this means that we put things we are saying in the appropriate order so that the meaning is made clear all the way through. An initial simplified example will be useful:

Below is a series of simplified statements for the purposes of demonstration:

> *Sam ran away.*
> *John shouted out loud.*
> *John has a dog.*
> *Sam likes bones.*
> *Sam bit John.*
> *The dog is called Sam.*

Clearly, in the above flow of statements, things seem to be out of order and difficult for the reader to follow and understand in an easy and ready way. As you move through the sentences you are possibly hoping or anticipating that the next sentence will bring more information that will allow you to make sense of the earlier informa-tion. However, in the above series of sentences this is not necessarily that easy or apparent.

Now if the statements are re-ordered using the principle of 'new information fol-lows old information', the following result can be obtained:

*John has a dog.*
*The dog is called Sam.*
*Sam likes bones.*
*Sam bit John.*

*John shouted out loud.*
*Sam ran away.*

Here, in the second layout format, new information builds on, and follows, old information. Each statement, and crucially the information it contains, logically follows on from the previous one in terms of both time and content. Effectively, we are 'guiding the reader' through our narrative. We are not seeking to 'surprise' or unsettle the reader as is certainly likely to be the case in the first series of sentence ordering. Writing in the style of the first example is more likely to be found in, for example, creative writing, novels and thriller stories where the express purpose of the narrative is to entice, surprise and thrill the reader and keep him or her guessing what will happen next and on the edge of their seats.

Having initially provided a simplified example in order to demonstrate the core principle of 'new information follows old information', it will be useful to take an example from an organisation and management context. The text below analyses the role of pharmaceutical sales representative in connection with GPs:

This study considers the sales and marketing activity of pharmaceutical industry representatives in relation to the UK family doctor medicine prescribing behaviour. Family doctors in the UK context are known as 'general practitioners' (hereafter referred to as GPs) and work within the National Health Service (NHS) framework of the UK. GPs are independent contractors to the NHS. Since 2004, contracts have been negotiated between the governmental intermediary of primary care trusts (PCTs) and GPs rather than between the Secretary of State for Health and individual GPs (Pollock, 2005). PCTs originated in the period 1997 and 1999 and initially, PCTs had an advisory role but from 2003 they assumed responsibility for 75% of the total NHS budget including the prescription budgets of all general practices in their areas. Prior to this, local health authorities had endeavoured to persuade GPs to limit their medicine prescribing to a National Institute for Clinical Excellence (NICE) approved list of drugs but had generally not controlled what GPs prescribed. PCTs currently have a fixed drug budget and have powers to ensure that their GP practices stay within it (Pollock, 2005). Scott, McIntosh-Scott and Stokes (2013: 38)

You will see that the opening sentences set the overall scene so that the reader is completely clear what is being dealt with and talked about. Notice how each sentence actually introduces the terms and issues that will be picked up, and treated, by the next; for example, see the highlighted sections:

> Family doctors in the UK context, are known as **'general practitioners' (hereafter referred to as GPs)** and work within the **National Health Service (NHS)** framework of the UK. **GPs** are independent contractors to the NHS. Since 2004, contracts have been negotiated between the governmental intermediary of **primary care trusts (PCTs) and GPs** rather than between the Secretary of State for Health and individual GPs (Pollock, 2005).
> **PCTs, originated** in the period 1997 an …

In a subject context such as this, abbreviations can also be a very useful way of condensing technical terms and names and avoiding cluttering up the writing with the need to repeat long labels and terminology.

If you read carefully over the case study Vignette 2.3 below, you will see that the authors have been very mindful to employ this technique in both the structuring of their argument and the overall text.

---

### Using word counts to map out the ideas in your writing

One way to plan out your work is to think about the approximate amount of words that are going to be in the given section. Self-evidently, in order to express ideas you need to use words. If you have a word limit then this means that there are likely to be only a certain number of ideas that you can reasonably and adequately explore within that limit.

For example, typical word limits may be (however these are only approximations):

10,000 word undergraduate dissertation – literature review = 2,000 to 3,000 words;

20,000 word postgraduate dissertation – literature review = 5,000 to 7,000 words;

80,000 word doctoral thesis – literature review = 15,000 to 25,000 words.

If you take 3,000 words for the literature review for an undergraduate dissertation a general indication and, for ease of example:

A sentence = 10 words

A paragraph = approximately 10 sentences = 100 words

VIGNETTE 2.3

A paragraph = one idea or issue, introduced, developed and expanded.

This means that 3000 words divided by 100 (words) = 30 ideas or expansion points on ideas developed in relation to other key points.

Then we can use sheets of paper or Post-its™ stuck on a wall and map out the points and argument structure, narrative and flow that will be employed in the literature review. The good thing about using something akin to Post-it™ stickers is that they can be moved around as ideas develop and the structure of your argument is formed.

## *Using a thesaurus and awareness of register to enhance your literature review*

In addition to checking in your text for the points above, there is also a need to do a re-reading in which you hone, craft and fine-tune the text. When you are convinced that there is no need for further major structural or layout change in your literature review, then it is time to move on to the next stage of reading. In this stage, you can re-read the entire text. On this reading you are looking at the word choices you have made in each sentence. Here it is very helpful to make extensive use of an electronic or paper-based Thesaurus and begin to veritably 'craft' each and every one of your sentences. A Thesaurus is a document that identifies synonyms and derivatives of words. This allows you to look up a word and to identify alternative words that you might use in a sentence. Quite often it is possible to identify one word that will work in the place of a few. Equally, on occasion it is possible to locate a word that captures perfectly the inference you are trying to make in a sentence or passage (McMillan and Weyers, 2012).

At this stage, you might also think about varying other features of your writing such as sentence length. A further thought to keep in mind is what your readers are looking for when they read your work. Try to put yourself in the reader's position. If you can see the world from the position of 'their shoes', this may help you write more engaging arguments. This can be very important for making your text appealing and engaging, and it will work better to draw your reader in and convince them about the argument in your literature review.

At this time it is also useful to pay attention to register. Register is the choice of words and 'level' of formality in the language employed. For example, if you were asking someone to leave your presence you could ask:

- Please would it be possible for you to leave us alone for a moment?
- Please leave us alone.

- Leave us.
- Go away.
- Get lost.

You can see that as the statements move along, the informality and directness increases, but the politeness diminishes. This change in register can be employed for a wide range of words and expressions. A literature review is generally a formal academic text, and therefore, it is important to ensure that you consistently use the appropriate level of language in your text (Hickey, 1993; Hickey and Stewart, 2005). An example of where this did not happen was in the following sentence taken from a student draft literature review (which of course had to be modified following feedback):

> The retail sector in X is booming and there are now loads of opportunities for investors and people with lots of cash to spare.

In the general context of a literature review, in terms of register, this would be more appropriately written as something akin to:

> The retail sector in X is growing substantially and there are many opportunities for investors at the present time.

## Use of first person in dissertations

Historically and conventionally, it is considered usual to use the third person singular in formal academic writing. For instance, this means using 'he', 'she' or 'it' forms of verbs and expression in your writing. One way of describing this is to use the term 'voice', in other words, whose voice in which your dissertation is written and spoken. An example of writing in third person singular style is exemplified in Vignette 2.1 above.

Extensions of this are the use of the second person singular and plural, 'you'. Indeed, this very book is written in this voice or style. The reason for this is that we, as authors, would like the book to speak directly to you, the reader.

In contrast, it has become increasingly common in articles, books and indeed in student dissertation writing to see use of the first person singular, that is, 'I', 'my or 'me'. This tendency might be for a number of reasons. It could be seen as being reflective of a more informal and direct nature of communication in the contemporary era. Such styles of communication have been encouraged through, for example, wider social media usage. Equally, it might be associated with the influx of news schools and traditions of writing such as, for instance, CMS which often employ the first person singular. In the case of CMS, this is done as a deliberate and mindful act of taking power over the act of writing directly for the author rather than abrogating it to an anonymous third person.

In the case of your dissertation, you will need to verify whether or not your college, university or faculty, or more importantly your dissertation supervisor has a view on whether or not it is appropriate to use first person in your writing. Many tutors will have been trained and will have developed the practice and habit of writing in the third person. Tutors may have strong views on what constitutes appropriate practice and you will need to listen to their advice.

### Critical analysis in the literature review

Maylor and Blackmon (2005: 117–118) appropriately underline that it is important to remember that a literature review is more than just a summary of the literature that relates to your chosen topic. It is essential that you have a critically analytical mind-set and approach to the task. Prompts to keep in mind while you are doing this are:

1. *What are the arguments that are being employed and developed in the paper, article or book you are reading and incorporating in your work?* – To what extent are they reasonable and justified?
2. *What are the key points that the source text makes?* – Has the author missed some important points or dealt with them too lightly?
3. *Has the text employed assumptions that he or she has not fully explored?* If this is the case usually these assumptions are implicit rather than explicit in the work. Often these assumptions will be based on some conceptual or philosophical approach, belief or paradigm. For example, if an author were operating in line with a positivistic methodological approach, then it would be usual to anticipate that they would be simplifying complex data into more isolated variables (the principle of reductionism), identifying linear cause and effect behaviour between these variables (the principle of causality) in order to draw objective conclusions on the data.

Other researchers using alternative, conceptual and methodological approaches, such as interpretivism, may well take issue with such principles. Interpretivism considers the research field in a more naturalistic manner. To achieve this, research methods such as participant observation, interviews and ethnography are used. These approaches within interpretivism acknowledge and embrace the subjectivity and complexity of respondents' perspectives.

To summarise, paraphrasing Hart (1998), upon the completion of a literature review, it should accomplish the following:

- A clear comprehension of your chosen topic;
- Ensure that all the key works for a given topic have been included;
- It should argue, build, assert and defend definitive conclusions – it should not be ambivalent or weak;
- A gap in knowledge or a focal point for examination – often leading to the generation of research questions at this end stage of the literature review – should be identified;
- A possible approach or methodology to tackle the identified gap and focal point may also be pointed at;
- Underlines why the identified gap or issue merits attention and examination.

In tandem with this, be wary of the following classic oversights, faults and pitfalls (paraphrased and adapted from Berman Brown, 2006: 80):

- Omission of well-known and important publications that relate to your title and topic;
- Overlooking adequate and appropriate referencing of your arguments;
- Misspelling authors' names and writing down key referencing and bibliographic details incorrect;
- Writing in a manner than is primarily descriptive rather than critically and analytically;
- Overusing jargon, technical or elaborate words;
- Writing about a topic that strays from your chosen title or your research questions.

## THOUGHTS ON USING REFERENCING AND SOURCES

Referencing in an academic piece of work is required and essential. There are a number of key things to ensure you observe in carrying out referencing.

Firstly, there are several different referencing systems in operation in the world. Find out which particular referencing system is required for the work you are producing. Two of the most common systems in use in the world are the Harvard

Referencing System and the APA system. If you are producing a dissertation then your department or institution will usually have clear indications which system you should use. Quite often they will also have teaching and learning support materials and websites in relation to it (Pears and Shields, 2013).

Secondly, you need to use the identified and required system of referencing correctly. This involves thinking about using referencing in a stylish way and as an integral part of your argument/the appearance of your paper (look at articles and books and see how they manage the use of referencing in their texts). Also, when citing editors, remember to take account of the debates and authors about whom you are writing. It may even be considered a discourtesy to overlook certain writers.

Furthermore, at the end of general statements you can use a collection of authors to show the flow of history and development, for example, see the opening sentence of the Introduction in Vignette case study 2.1. Moreover, the placing of a reference at the end of a first sentence of an argument – when you have made a topic sentence at the start of a paragraph (see Vignette 2.1) – has the effect of putting a 'marker' reference in order to show the territory and literature base you are entering. Finally, as a general guide, it is best to put references at the end of a sentence rather than positioning them in the middle of the sentence. This improves the fluidity of scanning and reading the text (there are multiple examples of this in Vignette 2.1).

A range of software is available to help you with recording, organising and recalling your references. End Note™ is one such example. These can be very useful for large and complex projects such as theses or book writing (Edhlund, 2007; Agrawal, 2009) However, they can also take a considerable amount of time to load up the data.

## GLOSSARY OF TERMS

**Argument** An argument is when you express your opinion in a piece of writing in a balanced and structured way so as to persuade the reader of the case you are making. The balance is usually achieved in two ways: firstly, you ensure that you examine the various sides and aspects of the situation you are discussing and, secondly, you draw on and relate your thoughts to the ideas and thoughts of those writers who have looked at the issues before you, that is, the topic literature.

**Conceptual framework** The notion of a concept links to an idea, a theory or an outline of thought processes. In other words, how do the ideas you are dealing with connect together and what is the relationship between one idea and another? Quite often it is common to produce a diagrammatic representation of the ideas and where they sit in relation to each other. This will quite often show causal links, impacts and effects. A look through any range of business and management papers will reveal a host of attempts to produce conceptual frameworks for the arguments the papers are making.

Whenever you write a literature review, or indeed any piece of text, you are involved in thinking about how you will shape and structure your ideas, argument and general form of the piece. This is the structure and is determined by a set of ideas you are using. Sometimes this framework will be linked with formally established theories and sometimes they will be structures that have been developed as part of your work.

**Critical analysis** Critical analysis means the process of challenging and questioning the ideas and theories in the articles, books and web materials you are examining. This is an integral part of building up an argument. Critical analysis often involves a process of finding and identifying information – presenting the idea to the reader; inference – then telling the reader what you would like him or her to understand from this information (this is the translation of the information into how it sits in relation to your argument); then, implication – this is the 'so what' point of the critical analysis process – what are the consequences and outcomes of this understanding (i.e. inference) of the information. The act of analysis flows through the inference and implication aspects of these steps. Thus, analysis can be summarised as weighing up different arguments, working out their strengths and weaknesses, and how they fit together and relate to each other (or do not). Ultimately, analysis produces a new statement about what you think a given situation is and what it means. Sometimes this overall process is represented alternatively as – thesis, counter-thesis and finally synthesis (i.e. what is being claimed, what are the arguments against what is being claimed and what are the alternatives, and what is the fusion or resultant argument between all these various points).

**Double-blind review** A blind review refers to the process in producing journal articles and sometimes books, whereby the paper, or the book text, is sent to an expert secret reviewer by the publisher or journal editor. Double-blind review refers to the process whereby it is sent to two reviewers in order to secure a cross-section of views and feedback. The purpose of this is to ensure that the quality of the piece is enhanced and maintained.

**Edited volume** An edited volume refers to a book which is comprised of chapters or sections each of which is written by a different writer. The role of the editors of the book (who will have their name on the cover and spine) is to co-ordinate and harmonise the style of the different chapters into a co-ordinated and integrated overall result. Quite often one or more of the editors may contribute a chapter and also write an introductory section.

**Monograph** A monograph is a book that consists of a holistic, coherent, discussion and argument that occupies the length of the text and is written by a single author rather than by a two or more people.

**Narrative** Narrative means the flow of events and plot in an account. This will embrace and relate the facts and sense to the reader of a piece of writing. Another way of thinking about it is as storytelling, although some people like to draw a clear distinction between the two. A way to think about narrative is that it is akin to choreography on the stage – it shapes and drives the interest and dynamics of your writing. Students and writers of research reports often overlook the benefits of investing time in learning about, appreciating and developing narrative and its application.

**Search terms** Search terms are the key words that identify the areas you are investigating in your research. Often your search terms will start out from words used in your title or research aims. As the work develops it is normal to gradually expand your list of search terms as the argument broadens and deepens.

## KEY POINTS

1. The literature review is completely achievable and 'do-able' by any student;
2. Look to your title, aims and objectives to tell you what you should be looking at in terms of strands or areas of the literature;
3. Be clear about your (working) title and your research questions (even if only in sketch form) before you embark on the literature review. This will help avoid going in wasteful wrong directions and economise your efforts;
4. Be prepared to use a wide variety of sources as potential information sources ( in a discriminatory and analytical manner) – in order to complement and build on books and journals;
5. Do not write just a descriptive account of the ideas, concepts, articles and books you find. Work out your own point of view and beliefs in relation to what you are reading and write a well-informed, balanced, engaged and critically analytical argument;
6. Your completed literature review will demonstrate to readers that you are familiar with the subject and that you have identified the key themes and gaps in the literature that you are studying;

7. A literature review conducted in an article helps you to develop rapidly an overview of writings that already exist. In other words, to coin a well-known everyday phrase, 'you do not have to reinvent the wheel'. Nevertheless, you do have to craft and adapt these ideas to your own argument;

8. Remember to respond to the expectations of level and the type of output depending on whether it is undergraduate, postgraduate, dissertation or project.

9. Remember new information follows old information;

10. Remember to build your arguments on the structure of information, implication and inference.

## REVISION QUESTIONS

1. Have you gone back over your literature review and read through it in the range of ways discussed above?

2. Have you checked that each section truly has a beginning, middle and an end?

3. Have you re-read the chapters to check that they address the subject matter and material that they are meant to be addressing?

4. Does each paragraph and section convincingly and coherently fit in relation to the adjacent or the next one? (Remember – new information/old information – see above. Remember, logical argument and narrative).

5. Is your work largely descriptive? If so have you introduced enough critical analysis into the literature review?

6. If your work is a Master's dissertation – are you not only critically analysing theory but also developing the theory and building new theory as a consequence?

## FURTHER STUDY

The following texts, many of them established and well known, have helpful and more extensive commentaries and treatments of literature reviews:

1. Bryman, A. and Bell, E. (2007) *Business Research Methods*, Oxford: Oxford University Press.

2. Hart, C. (2001) *Doing a Literature Search: Releasing the Social Science Research Imagination*, Sage: London.

3.  Rugg, G. and Petre, M. (2004) *The Unwritten Rules of PhD Research*, Maidenhead: Open University Press.
4.  Dunleavy, P. (2003) *Authoring a PhD: How to Plan, Draft, Write and Finish a Doctoral Thesis or Dissertation*, Basingstoke: Palgrave Macmillan.
5.  Fink, A. (2009) *Conducting Research Literature Reviews: From the Internet to Paper*, London: Sage Publications.
6.  Ridley, D. (2008) *The Literature Review: A Step-by-Step Guide for Students*, London: Sage Publications.
7.  Thody, A. (2006) *Writing and Presenting Research*, London: Sage Publications.
8.  Williams, K. (2014) *Getting Critical*, 2nd edition, Series: Pocket Study Skills, Basingstoke: Palgrave-Macmillan.

# 3

# RESEARCH METHODOLOGIES

## OBJECTIVES

*Successful completion of this chapter provides guidance on:*
- How to better understand what methodology is;
- How to develop and use it in your research;
- How to develop the ability to produce research which considers reliability, validity and generalisability;
- How to realise that research methodologies and philosophies are not uniquely about doing research – they may also reveal a considerable amount about your personal values and beliefs.

## INTRODUCTION

Research methodology is one of the most fascinating aspects of being involved in research. Research methodology involves the conceptual framework (see Chapter 2) of ideas, philosophies, approaches and concepts that are brought together in order to conduct your piece of research. The act of research is intrinsically linked to choices about the way you see and form opinions about the world. This section provides some ideas and strategies with which to approach research methodologies. It also invites you to consider your value system in relation to the research you conduct.

Although it is difficult to generalise, different levels of course tend to approach research methodology in varying ways. In most undergraduate courses that provide sessions on research methodology for dissertations, quite often, but not always, they tend to illustrate a couple of contrasting methodological options (commonly and conventionally positivism and interpretivism). However, in the case of postgraduate or doctoral-level work, the expectation will be that there is a much more in-depth and detailed understanding and fluency concerning the treatment of a wide range of methodological options and their complexities (Bryman and Bell, 2007). On the

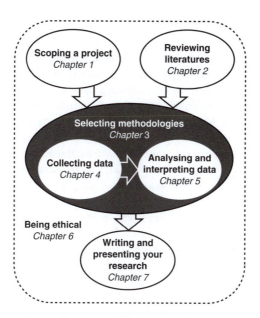

Current location within the research process

other hand, project work may or may not feel that a detailed discussion on methodology is important for the document and target audience (McMillan and Weyers, 2011). In a project, where a decision is made to incorporate comments on methodology these are likely to be of a general background and concise nature.

Some students seem to find issues and questions around methodology quite daunting. This is possibly because it requires dealing with, to some greater or lesser extent, philosophical ideas and systems of thought. There is no reason why this should be the case and this chapter aims to assist in developing your understanding.

## RESEARCH METHODOLOGY – DEVELOPING THE STRUCTURE AND ARCHITECTURE OF YOUR STUDY

### What broad considerations should you be aware of when considering the design of a piece of research?

Your research design, which can be seen as the overall planning, structure and conduct of the research (and thus embraces research methodological choices), will be governed by a number of factors which are gradually elaborated below. Leading on from Chapter 1, which discussed titles, aims, objectives and research questions (in conjunction with Chapter 2 on literature reviews), your research questions will have a powerful role in shaping the design of your study. The question of what you aim to discover, and how, will very much determine the most appropriate way to design your research. It is also important to understand that in discussing research methodology you are looking at both (research) philosophies and research methodologies. In other words a range of both philosophies and methodologies exist and are available to be employed in your work. In its most simply stated manner, for the purposes of developing an initial understanding, research philosophy points at the overall or over-arching values and beliefs in a given system of thought (i.e. philosophy). A given research methodology will operate within a system of philosophical thinking. Together the research philosophy and methodology will fuse to create your research design.

Designing a piece of research is very much a matter of making choices and decisions about what you are interested in and what might be the best way to research it. For many students/researchers these choices are often discussed, at an initial level, in terms of, for example, 'doing either a qualitative or a quantitative piece of work'. Alternatively, the debate might involve whether or not you should choose between positivism and interpretivism (The core principles of these were introduced in Chapter 2, but they are also elaborated further below). Indeed, thoughts and conversations on research design often do not go much further than this for many people. This is not necessarily a problem and often rather a *question of the level* being undertaken as already alluded to above. For example, if you are doing a dissertation for an undergraduate degree, then in your Methodology chapter you will need to provide an exploration of a limited number of methodological options and positions and a rationale for your methodological choice. This will be underpinned by a discussion of relevant literature. However, for Master's level your treatment and discussion of methodological aspects will be expected to be considerably more in-depth and should also recognise and demonstrate an ability to handle more complexity of the field (Furseth and Everett, 2013).

Overall, research design can, and often should, involve a wider range of choices and potentially rich and complex options and decisions. The intention of the following sections is an attempt to move beyond some of the more binary thinking (i.e. the all too often choice presented to students in research methodology classes of positivism or interpretivism to the omission of wider options and considerations) outlined above and to explore some of these possibilities. In line with the advice in Chapters 1 and 2, the first thing to do is to identify the broad area you want to investigate (Collis and Hussey, 2009). This will involve following the steps and advice provided in those earlier chapters which will provide you with the research focal topic and research problem and/or questions that you aim to consider.

Subsequently, when thinking about a research design that will suit your chosen question and area of investigation, it is often useful to think about it in terms of *high-level* theoretical design and then *detailed* methods and data level within the overall higher level choices. Various authors present different ways of describing and talking about frameworks for research design (see the example of Wilson below). None of these typologies or classifications is categorical but rather represent differing ways of mapping out the research design domain. This can create confusion because different authors in textbooks might use different terms to encapsulate and refer to different approaches to research. For example, Wilson (2010: 104–105) suggests choices between three broad types of study when designing and conducting your research:

1. *Exploratory Research* – which aims to fill missing gaps and under-researched areas of knowledge in particular fields;
2. *Descriptive Research* – which aims to elaborate current or historical topics with a view to deepening understanding of them. This is often achieved through instruments and methods such as surveys and observation;
3. *Causal Research* – which involves gathering empirical data in order to determine why something happens or occurs.

While such descriptive frameworks are helpful up to a point, in another way they often are difficult to relate to commonly used and well-known methodological approaches (such as positivism or interpretivism). In relation to this issue, one of the things that it is useful for you to be able to do when reading methodological textbooks and writings and their varying and differing ways of talking about methodology is to try gradually to develop an awareness and ability to identify the shared characteristics of the different labels writers use.

For example, in relation to the three terms employed by Wilson above (Exploratory, Descriptive and Causal), it will be seen (as we progress and expand the discussion below) that Wilson's term '*Descriptive Research*' echoes similar characteristics of interpretivism. It indicates rich and deep accounts based on classic ethnographic methods such as, for example, observation (Hammersley and Atkinson, 2007).

On the other hand, '*Causal Research*' resonates much more with positivism. It employs the term 'empirical' and the notion of clear 'Causal' (… and effect) judgements are kindred with this approach. Finally, exploratory research is more difficult to align with, for example, either interpretivism or positivism. The key indications that describe it are 'exploratory' and gaps. One might argue that this form of language suggests a fixed, categorical and delineated view of the world (which has shades of positivistic approaches), but this is too remote a connection to suggest that the term 'Exploratory Research' is particularly connected to any particular methodological stance (Stebbins, 2001). Nevertheless, overall, the typology Wilson conveys to the reader provides an interesting illustration of how different categorisations are employed in the field and how you might seek to understand and engage with them.

In the range of texts available on research methodology there is a wealth of ways to describe and talk about possible frameworks, structures and approaches that might shape your study. How might you glean and understand the myriad and often confusing world of choice in relation to research design? There is a need to develop an understanding of the underlying characteristics or 'species' of methodological approaches. It will be useful to consider some of the defining underlying foundation principles of the overarching areas of various disciplinary domains. In the very broadest of terms, and from one perspective, it is possible to view the methodological spectrum as comprising natural science and social science approaches. Business management and organisation is usually considered as residing within social sciences, although it is important to remember that it is difficult to be completely categorical. The two spheres are elaborated below.

## Natural science approaches and terminology

*These approaches are commonly aligned with, and characterised by, the following principles, assumptions and mechanisms:*

- *Deductivism* – involving reasoning and rationalising from a general notion to a specific focused notion often through the use of hypotheses;
- *Objectivity* – wherein supposed human bias and subjectivity is removed from judgements concerning the research;
- *Reductionism* – which suggests that an entity or whole object, domain or phenomenon can be readily dissembled into its constituent parts;
- *Causality* – which claims that one event or set of circumstances brings about another event or occurrence as in 'cause-and-effect';
- *Determinism* – determinism is linked to causality and points at the recognition that one set of circumstances may pre-determine another set of circumstances.

These are the principles that underpin areas such as biology, physics and chemistry.

A commonly used methodology that embodies and employs these principles is positivism. Positivism and the above principles are elaborated further in the discussion and glossary of key terms below. In terms of business, management and organisation, the methodological approaches that underpin much of the natural science domain were also used in early waves of research in the business arena. This situation continued from the 1920s through to the mid-1950s and 1960s. This is not to say that other more inductively inspired (see the next section) methodological approaches were not employed and adhered to (see the classic studies of Mayo (1933) The Human Relations Movement and the Chicago School of Management), but positivism remained the overall dominant paradigm. It was, broadly speaking, during the 1960s onwards and particularly during the 1980s, that critical management ideas drawing on longstanding Critical Theory, postmodernism and poststructuralist methodologies from the wider social sciences (see below in the next section) began to become more common (Alvesson, Bridgman and Willmott, 2011). These approaches offered alternative, inductive, ways of viewing situations, events and relationships through research.

## Social sciences approaches and terminology

These approaches are commonly aligned with and characterised by the following principles, assumptions and mechanisms:

- *Inductivism* – This approach typically uses observational-style methods on small-sized sample in order to be able to make emergent sense of what is taking place in relation to the phenomenon under examination in the sample.
- *Subjectivity* – This is the recognition that individual perspective will play a role in the creation of meaning from data. In other words, while various individual people and groups of people may share a view on an issue, there may well still be variations between them.
- *Multiple factors and causalities* at play and influencing the researched phenomena – Unlike the deterministic and causal stances of the natural sciences, social sciences tend to be open to seeing many factors playing a role in the creation of the data or the situations that are observed and recorded.
- *Rich and expansive description* – Social science approaches tend to encourage extensive elaboration around the situations and phenomena under investigation. This paints a fulsome and in-depth backdrop and portrayal of the research situation and allows readers to have a vivid and clear insight into how the research was undertaken.

These are some of the principles that are likely to underpin areas such as sociology and many of the humanities including business, management and organisation. A commonly used methodology that embodies and employs these principles is interpretivism (which believes that 'realities' concerning field research emerge from the data in processes that acknowledge a role for the subjectivities of the researched and the researcher). This is outlined further in the discussion below.

However, this is a brief attempt to reflect a complex set of methodological communities and practices, and it is indeed still the case today that in some parts of the business and management discipline, and in some geographical arenas and national business and management academies, particular approaches are dominant. For example, in many sections of the North American Academy of Management, positivistic (i.e. natural science methodology influenced) approaches are applied to organisations. However, in the Scandinavian Academies of Management more often than not, interpretivistic approaches using qualitative data are employed. The UK business and management research community tends to comprise a mixture of methodological approaches rather than one particular approach dominating.

Within your choice of methodological domain, many of the *design choices* available to you in the development of your study are not actually necessarily philosophical schools or specific theories but are rather 'boundaries', 'structures' or more styles of study that you might consider relevant for your research. Some of these include, for example:

- *Case Study*
  A case study is a specific and focal examination of a particular organisation or a situation within a particular organisation (see below for key word definition). Case study could be used in either positivistic or interpretivistic studies (Hancock and Algozzine, 2012).
- *Cross-Sectional*
  This involves looking at particular factors across various settings or parts of a research area or topic. For example, it might be possible to conduct a study across the firms of a particular industry. Alternatively, it might even be possible to look across a range of different industries in relation to a particular phenomenon. An example here might be a study on the factors that cause and underpin absenteeism at work in different organisational contexts. Some researchers might tend to consider cross-sectional studies as more of a positivistic/deductive approach because of the need to develop comparative benchmarks and measures across a large sample; however, the approach can be employed in inductive studies also.

For instance, it might be equally possible to conduct semi-structured interviews with a range of human resources managers across the various firms and industries (see Eggert and Helm (2003) for an illustration).

- *Longitudinal*

  This simply means a research design and study that is to be carried out over a substantial period of time (see Tengblad and Ohlsson, 2010).

- *Archival Analysis*

  This form of analysis usually involves investigating large collections of stored secondary data. Quite often this will be in well-organised collections. They might be in major central repositories in major cities such as The National Archives or the British Library in London, UK. This form of approach can be employed in any piece of research; however, within the business management and organisation area it is particularly popular with business historians (Larson, Schnyder, Westerhuis and Wilson, 2011).

- *Comparative*

  This style of research is conducted by comparing and contrasting two or more cases, situations or instances of the phenomena in which the research is interested. Comparative studies need to exercise great care and attention in laying out the context for each of the cases that will be compared. If this is not done then there is not enough detail for the reader to make sense of, or appreciate the full significance of, the deliberations and discussions (Etzioni, 1975).

It is possible to use any of these above approaches in either inductivist or deductivist research (which have been outlined above). The important difference and the challenge centres around *how* they are used and the manner in which data should be interpreted in relation to them. For example, if you were to conduct a *deductive piece of research* involving a comparative analysis, then you would be looking for similarities and differences between the cases. Such a study may well employ some statistical or numerical assessment in order to gauge issues of size, performance, scope, etc. Typical methods employed might be survey, structured questionnaire and structured interviews. The subsequent chapters will be revealing more detail in relation to research methods.

The contrast with conducting a similar comparative study *with an inductive approach* would mean that the study would be seeking, for example, to surface and explore competing meanings of actors and boundaries of sense-making in relation to the issues (Weick, 1995). The focus would be on using concepts, ideas and language to explore these issues. Typical methods used, by way of example, might be participant observation, ethnography, focus groups or unstructured interviews.

The discussion hitherto has provided a broad outline of the methodological positions and spheres that are in operation within the world of research. The subsequent sections begin to explore in greater detail the dimensions and character of the different methodological approaches and, in particular, will work to assist you in understanding some of the factors on which you will base your choices as you approach your research.

## RESEARCH METHODOLOGY – ACHIEVING A MORE IN-DEPTH UNDERSTANDING OF VARIOUS METHODOLOGICAL APPROACHES AND STANCES

### What are epistemology and ontology and how should I engage with them in my work?

Epistemology and ontology are words that you are likely to encounter when you start engaging with research methodology (Audi, 2011). They are typical of the complex-sounding forms of terminology that can occur in the realm of research methodology, and it is important that you develop an understanding of them. Epistemology and ontology affect every aspect of the natural and social science domains, and in the case of the latter, this also applies to business, management and organisation. One way to think of epistemology and ontology is as being something akin to the DNA mechanisms that assist in classifying and characterising a particular methodological approach. When you appreciate the epistemological and ontological aspects of a particular philosophical and methodological approach you begin to understand how it forms the views of the world and the people, things and situations within it.

### *Epistemology*

Epistemology is the study and the consideration and development of theories about how and why knowledge is made (Audi, 2011). This is important because when you are undertaking a piece of research, whether for a dissertation, project or article, you are in the process of trying to develop new knowledge. In other words, with your study, one of your ambitions will be to say and contribute something new to the field you are examining and researching. Epistemology tells us that 'knowledge is made'. An understanding of the presence and the role of epistemology is indicative that you should not accept as a given, or take for granted, the processes of the formation of knowledge. You must always ask questions about how, why and when any knowledge came into being and was accepted as valid. Through these processes, it can be seen that epistemology also touches on issue of power and who is holding it (Knights and Willmott, 1999). By understanding the drivers and forces that cause knowledge to be shaped in various ways, we better understand the overall patterns of how knowledge is formed.

## Ontology

Ontology is an aspect of research philosophy that is concerned with varying perspectives on the nature of reality and of states of 'being'. Alternatively expressed, ontology concerns matters of 'what exists', 'how do we know it exists', 'to what extent can the nature of its existence be verified or confirmed?'

As Stokes (2012: 90) indicates:

> It might seem strange to question the nature of reality; after all, to our empirical senses reality might seem clear, uncomplicated and self-evident in so many ways. For example, we feel heat or cold with our skin, we smell a nice or unpleasant odour with our nose, and certain objects apparently self-evidently exist – houses, walls, cars, people, planes and so on and so forth. However, there *are* differing and alternative views concerning what reality might consist of in relation to experiences and phenomena. Different sensations might be associated with different reactions and emotions for different people. Reality varies, for example, through individual perception. What might seem a 'fact' to one person is not necessarily apparent or acceptable as a 'fact' to another individual. An everyday illustration of this might be contrasting views people hold about religion or politics. Some individuals may hold beliefs that will not be valid or constitute 'facts' for other individuals or groups. As such, one person's *view* of reality constituted by 'facts' (and the consequent actions he or she takes following these beliefs) will not necessarily be another person's view or construction of reality and 'facts'.

Within research methodologies, each particular approach has a particular stance on ontological issues. One way of talking about ontology is to use the term 'realist ontology' and the alternative term of 'relativist ontology'.

- Realist ontology sees reality as solid, fixed, permanent and, most importantly, external and objective to the observer. In general, deductivistic and positivistic approaches adhere to realist ontologies (Fleetwood, 2005).
- Relativist ontology sees, to a varying degree, reality as being created by the perception of the observer. In other words, if you think 'X' is occurring then this may

become a solid belief in your opinion. In general, inductivistic and interpretevistic approaches incline towards relativistic ontologies (Whittle and Spicer, 2008).

## A final note on epistemology and ontology

One of the questions that you will need to address during your research is: to which particular philosophical and methodological approaches do you subscribe when you are in the process of developing new knowledge? Any methodological approach will be underpinned by particular epistemological and ontological values. This question involves discovering your own approach, attitudes, beliefs and assumptions in relation to how much of the wider world operates and functions particularly in relation to ideas such as subjectivity versus objectivity and realism versus relativism (see examples in Hill and McGowan, 1999). For example, do you believe that there are such things as unquestionable 'facts'? or, again, do you believe that you might arrive at different perspectives on the 'truth' depending on which individuals or group of people are interviewed? Each of these two examples point at underlying assumptions and beliefs being in operation in your mind (and the minds of the individuals you are researching) and the way you (and they) see the world. These particular beliefs and viewpoints will often align with particular viewpoints and perspectives of particular philosophies and methodologies. In this way, a consideration and exploration of research philosophy and methodology can begin to provide a window through which you are able potentially to better understand many aspects of life in general. This underlines that it is useful not to think of the act of research as being separate to life but rather an integral and implicit perspective on life.

The discussion thus far has indicated the broad structures and principles that underpin all research studies. The discussion now moves on to consider in great detail the role, and character, of inductivism and deductivism in relation to epistemology and ontology. In particular, the subsequent sections provide ideas on how you might translate some of these ideas from theoretical and philosophical ideas into the operational fieldwork and detail of your research.

## WHAT IS INDUCTIVISM AND HOW DO ISSUES OF SUBJECTIVITY, 'TRUTH CLAIMS' AND REPRESENTATION PLAY A ROLE IN THIS METHODOLOGICAL APPROACH?

Inductivism is the name for the methodological approach and set of principles that underpin widely used methodologies such as interpretivism. Inductivism and interpretivism (which were outlined above) predominantly, indeed almost exclusively, tend to develop and employ qualitative data.

Inductive approaches are characterised generally by the following points:

*Small Samples*

Inductive approaches generally involve small samples, but not necessarily. There is a debate on the use of the term 'small' in relation to samples within research communities. It should be noted that in the eyes of researchers who conduct inductive research the sample is not necessarily considerate and small but 'normal' and usual for that approach to research. Deductive researchers generally require larger samples for their methodologies and it might be from this quarter that the critique perhaps emerges. Indeed, some inductive-style researchers might go as far as to consider the very term 'sample' as inappropriate in anything but a deductive study. This would be because for them the notion of 'sample' and its underpinning rationale are based on deductive and positivistic assumptions.

*Data Analysis*

*In data analysis, inductive approaches tend to use techniques* like narrative analysis, Grounded Theory – an established inductive research methodological domain aimed at generating a comprehensive system of coding and understanding on qualitative data. It can also include other less formal forms of theme coding, content analysis and, in general, the identification of the recurrent and salient themes and key moments by careful reading and re-reading of the data by the researcher(s).

In terms of *undertaking data analysis*, inductive approaches tend to formulate a series of research questions and/or identify an area to examine as an initial stage of the research. A body of data is gathered using naturalistic approaches and methods, that is, observation or interviews, photographs, focus groups, emails, text messages, etc., whereby you actually go into the research field or a setting rather than staying at your desk. From these data the salient issues, recurrent terms and themes are identified.

*Hypothesis*

Inductive approaches tend not to use the term and language of *hypotheses* although it is possible to do so. A hypothesis can be understood as a statement about the nature of a certain situation or phenomenon (see the example of MacCormack, Carliss, and Rusnak, 2012). In this way, a hypothesis seems more aligned to positivism because, by its very nature, a hypothesis can be seen to be an attempt to make a (truth) claim about the nature of 'the world out there' and outside the researcher's identity and senses. This implies that an objective truth can exist outside the perception of the researcher. Inductivism commonly sees the world as being constructed, and made sense of, by the research respondents and participants (i.e. and not existing outside of the human perception) and so the idea of hypothesis sometimes seems challenging for inductivism.

So, *can you use hypotheses in inductive research*?

The answer is 'yes' sometimes, however they operate in a slightly different manner to their use in positivistic research. In inductive research using qualitative data, hypotheses can be used. Sometimes, authors use similar words such as 'propositions'. Within inductive research, hypotheses and propositions tend to be postulations about the relationship between two items, situations or aspects in the research and this leads to rich descriptions rather than categorical statements of 'right' or wrong' or proven/unproven as they might within positivistic research.

Two illustrations are provided below:

1. Proposition 1: Quasi-public contexts are an under-explored context and novel, specific and valuable data will be able to be determined.
2. Proposition 2: Application of a critical perspective lens on organisational ambidexterity will be effective in identifying behavioral shifts from relatively conservative modernistic exploitative states to more radical critical explorative conditions.

Often, in inductive research, the purpose is not to categorically prove or disprove the hypothesis, rather *the purpose is to elaborate and deepen and broaden understanding* around the hypothesis (Silverman, 2011).

*Subjectivity*

*Subjectivity* – within inductive research the role, presence and operation of subjectivity in the research, is readily and openly acknowledged and embraced by the researcher. Moreover, subjectivity is an important aspect of reflexivity (remember that this contrasts sharply with deductive and positivistic views). In inductive research, a need by the researcher to understand human perception, opinion, point of view and the processes through which these emerge and are constructed is seen as rich, varied and relevant for making sense of what is occurring in the research setting and environment (see an example in McMurray, Pullen and Rhodes, 2011). As a consequence, (subjective) meaning and significance are seen as being attributed to events, places, language and discourse by individuals and groups in ways that are pertinent and relevant to the particular context(s) in which they live and operate.

In the subjectivity of inductive research, you do not stand objectively apart from this process because through processes of reflexivity (see below) you are a co-creator of the data. You listen to and observe the respondents who act out their meanings and significance in the research field. You make choices and decisions regarding recording respondent utterances and actions. Then, you interpret these data and finally you write up an account of the findings and study. This type of research is often termed as ethnography. Ethnography is the study of people and communities in their natural settings by researchers who enter those settings and live and work closely with the research respondents. All of these stages involve choices and decisions which invite and involve the views and subjectivities personal to you (see Bergström and Knights (2006) and Böhm and Batta (2010) regarding discussions and presentations of subjectivity in operation in research contexts). It is true that you are exercising professional judgement and operating a particular logic in making the decisions you make. However, inductive approaches to research do not purport that there is only one way in which to undertake all of these steps and stages.

### Reflexivity

*Reflexivity* is also centrally important in inductive and interpretivist approaches (in stark contrast to deductive/positivistic approaches). In inductive approaches the need is overtly acknowledged and encouraged, throughout the research, for you to recognise your own role, values, beliefs and perspectives in generating the data and writing research. For example, if you were conducting research into the organisational structures and business practices of political parties, you may enter the research with quite fixed prior beliefs regarding the relative messages of their manifestos. Alternatively, if you are studying working conditions and practices of factory employees you may (or may not), for instance, have quite strong views on the identity, role and merit of workers conducting manual labour stemming from what work your parents do. All the way through the research design and execution you are making choices and decisions about how to shape the study, gather and most importantly interpret the data to produce findings. Many of these actions are undertaken in direct or close proximity to research respondents and the data they have generated (Alvesson and Sköldberg, 2009; Bryman and Bell, 2007; Jankowicz, 2005; Kuhn, 2009; Silverman, 2010a; 2010b; Whittle, 2008).

### Representation

Finally, *representation* is important to consider in connection with reflexivity although often not discussed and overlooked. While you may not engage knowingly or consciously with representation, it is nevertheless part of the processes whereby the world is labelled, named and categorised. You and other people use labels and descriptions constantly in order to portray the world. For example, we use everyday labels like chair, car, bus, food and holiday. We often take these terms for granted and at face-value. However, they are all *human creations* and, frequently, labelling has power effects and implications of which we need to take account. We see this in the media and everyday life when a celebrity is given a label, and it seems to become a significant part of the public identity with which they are associated. As such it becomes socially constructed into 'fact' and famous and infamous reputations are ascribed (see Ellis, 2008; Mescher, Benschop and Doorewaard, 2010). As mentioned, representation is not talked about that much in relation to research but it is worthwhile to dedicate some consideration to it because by appreciating the fact that 'labels', 'names' and nomenclature are created by humans, this makes us further aware of the need to 'unpack' the motives, roots, origins, politics, identity issues and so on and so forth in relation to the terminology we encounter, deal with and generate in our work. This is a central part of creating an argument and conducting critical analysis.

## THINKING FURTHER ABOUT SOCIAL CONSTRUCTION AND THE PROCESSES IT MAY INVOLVE ...

Social constructionism is a sociological set of ideas and philosophical approach that seeks to understand the processes and ways through which people relate to each other and the situations and environments in which they live and interact. These interactions create meaning, discourses, knowledge and a range of wider effects and implications.

Berger and Luckmann (1966) authored one of the most influential texts on the subject: *The Social Construction of Reality*. They suggested the following regarding the process:

- *objectification* (i.e. representationalism); This involves a process of identifying 'object', 'people', 'effects' indeed anything as something that could be readily recognised as being separate from other artefacts. For example: 'good' employees are noted as being different from 'bad' employees.
- *typification* (classifying objects); This involves the subsequent stage of grouping things together. So, for example, a particular group of workers appears to emerge as discernible – the 'high flyers' or the 'dead wood' to use two populist colloquial terms and examples.
- *habitualisation* (repetition and reinforcement); People engaged in the process of objectification and typification use the labels high flyers and dead wood as if they are valid, useful and legitimate terms;

- *internalisation* (of the objectified, typified, habitualised people and things); This results in a "reality" in that: "A world so regarded attains a firmness in consciousness" (*ibid*: 78). Consequently, everyday human interactions and behaviours become seen as 'legitimated' (*ibid*: 111) or 'representations' (Chia, 1996) rather than being "humanly produced" (Berger and Luckmann, *ibid*: 78) and based on choice, decision, politics and behaviour.
- *externalisation* (reproducing the internalised knowledge and behaviours); Herein people have largely inculcated and imbued the knowledge and behaviours created through objectification, typfication, habitualisation and internalisation.

In appreciating social constructive patterns it is important not to envisage them as a clean, logical step-by-step process. Rather than seeing them as a 'temporal sequence' (*ibid*: p. 149), it is perhaps preferable to view them as an iterative and relational manner (see also Watson and Harris, 1999: 18, and Chia, 1996: 581). In other words, social constructionism is not necessarily simply cause-and-effect but rather outcomes and events stemming from many and varied interactions and moments over time. It can, indeed, be quite difficult to determine how occurrences and events emerge.

One of the cumulative effects of processes, such as social constructionism, is that it fuses into what can be termed a *weltanschauung*. This is a term taken from German meaning 'world-view'. In essence, it refers to the holistic, integral and overall manner in which a given individual views the world. Each person has a 'world view' or indeed often groups of people share a world view in some regard or other. Because of the many, often unique, individual experiences people have, while people share ideas and views, it is highly improbable that they will be identical. So, while social constructive processes are based on shared interaction, it does not necessarily mean that shared views are identical or held on the same basis of understanding or sense-making. In interpretive and inductive research the idea of *weltanschuung* is important because these forms of research are centrally concerned with understanding the subjective ways in which individuals and groups arrive at their viewpoint of the situations they experience. When you are in the field conducting research it is important to be mindful and observant regarding the ways in which people invoke their world view in order to make sense of experiences.

## A WAY OF SUMMARISING VARIOUS WAYS OF VIEWING QUALITATIVE DATA

The above described principles and approaches have led inductive and qualitative management research to be variously characterised by researchers who employ them.

Cassell et al. (2005: 12–16) conducted an examination of qualitative approaches and identified the following categories:

As *verstehen*

[Understood as having:]

> a direct concern with accessing the actor's subjective, culturally derived meanings in order to explain their behaviour through *verstehen*. In other words qualitative methods are defined in terms of an interpretive understanding of the meaning of a set of actions has to an actor through some form of contact with how they experience their experience.

As *verstehen* but with reflexivity which:

> While still emphasizing the aim of *verstehen*, a new mutually exclusive category emerges where … a significant characteristic of research was reflexivity on the part of the researcher … [who] critically scrutinize the impact of their field roles upon research settings …

As a general bags of tools that;

> … implies the possibility of rapprochement between quantitative and qualitative methods since different kinds of information … are gathered in different ways. Therefore, it is the nature of the research question and what is under investigation that should pragmatically dictate the correct methodology to use.

As a specific bag of tools that;

> … enables 'depth of insight … into the workings of organisations that you simply don't get from quantitative research' or that 'gets behind the surface of things … so that you get a more rounded picture of what you are faced with' or 'tries to grasp complexity … by being close to actual management practice'.

As exploratory research;

> Here qualitative methods are seen as being useful … to develop concepts and theory while quantification of those data using content analysis and statistical techniques enable theory testing and evaluation. The result is that all qualitative management research is relegated to a preliminary role prior to the use of more rigorous, that is quantitative research.

As a disposal category;

> Here qualitative research is condemned as something that isn't compatible with proper management research because it is something which inherently lacks rigour and is unreliable due to its subjective nature ...

As specific data collection techniques ... [this sees ...]

> Qualitative research in terms of an array of specific data collection techniques such as case study research or 'in-depth interviews, focus groups, in-depth probing, semi-structured interviews'. Therefore, it was the technique used that defined something as qualitative.

Cassell et al.'s (2005) research is useful because it was based on an extensive range of interviews with established researchers. In other words, the views and positions that they were able to glean and establish were those of the expert community engaging with and employing inductive and interpretivistic approaches. Their research underlines the rich and diverse tradition of working with qualitative data and equally point at the challenges that such work might involve.

In summary to the above discussion on inductivism, it can be seen that, as a methodological approach, it has its own distinctive stance and characteristics. When conducting a piece of research using inductivism, it is vital to try to remain open to the ways in which individuals are making sense of the situations in which they find themselves – respondents and wider actors, participants and fellow researchers. They are all co-constructers of the final product of the research you are undertaking.

## WHAT IS DEDUCTIVISM AND HOW DO ISSUES OF OBJECTIVITY, CAUSALITY, DETERMINISM AND REDUCTIONISM PLAY A ROLE IN THIS METHODOLOGICAL APPROACH?

Deductivism is the name for the methodological approach and set of principles that underpin widely used methodologies such as positivism:

- The deductive approach is generally associated with *positivistic and experimentationalist-style philosophies and methodologies* that value objectivity and therefore quite often, but not always, statistical or numerical data may well have a role in the study.
- *Hypothesis* As a methodological approach deductivism tends to develop *categorical hypotheses within a positivistic-style framework*. These can be tested

by gathering data through a range of firmly structured methods in the field (Cameron and Price, 2009: 74–78). These methods tend to include questionnaires that are likely to involve, for example, a range of closed-style questions and/or structured or semi-structured interviews. In relation to the hypotheses the aim is to determine a 'proven' or 'not proven' (or on occasion partially proven) outcome to the research that has been conducted.

- In addition, it is important to be aware of the concept and operation of a null hypothesis. When you have a hypothesis, in order to able to be sure that you can prove if it is correct, you also need to be able to verify whether or not it is not valid. For example, if we say as a hypothesis:

  a given (sample) group of managers become most stressed on Monday rather than any other day of the week due to email catch-up and overload.

Then equally it may be important to establish a null hypothesis of:

  a given (sample) group of managers do not become most stressed on Monday rather than any other day of the week due to email catch-up and overload.

Usually, or often, statistical techniques are employed to prove or disprove these hypotheses. By establishing the null hypothesis you are categorically trying to isolate and determine the factors that are actually causing the events by directly challenging your hypothesis that states what the cause might be.

### Samples

Deductivism generally involves *relatively large samples*, but not always. The need or desire for large samples is often connected to the requirements of certain statistical methods and techniques. These require particular sample sizes in order to ensure important criteria such as validity and generalisability can be achieved. It can be seen that the larger proportion a sample represents of a given population the closer you are to actually working with the whole population and achieving representativeness (Thompson, 2012).

### Objectivity

*Objectivity* is a major principle and characteristic of deductive (positivistic) approaches. Objectivity can be seen as the aim to secure data that are intended to be free from bias, emotion and prejudice. For deductive research, it is imperative that objectivity be factored into the research design. You will remember that in this, deductivism differs from inductivism because the latter actively claims the inevitably of subjective factors being in play in the research environment as part of its methodological commitments and principles (see a counterpoint in Letherby, Scott and Williams, 2013).

## Reductionism

As part of embedded objectivity and rationalism, deductivistic and positivistic approaches also *involve processes of reductionism*. This inevitably means defining and categorising data, respondents, artefacts and situations as being distinctive and labelling them with a term to *represent* them.

## Causality

*Causality* is another significant feature of the assumptions underpinning deductivist and positivistic approaches and is linked to the idea of variables. Causality refers to the direct affect one variable may have on another, thus causing the variable to act in a particular way. The purpose of this is to be able to see and understand the precise effects and impacts that might exist in a localised space (Maylor and Blackmon, 2005: 200–206). For example, a study might wish to examine the relationship between the decrease in the price of a product and the number of items sold over a given period. Alternatively, a study may wish to consider staff turnover and the shift patterns, or the number of hours staff are asked to work in a given period. Causality is linked to the *notion of determinism* and both play a role in deductivism and positivistic-style approaches. Determinism is a central principle of the scientific approach that underpins methodologies such as positivism. In essence, determinism suggests that one event or action is determined by another event or action.

## Variables

In order to be able to examine focused and sharply defined hypotheses, it is necessary to identify specific items as *variables* that will be examined and measured. This usually means making decisions and assumptions about simplifying a very complex world into a number of clearly defined set of categories. This involves employing reductionist practices by delineating categories and types so that these can be examined as variables. While it may well be acknowledged and recognised that the world is complex it is felt that the only way to understand that complexity is to consider the relationship between certain variables and by looking at them in relative isolation. This notion is partly captured by the Latin expression, *ceteris paribus* – meaning 'all things being equal'. In other words, in so delineating, categorising, and isolating variables for examination and, in order to develop understanding, you temporarily suspend the complexity of the world for the purposes of the study. The reason for this is that if we tried to look at all the complexity at once it would be impossible to see the effect of one variable on another. It is common practice in deductivistic research to identify one item in the study as an independent variable. The independent variable might cause actions and effects upon the item designated as the dependent variable. The dependent variable is an item which reacts and which is affected by the independent variable. For example, you could examine the effect weather has on absenteeism. Within this a potential independent variable could be designated as the temperature. This could then be observed and staff absenteeism would constitute the dependent variable. As the temperature rises it would be possible to measure the extent to which staff absenteeism increases.

It should be remembered that, in contrast, inductivist approaches may not employ the terminology of variables. Inductivism tends to be more wary of clear boundaries and categories and is more likely to see the phenomena not in terms of variables but as socially negotiated and constantly forming and transforming over time and different contexts. Examples of typical inductive phenomena might be aspects of behaviour, identity or personality. Therefore, the idea of reductionism tends to be refuted in inductive approaches as it is not conducive to the in-depth description and richness of the data. Also, for inductivist approaches, a further critique is the risk and danger of a powerful attempt by the researcher(s) to over-categorise and suggest a pre-judged or even over-structured construction of the field rather than permitting the story of the field to evolve naturally (Al-Amoudi, 2007; Fairhurst, 2004).

## WHAT IS THE HAWTHORNE EFFECT AND HOW DOES IT PLAY A ROLE IN RELATION TO INDUCTIVE AND DEDUCTIVE RESEARCH?

When researchers use the term 'Hawthorne Effect' they are referring to the notion of some kind of interaction taking place between the researcher and the people being researched (Birkinshaw and Caulkin, 2012).

The Hawthorne Effect was recognised and coined as a phrase at the beginning of the twentieth century. It was invoked in relation to research carried out at the Hawthorne Plant which was part of the Western Electrical Company (Chicago, USA) (Roethlisberger and Dickson, 1939). The research team wanted to observe if, or to what extent, changes introduced in various conditions such as lighting and temperature in the workplace would impact on the levels of production at the factory.

The experiment worked in the following manner. Researchers gained access to the factory and they planned to adjust a range of environmental factors such as, for example, variations in the degree of lighting and the temperature in the work areas. The aim was to gauge what effect, if any, a specific adjustment in a given work environmental aspect would have on the level of productivity members of the workforce under examination. The assumption, or hypothesis, would be, for example, if a greater or lesser measurable degree of light were to be allowed over the work area, then what increase or decrease would result in the output of the workers?

In the typical research conventions for the period, the research followed a deductive, positivistic scientific experimental design. This involved the setting up of control groups with different sets of workers. These control groups were put in place to see whether the same change in production would take place even if the changes in environmental conditions were not made. The results of the research were difficult for the researchers to comprehend. This was because, independent of the various changes made in the environmental conditions, production appeared to improve. It was realised that other effects were taking place. Among the factors considered as potentially influential were the social interaction and interplay that was taking place between the researchers and the researched groups. In other words, the presence of the researchers in the workplace seemed to be creating an effect in production linked to the workers' behaviour – see Gill and Johnson (2006: 47–65) for an interesting presentation on the Hawthorne Experiments and the associated consequences.

Here, a brief example of the Hawthorne effect taking place within a positivistic study could be:

> Imagine you are interviewing respondents in a firm. You identified the firm and, subsequently, the respondents in the firm through a pre-determined sampling process so as to ensure objectivity. Then you secure the interviews, produce transcripts and start to analyse them. Say you have a tendency to pay more attention to the respondent transcripts of the individuals you liked and enjoyed meeting more than the ones you did not like so much. This is an example of the Hawthorne process in operation.

This interaction may be considered in a negative light or in a more accepting manner depending on the methodological approach through which the effect is considered. For adherents to positivistic and deductive research, the interaction and effect between the researchers and the research participants was viewed as highly problematic. This is because the deductive approach values objectivity as a central principle of the research design and associated data collection. Clearly, the objective of the Hawthorne Experiments was drawn into question and this challenged the value of the findings.

However, for inductive methodological approaches, the view of the Hawthorne Effect is rather different to the deductive view. Inductive approaches acknowledge the role of reflexivity and subjectivity in the research design and execution. This means that it is recognised that interaction between the researcher and the research participants is inevitable and plays a central role in the sense-making of the data.

Stokes (2011) comments:

> Moreover, the case of the Hawthorne experiments and the subsequent creation and labelling of the *Hawthorne Effect* also underlined potential shortcomings and pitfalls in experimental design both in terms of the specific Hawthorne experiments but also in its general methodological approach. Simply stated, it is very challenging to observe complex human social contexts and be able to easily isolate 'variables' and their effect on one another. In a complex and messy social fabric of human society a multiplicity of factors may be at play at any given time in a given social setting (Monahan and Fisher, 2010; Stovall, 2010)

In summary, if you are conducting your work with a positivistic approach then the presence of the Hawthorne effect in your work is likely to be considered to be problematic and will need to be addressed. However, if you are conducting an interpretivistic approach then the Hawthorne effect will most probably be viewed as an implicit and inevitable aspect of the research design, data collection, analysis and discussion.

## BRINGING TOGETHER PHILOSOPHY AND METHODOLOGY

*What should you be mindful of when using your chosen methodology?*

The discussion above underlined that when you read about, identify or connect with a particular research approach for your proposed study then:

- You need to ensure that the methodology you chose for your study, and the way the given approach builds up knowledge (i.e. its epistemology and sense-making) matches the way you make sense of, and see, the world. For example, if you believe that it is important to be as 'objective as possible' in all the decisions you make in life, and, moreover, you believe in the possibility that 'an objectivity' is obtainable and can be shared by people, then positivism and deductivism are likely to work for your study. Furthermore, if you are a person who believes that problems can readily be broken down into boxes, typologies and categories (i.e. through process of reductionism and representation), then this too suggests a leaning towards deductive reasoning.
- Alternatively, if you believe that people and their beliefs and perceptions play an important role in creating what are taken to be 'facts' and 'understandings'

of things and situations, then you are identifying a role for subjectivity in the creation of knowledge and a propensity towards inductivism and methodological approaches such as interpretivism (Letherby, Scott and Williams, 2013).

- Once you have made your choice you need to adhere strictly to the principles of the given methodological approach. For example, a common error on the part of some students and researchers is to state that they are adopting an interpretivistic approach and then, in writing up the work, say how it is crucial to ensure that they ensure the unbiased approach and maintain objectivity in the data collection, analysis and interpretation. This is simply inappropriate and inaccurate because the central principles of interpretivism include inductivism which involves acknowledgement of the role of subjectivity in the work. Therefore, it is important to maintain the principles, commitments and characteristics of each approach.

- A good way to see methodology and philosophy working together is to look at published papers and studies that have employed your chosen approach and emulate them. You need to be careful because, quite often, studies will not explicitly state their espoused methodology. This is very often the case with positivistic studies employing numerical and statistical techniques. These studies sometimes seem to take their approach as being the obvious 'right one' because of the emergence and dominance of that particular scientific paradigm in the last two and a half centuries across natural and social sciences (see Stokes, 2011, and Bamel, Rangnekar, Stokes and Rastogi, 2012, respectively, by way of further discussion and an illustration of a paper conducted in this manner.).

- It is also important to be aware that political and ideological commitments may guide epistemological and ontological philosophical choices. By way of example, it might be the case that you wish to adhere to, and follow a feminist (see, for example, Kleinman, 2007; Ackerly and True, 2010), Marxist, humanistic, conservative, socialistic, environmentalist, critical realist, postmodernist or post-structuralist philosophical perspective. This would mean that your research will be planned, conducted and written up keeping in mind the conventions and beliefs of your elected philosophical domain. In other words, your work will be produced through the lens of that paradigm and philosophy. This means that you will need to seek out texts on these approaches and study them as part of your research approach.

### How do methodological considerations link to realism and relativism?

It will be useful to reflect on notions of realism and relativism in relation to inductive and deductive approaches. This is a complex area but there are some interesting guidance points to be made. When you talk about reality and realism you are involved in making statements about what 'is' and what 'is not'. In other words, you are alluding to concerns and questions about the very nature of existence and being. These matters are at the heart of the philosophical area called *ontology* (Stokes, 2011, and also see Medlin, 2012, for an illustration of its usage).

In relation to *realism*, if you are doing a dissertation or piece of work from a deductive or positivistic methodological approach, you are unlikely to ask many questions regarding the actual, or the degree of, 'reality' of events, people, ideas or things. That is to say that the idea of 'reality' generally tends to be taken for granted and as a given. In philosophical terms, this tends to be called 'naïve realism' (Russell, 1995). Naïve is usually a pejorative term but it has no such connotation in this usage. Rather it means that the observer or researcher sees the world empirically and takes it at face value using the human senses. Institutions, processes and structures are recognised as being present and in operation and yes, of course, research will analyse the histories, trajectories, impacts and consequences of such phenomena, but they are unlikely to be discussed in terms of as being human constructed, impermanent and ephemeral. Rather, they will be described as being outside and independent of human perception, permanent, fixed and unchanging. Once accepted, such a perspective allows you to believe that you can, and should objectively gather data in a research setting and subject it to representation, reduction, determinism and causality (see above). In recent years there has been an emergence of the field of Critical Realism which many researchers argue as bridging some of these tensions between these views on realism and the counterpoint of relativism (Ackroyd and Fleetwood, 2001; Woźniak, 2010).

*Relativism* contrasts with realism. Relativism has come to the fore to a much greater extent during the latter part of the twentieth century and in the contemporary era. It has become associated to a greater or lesser extent with philosophies such as postmodernism, post-structuralism and Critical Realism (Al-Amoudi and Willmott, 2011). Relativism challenges, or is at the very least questions, the notion and possibility of fixed facts and truth. Rather, it tends to see events, identities and meanings as constructed and negotiated through, for example, mechanisms and phenomena such as discourse, signs (semiotics) and language. In many instances, these meanings are emergent, ephemeral and shifting which renders them elusive and difficult to pinpoint with a specific answer. Much of the research carried out under the banner of critical management studies more or less relates to, or directly espouses, relativistic approaches (Stokes, 2011). For students and researchers, one of the advantages of viewing the world through a relativistic lens is that data and observations from the field research are not portrayed in a reductionist manner.

Vignette 3.1 below provides an illustration of how realism and relativism can be conceptualised in relation to each other.

IMPORTANT: Many students or researchers do not explicitly state any position in relation to ontology and epistemology in their research. While this is not necessarily essential it is a potential opportunity to develop a deeper and more meaningful presentation of your work.

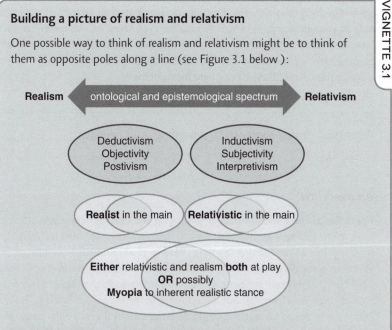

## Building a picture of realism and relativism

One possible way to think of realism and relativism might be to think of them as opposite poles along a line (see Figure 3.1 below ):

Realism ◄ ontological and epistemological spectrum ► Relativism

Deductivism
Objectivity
Postivism

Inductivism
Subjectivity
Interpretivism

**Realist** in the main    **Relativistic** in the main

**Either** relativistic and realism **both** at play
**OR** possibly
**Myopia** to inherent realistic stance

**Figure 3.1** An example of a realism–relativism spectrum

VIGNETTE 3.1

It will be possible to identify varying degrees and perceptions in differing contexts in-between the two poles. In relation to the pole positions of realism and relativism, it is then possible to chart various epistemological, ontological and methodological positions and characteristics along the spectrum. These would of course be approximations and indications rather than specifically marking a specific point. This figure is intended as a visual means to understand the positioning and interplay of these concepts.

## PAUSE FOR THOUGHT: A ROLE FOR COACHING AND QUESTIONS?

The section of the discussion below by Wall (2014) offers one particular valuable and complementary discussion and approach to many of the points raised above. Interestingly and in a timely manner this employs a coaching method through which to pull together many of the issues that have been raised and discussed in Chapter 3 and, indeed, it sets the scene for further issues to be raised in subsequent chapters. Coaching approaches and techniques are playing an increasing role in the training of young researchers as well as business executives. As this present chapter has sought to pull together the notions of methodology and methods, so Wall's 'question-driven' argument and approach offer an alternative and innovative way of considering these issues through coaching methodologies.

### A *question-driven* approach to designing your research

Dr Tony Wall

#### An overview

The power of questions in stimulating thinking and moving people towards an outcome has been at the heart of some forms of action oriented research for some time. Within Action Learning (Revans, 1980, 2011), for example, questions work alongside solutions known to work in similar contexts, or published theory. Here, the questions serve to help people develop and embody their own learning, and test solutions in the real world. Similarly, within the professional coaching world, questions are at the hub of helping people move to, or at the very least move more quickly, to bigger and better things in their life (Whitmore, 2009; Linder-Pelz, 2010; Starr, 2011; Thomson, 2013).

Questions help guide you to find your own answers but drawing on other knowledge sources to find solutions as and when you feel necessary. Connecting this principle to the process of designing research proposals, Wall (2011a, 2011b, 2013a, 2013b, 2014) and Wall and Leonard (2011) have developed key questions that have proven to facilitate the clarity in thinking to achieve more focused, coherent, relevant and strategic research proposals.

The questions move logically between the strategic thinking aspects of design (in which wider problems are being addressed), through to the specifics of when you will actually be asking the questions in an interview (if you choose this method).

When you first use the key questions, try working logically through them, jotting your thoughts under each heading. Pay attention to the thread of logic (what some people call the golden thread) that develops through answering the questions, and notice any contradictions. For example, if you argue that there has been no exploratory qualitative research in your area of focus, and then do a quantitative descriptive study, the thread is broken. After this first usage, and when your confidence grows in using the key questions, you may find it useful to be more fluid in your usage of the key questions. At this point, they become pointers, prompts or reminders of the particular areas you need to ensure you cover for a persuasive proposal.

## Persuasive designs

One way of conceiving of research is that it is different to personal learning. Personal learning is about changing yourself in some way, to see new perspectives that become part of how you see the world. You know you have learnt when you look at things differently. Research has this element, but it is also wider than yourself; you are trying to convince others that your findings are valid, and they are valid because of the way you have designed and implemented your methodology (and of course, the way you have communicated the design and implementation). So research is about persuasion. There are two key principles to note when designing research. The first is to become familiar with Occam's Razor (see Cathcart and Klein, 2007). There are various explanations of this concept, but here, the idea that the simplest solution will usually get you something fairly useful – think of Einstein's 'aha!' moment when thinking of gravity. In other words, keep your methodology simple enough for you to be able to handle it, and for others to understand it. The second principle is linked to Occam's Razor, and is referred to as the dilution effect (Huczynski, 2004). Here, with each bit of additional information that is presented and which is seen as irrelevant, the influence of the researcher is reduced. So it is important to have a sharp clarity of focus and retain this throughout (i.e. the golden thread).

There is one *caveat* in using the questions to help you design a persuasive research proposal as part of an academic or professional award, or whether you are conducting the research as a professional activity. That *caveat* is to ensure you make yourself aware of *who* exactly the proposal is for, *what* exactly is being asked of you in the proposal and *how* it will be judged. Though the key questions are generic and do help facilitate research design, the potential impact can be minimal if you do not specifically address your audience and any explicit requirements. Each of the key questions is now presented with a short explanation.

## A summary:

1. What alternative *perspectives* or *positions* are available to you here?
2. What needs to *change* or *develop* in your research setting?
3. *Who* has said *what* about your focus?
4. What are you trying to *achieve* with your enquiry?
5. How could you *approach* this purpose realistically and persuasively?
6. What specifically are you trying to *find out*?
7. What *data* do you need to answer these questions realistically and persuasively?
8. How can you *collect* these data, realistically?
9. How can you *analyse* and interpret the data, realistically?
10. What specifically will you do to ensure the *ethicality* of your research?
11. Realistically, *who* needs to do *what*, *when*, to implement your research?

### What alternative perspectives or positions are available here?

If you look at something you will always look at it from a particular angle. Let us take the example of if you are walking along a path, facing forward. This angle will reveal some things (the path ahead), and hide other things (what is behind you, what is around the corner). Within research, this might be called a standpoint, and it is awareness of this standpoint that helps you make decisions about what routes to take in your research. This key question is one that should always be present, and is a way of being a critical thinker. It is important because it helps you check the ethics and validity of the methodological decisions you are making.

For example, if you are doing research as an employee (an insider researcher), your particular position in a work context might reveal certain issues but hide bigger issues which might be more easily visible to management. Or as someone doing research as an outsider, you may make assumptions about what is important to an organisation. This is not necessarily about making a value judgement about which is right or which is wrong; both are just different angles on the same thing. Rather, it is about becoming aware of the different angles that exist to help you make a decision on which angle you want to take. Importantly, some angles may give you more potential to make a difference or contribution to an area of investigation, because it is framed in a less directed way. In the same way, some particular angles may negatively impact certain groups, which are ethical problems.

Similarly, you may already have pre-conceived ideas of how something should be (a way of operating) or should be done (a solution) based on your own opinions. Or you may *believe* that something should be different. These 'shoulds' and beliefs are all forms of bias which are useful to become aware of and consider whether they are ethical and appropriate for the ultimate purpose for your research. This allows you the opportunity to accept or change the perspective or position to enhance the validity and persuasiveness of the research. Some of the additional prompt questions that might be useful checks are:

- How *is your own position affecting your choices?*
- *How is your own perspective affecting your choices?*
- *What assumptions are you making?*
- *Who may benefit and who may not?*
- *Who may be disadvantaged?*

### What needs to change or develop in your research setting?

In thinking about the focus of your research it is useful for you to think specifically about what needs to change or develop practically in your research setting. Let us be precise here – this is not asking you to think about a gap in the literature – it is about asking you to focus on an important issue that needs addressing in some way. As examples, the issue may be important to society (but to who specifically?), a particular industrial category, a particular group of organisations, a particular type of organisation or particular group of people. In asking what an important issue is, this assumes two things. The first is that there is an audience, that is, that you know *who* the issue is important to. Is this specifically managers? Is it marketeers? Or is it academics? This helps you become clearer about what the issue is for this group, and inform other methodological decisions as you progress your thinking about research design.

And the second assumption is that you have come to *know* that it is important. *How you know* it is important is a crucial aspect. This is about the critical evidence that supports your thinking that it is important – this might be other authors, or it might be statistics that demonstrate that it is an important issue to investigate. The latter might be called a 'killer statistic', something that is so powerful; it cuts straight to the heart of something (killer in the sense of it having such an immediate and direct impact).

Using statistics to demonstrate the importance of your focus is a double-edged sword. On the one edge, it can quickly communicate the significance of something, but on the other edge, the fact can be used at face value without being critical of its context and meaning. For example, the striking statistic that '80% of social media marketing managers use Facebook in promotional tactics' (a fictitious statistic) indicates the importance of investigating Facebook as a promotional tool. Yet, you may want to question the source of the statistic, its currency, which types of organisations, where they were located, which managers were being asked, and so on.

For example, social media marketing management practices in Australia might be very different to those in Russia, China or Ethiopia. This statistic may also have been produced as a promotional tactic based on a small sample of its customers using its social media marketing products, perhaps based in Silicon Valley in the US. So it may not be valid to generalise to other contexts – its validity is questionable. Again, it is important to ask the first key question when thinking about what needs to change or develop, that is, 'What alternative perspectives or positions are available to you here?' The outcome of asking this question is a statement of focus. The broad area of what you are looking in terms of what needs to change or develop (according to who) becomes your research focus and needs to be phased simply, for clarity and consistency of thinking from hereon in (the golden thread).

## Who has said what about your focus?

Once you have reviewed the situation, you will have identified a focus, and will have examined it to ensure it is ethical and appropriate from the perspective of the people you are trying to convince. The next step is to examine the literature to identify what people have said and done in relation to this specific area. This is not about paying attention to everything that has been said about things related to it, or examining all of the linked debates. This is tempting for those who are passionate about their focus – but can lead to delays and wasted energy. It is about directly tackling the specific focus you have just identified, and particularly what people have said and done about addressing your specific focus.

A useful way of thinking about this is that it is a conceptual toolkit which enables you to think more in depth about your focus, and therefore, help work towards a clearer methodological approach (the next part of this research design process). As part of this toolkit, you are specifically looking for different frameworks, processes and models. For example, if the specific focus is to identify the talent development practices that might help fast-growing high-tech businesses, you are looking for that (e.g. talent development + fast-growing high-tech businesses). This might appear simple, but so many researchers spend too much time examining a much wider boundary that leads to wasted efforts.

Of course, if this search does not provide a literature that provides you with a useful conceptual toolkit of frameworks, processes, and so on, it is then – and only then – useful to widen the scope of your research. In this example, it might be useful to search for 'talent development + fast-growing' or 'talent development + high tech'. 'Talent development practices' might be the highest-level search, but you would be taking a lot of time to sift through a wide research base. The more you focus, the more efficient you will be in dealing with the results from your searching – and remember, you are wanting to find a toolkit which you will actually *use* in the coming stages. Spending time debating definitions is useful only if it helps you clarify your thinking – move on to the frameworks, processes and models that you will use.

## What are you trying to achieve with your enquiry?

Having read and examined the literature, you will have built your conceptual toolkit about your particular focus. These may be frameworks, processes and models from academic and practitioner sources. Each will provide alternative views (or angles) on your chosen focus. This now allows you to consider two interlinked decisions: the first is **deciding which specific angle of the toolkit would be useful to take**, and the second is deciding **what specific outcome you are seeking to create with your research**. The linkage is in the idea of *use* (or utility) – the use will partly be determined by the outcome you are looking to create. To help think directly and explicitly about use, or the utility of your research, try finishing off these sentences in your area of focus:

- *To identify recommendations …*
- *To enhance …*
- *To recommend a course of action …*

This statement then becomes your **research purpose**. An example might be to *identify recommendations* for improving the *lead generation success rate* of social media promotional campaigns. The 'identify recommendations' is the actionable outcome, and the *'lead generation success rate'* is looking at a particular part of the sales process (as identified by the researcher in the literature).

To achieve the clarity and sharpness of your thinking, use this as a more precise 'golden thread' that helps you make decisions about your approach, methods and other methodological decisions. This replaces the need for other terms such as 'research aims', 'objectives' or 'outcomes', enhancing the clarity of your thinking. However, there may be occasions when you are asked to write these for your research.

## How could you approach this purpose realistically and persuasively?

Knowing what specifically you want to achieve (your research purpose) guides you in your thinking about a broad approach to designing your research. There are some very simple ways of thinking about your '**research approach**', but there are no widely accepted ways to describe it. Two alternatives will be shared here, but use the one that seem the most useful for clarifying your thinking about options. In using these ideas, it is not about mixing and matching them, but rather choosing one way to discuss your approach clearly – remember Occam's Razor and the dilution effect. Rather than being accurate descriptions of the reality of research approaches, treat them more as metaphors. Metaphors help us *engage* with the reality of something but are recognised as *characterisations* or *typologies* rather than *actualities*.

One way of thinking about approach is to think about the (over-simplistic) dichotomy of qualitative versus quantitative. Does your purpose require more soft data about people's thoughts, opinions and attitudes, or does it require hard data about measurable facts (even 'striking' statistics)? Or does it require a mix of these, for different elements of it? If so, which elements? And again, do not over complicate your methodology – flexible thinkers can easily design qualitative and quantitative studies in almost any topic matter. So be selective.

Another way of thinking about approach is investigating something *before* action, *during* action or *after* action (inspired by Chandler and Torbert (2003)). This helps you conceive of options in terms of an event that you want to investigate, and points in the direction of particular collections of methods. Again, it is intended as a metaphor rather than a precise device to help you make a decision (if X, then Y). Investigating something *before* action points to survey or decision analysis-type approaches. These might be more appropriate if it is impossible or too risky to investigate something in action, such as finding out customer preferences or trends before investing in a new product. Investigating something *during* action points to action research approaches, where you intend to make a change or need to trial something in the authentic context of a situation to be able to trust it. Cycles of action/evaluation are the basis of finding new insights. An example might be a change programme with a particular profession or community.

And, finally, investigating something *after* action might point to evaluation-type research approaches. This might be more appropriate when you need to assess the actual impact in practice, but where there isn't the opportunity to undertake a number of cycles in practice. But again, because this is a metaphor, it aims to aid thinking rather than depict reality – for example, a survey might be useful as an 'after action' approach, but where the focus is on what *has happened* rather than what *would or might happen*.

## What *specifically* are you trying to find out?

Once you have a clear idea of your research focus, have turned it into a more precise research purpose and have decided upon a research approach, the next step is to design some research questions. What *specifically* are you trying to find out which will take you towards your research purpose? The word *specifically* is intentionally italicised; it is not about turning your purpose in to a single broad question, it is about thinking through what you need to know to complete your purpose. For example, you may have a purpose to identify recommendations for improving the lead generation success rate of social media promotional campaigns. There might be questions related to how success is defined in lead generation, what the most successful social media campaigns are, what the factors are that lead to success, and so on. But answering these questions may not complete the full logic of your research purpose, that is, to actually *recommend* something. So it is important that you complete the logic of your research purpose with your research questions.

It is also important to note the difference between research questions and the questions you ask in collecting data, say an interview question. A research question specifically looks at the logic of your research purpose, and so is a broad question. An example might be 'what are the factors that are important to lead generation in social media campaigns?' Whereas if an interview was being used to collect the views of social media experts around the globe, there may be a series of interview questions, based on frameworks explored in the literature. These might include, for example, a broad opening interview question such as 'In your view, what is important in maximising the number of leads within a social media marketing campaign?', followed by a number of prompts, such as 'What about the use of blogging?', 'What about the use of micro-blogging?' and 'What about the use of networking sites?', and so on. The key point is to keep the research questions distinct from, but intimately linked to, the questions you ask people in data collection.

## What data do you need to answer these questions realistically and persuasively?

Once you have decided your questions, it is useful to work systematically through each question to identify what data you need specifically. The more specific you can be here, the easier it will be to identify relevant methods to collect the data. For example, if you are seeking to identify the impact of an advertising campaign, you might be looking at a person's thoughts, feelings and opinions towards the campaign (and more specifically, indicators of their attention, interest and desire towards purchasing the product). You may also be looking for whether a person acted or not: did they enquire, did they buy or did they recommend? The first set of data is soft, or qualitative, where there is no set answer or response, whereas the second set is hard, that is, yes/no, and more easily categorised as quantitative.

After taking this in to consideration, it is important to cross-check with each of your research questions. This process might identify additional research questions you may want to ask, or it might highlight 'scope creep' – the idea that you are collecting more than you need to, to answer the research question. It is also useful here to remind yourself of who the audience is for the research and any particular preferences they have for types of data. For example, figures or quantitative data can be very powerful in influencing higher level decision-makers, or certain industries/professions in which statistics play an important role, such as health care and medicine. Wenger (1999) makes a wider point to argue that this influence extends across levels of a hierarchy; statistics are a universal language up, down and across organisational structures.

## How can you collect these data, realistically?

By the time you get to this question, there is clarity about what and why data is being collected, in terms of research focus, research purpose, research approach and research questions. This key question is about how the data (specified in the previous key question) will be collected, and this includes methods such as questionnaires, interviews, focus groups, etc. Being an Occam's Razor is important here, to ensure the clarity of the method(s) you select, to collect all of the data you need to answer your questions and to work towards your research purpose. It is typical to jump between this key question and the next one to ensure the totality of your method(s) together will be realistic. It may be surprising to you that this explanation is smaller than many of the key questions before it; this is intentional. There is a lot of thinking and scoping that precedes the selection of methods to collect data.

## How can you analyse and interpret these data, realistically?

It is important to realise that methods to analyse and interpret the data are part of your total methodology. Often, people learning about research will think research is just about data collection (and some think the more data that is collected, the better!). However, moving from mountains of raw data to meaningful insights in order to recommend or take action is an important step. How *will* you move from the raw data to spot the patterns, trends or insights from the data? Part of the answer lies in *not* collecting mountains of raw data in the first place; designing research questions that specifically address your purpose, followed by designing methods that create a manageable amount of data. This includes a valid sampling strategy that gives you a persuasive set of data, data that will speak to those you are trying to convince with the findings. Again, analytical methods might be classified into qualitative ones, such as thematic and category analysis (picking up patterns in qualitative data), or quantitative ones, such as frequency counts, normal distribution analysis, trend analysis, and so on. You'll notice, however, that the golden thread of logic has been picked up from your selection of research approach, research questions, methods of data collection, through to methods of data analysis. Keep the golden thread pure.

## What specifically will you do to ensure the ethicality of your research?

Once you have designed your methods of data collection and analysis to work towards your research questions and broader research purpose, you need to check the ethics of your decisions. You will have been asking the first of the key questions through all of the other ones, that is, 'what alternative perspectives or positions are available to you here?', but it is useful to do a final check before you spend time on scheduling. As with all other stages of research, there are different ways of thinking about ethics. One useful and simple way of thinking about it is to refer to three concepts (see Sales and Folkman, 2000): autonomy, beneficence and justice.

- **Autonomy** is about treating human subjects in your research as decision-making beings rather than simply subjects without choice. People need to understand why the research is being undertaken, the possible advantages and disadvantages of being involved, and be given the choice to participate or not. In addition, a person's identity must be protected, with high standards of confidentiality. Beware of inadvertently revealing someone's (or an organisation's) identity through single cases.

- **Beneficence** is about seeking to maximise the benefits to human subjects while minimising harm and risk associated with the process or outcomes of your research. For example, if your research was investigating new protective clothing product, it should not put human subjects in danger of being burned in experiments with different types of chemicals.
- **Justice** is about the fair distribution of costs and benefits associated with the research, so that particular groups or individuals do not bear disproportionate risks or harm while others reap the rewards. For example, if your research was investigating facilities for elderly people, it should not result in extra provision for them, at the expense of young people. This may be tricky to deal with in some cases, so be aware of it.

*[n.b. More is written on ethics and seeking approval in Chapter 6]*

### Realistically, who needs to do what, when, to implement your research?

Once you have reached this stage, you know the types of methods you will be using and the implications of them. This stage is about deciding who needs to be involved, when and how. This may sound simple but involves coordinating people and their responses to requests for information or return of surveys. There are two important things to remember. The first is that your tasks will typically take longer than you originally expect – particularly in relation to data collection. Just because you ask for a response politely (or even demand it from people you know very well), this does not mean that the response is as important to them as it is to you. This needs to be respected; not everyone is involved or wants to be involved in the world of research. This means you need to build in buffer time to await responses, to follow up and then follow up again.

The second thing is that you probably won't get as many responses as you would ideally like; again, responding to your survey is not everyone's top priority. Buffer time helps the follow-up activity that is needed to obtain the number of responses you need. But also make sure you have a contingency in place to get the responses you need for a valid amount (sample) of data. Planning using a Gantt chart is very helpful to map out the tasks involved, and to identify which tasks are dependent on other tasks. Once you have a Gantt chart, you can also use it for monitoring your research as it progresses.

## CONCLUSION

You have now experienced a question-driven approach to designing research. You will notice that you will be able to answer many of the questions through thinking about what you already know. That is intentional. Your thinking is not likely to be clear straight away, but expect that and continue to craft it until you get the precision of a golden thread. It is also to be expected that you will need to seek answers and clarity from other literature. The idea is that you join clear thinking with what you systematically seek out in published sources so you can craft a *focus* which is then followed by *method*(s). In other words, method follows focus and purpose, rather than method being the driving force in design. Research design can be an exciting process, but also challenging, and a clear framework of questions can help you work through the methodological decisions you have as a researcher. Use the questions to determine your golden thread (focus, purpose) to then help you select choices which will convince others of the validity of your findings. This is where your research can really add value beyond personal learning, that is, to help move and improve things in organisations and communities: to create influence and impact the world around you.

## GLOSSARY OF TERMS

There are many terms which might be included in this section. Many of the terms related to methodological approaches are dealt with below.

**Action research** This is a large topic that commands a substantial and, at times, complex literature. The general principle and thrust of action research is that it is a piece of research that, by first identifying and distilling extant knowledge in a domain, is then able to identify potential for action and real improvement in relation to the research setting(s). Stated more basically, action research is research undertaken with the express aim of being directly used to change things rather than being research that is carried out and then remains in a book, paper, report and is not actively applied to a 'live' setting. Heller (2004: 349–360) provides a very useful and insightful overview on the approach.

**Epistemology**  Epistemology concerns the processes by, and through, which knowledge is made. The way knowledge is made or developed reveals assumptions and beliefs that researcher(s) hold about the world. Therefore, every piece of work will adhere to a particular epistemological stance or position whether or not this is explicitly stated in the work. It is quite common for different discipline areas, or indeed sub-discipline areas, to generally use a particular epistemological approach. One of the common central differentiators of various epistemologies is their adherence, or not, to subjectivity or, alternatively, objectivity.

**Case study**  Case studies are in-depth studies of a particular situation, company or organisation. The case study usually provides a short history, a synopsis of the current situation and then details of the most pressing issues or problems that are to be considered in the case. Above all, when a case is offered in a text book the intention is for student to come up with answers. When a case is presented in an academic paper or in a dissertation it is, of course, meant to provide data, but it is also intended for the student or researcher to suggest answers and recommendations for actions and solutions (Yin, 2003, 2011).

**Causality**  Causality relates to the idea that one event brings about another event. In the scientific paradigm, this is a central theme and assumption and it is common, as part of that approach, to identify variables (independent and dependent). These variables can then be measured and the effect of a change in one variable can be assessed on the other. Causality is therefore a feature of positivistic approaches to research. In contrast, while causality is at play in subjectivised and interpretivisitic methodological research approaches, these methodological perspectives tend to see research settings as context based and having potentially many causes rather than occurring through the (perhaps simplified and reductionistic) view of one variable impacting on another.

**Deductivism**  Deductivism is a methodological principle and approach (Cameron and Price, 2009: 74–78). Deductivism is prone to constructing hypotheses (see Chapter 1) which are then tested in an objective manner by gathering data which will demonstrate whether or not the hypothesis is proven or not. Deductivism is at the heart of the scientific method and the scientific approach to building knowledge (see epistemology above) (Cameron and Price, 2009). See Vignette 3.2 below.

## The 'reality' of many students early views of dissertations and research

Although it is difficult to generalise, it is the case that large number of dissertations and research undertaken still adhere to what can be termed positivistic and realist commitments and principles. This is largely because, due to historical influences and the philosophical hegemony of science and deductivistic scientific methods, a large amount of education has been imbued (to a large degree unilaterally) with these values. When teaching students in a classroom it is often the case that they are automatically using deductivistic and positivistic orthodoxies and rationale to make sense of ideas. It is profoundly imbued in a Western (and increasingly Asian) cultural mind-set.

However, here is the interesting irony. Once they have undertaken a course in research methods, when asked, a large number of students declare that they will be using a 'qualitative' approach. By this they actually mean an interpretivistic approach. For some students who have yet to deepen further their understanding of the research methodology sphere, they believe that 'qualitative' means using words and description rather than numbers and statistics of a quantitative approach. In fact, what students sometimes fail to grasp is that, rather than saying they are 'doing a qualitative' or 'doing quantitative approach', it would be more accurate to use the terminology inductive/interpretivistic or deductive/positivistic methodological approach. Many academics and researchers feel that it is inappropriate to use the expression 'qualitative dissertation' or 'quantitative dissertation'. It would be more pertinent to say that 'qualitative data' and 'quantitative data' are used within a dissertation methodological framework of either inductivism or deductivism.

**Inductivism** Inductivism is a methodological approach whereby data are collected and then, subsequently, the emergent theory and meaning is developed by the researcher in relation to the respondents. Inductivism recognises the subjectivities at play in these processes and takes account of them (Bryman and Bell (2007); Jankowicz (2005); Kuhn (2009); Silverman (2010a, b); Whittle (2008)).

**Interpretivism** Interpretivism is often seen as a collection of techniques and approaches that are characterised by inductivism and subjectivity with regard to the data they develop. Interpretivism and positivism approaches to research seem to be the most commonly presented and discussed approaches employed by students. As such, they are often presented as the dichotic choice available. As has already been discussed this is not necessarily the case (Fisher, 2010; Silverman, 2010a, b). See Vignette 3.2 above.

**Mixed method research** The expression 'mixed methods' is often used to mean that a piece of research uses both quantitative and qualitative research approaches. Alternatively, some researchers use it to mean the use of a combination of methods within a piece of research (Clark and Creswell, 2008; Creswell and Clark, 2010).

**Objectivity** Objectivity is an important principle of deductive and positivistic approaches. It is seen as critical for these approaches to be able to ensure that no researcher subjectivity or interference has impinged on the research data. This is in stark contrast to inductive and interpretivistic researches which openly embrace the idea that subjectivities are inevitably at play.

**Ontology** Ontology concerns a researcher's attitude to the nature, solidity and substance of reality. In this way ontology and epistemology for a given methodological approach might be considered to make up a large part of the 'DNA' of that approach. For deductive, positivistic approaches reality is simple and straightforward. A chair is a chair, rain is rain and a house is a house and so on and so forth. These notions, identities and concepts are not problematised beyond what can be empirically, objectively and externally observed. In other words, reality lives outside and independent of the observer's perception. However, for inductive and interpretive approaches, reality is seen as being perceived and constructed subjectively by the people including the research respondents and participants and the researcher (see, for example, Al-Amoudi and Willmott (2011) as an illustration of these issues).

**Positivism** Positivism is a methodological approach that values objectivity and is grounded in deductivism, reductionism and causality. It uses the notion of hypotheses (see above) as an integral part of its process (Bryman and Bell, 2007; Clegg, Kornberger and Pitsis, 2008).

**Qualitative** Qualitative is a term used by students and researchers to indicate types of data often associated with words, images, pictures and diagrams. This contrasts with quantitative data linked to numbers and statistics. The term 'qualitative' is also used to refer to a type of overall study as in, for example, the expression 'I'm doing a qualitative dissertation' usually implying use of interviews and semi-structured questionnaires (Eriksson and Kovalainen, 2008; Silverman, 2006, 2010a, b). However, in relation to this it is important to see the caveats mentioned elsewhere in relation to qualitative and quantitative data (see Vignette 3.3).

## Reliability, validity and generalisability

These are essential considerations for your research design and should be considered at the outset rather than during or at the end of the study.

Think of these three aspects as providing the safety and security checks on the value and usefulness of your research.

1. *Reliability* – In your research design, how will you ensure that your research design is clear and transparent to others in such a way that, should they chose to, other researchers could repeat your work and reasonably anticipate achieving the same result(s) – see Maylor and Blackburn, 2005: 157–159 for a useful overview).
2. *Validity* – In your research design, how will you ensure that your research design will produce results that can be considered true and reasonable, that is to say, valid.
   • Do your results seem plausible and credible?
   • Are you using your chosen methodology and methods correctly and in an appropriate manner?
   • Are you discussing, and portraying, your findings and results in a manner that is considered fitting for your methods and methodology?
   • In relation to all the above would the wider community of researchers favourably consider and review your study?
3. *Generalisability* – In your research design, how will you handle this?
   • You must show the extent to which you believe your results and findings can be applied to other similar related cases or settings.
   • How far and wide is it reasonable and pertinent to suggest that your results are relevant and pertinent?
   • As a general rule, the smaller the sample, the less generalisable the study will be.
   • In general, inductive and interpretivistic studies tend to use smaller more localised and focused samples because these approaches believe in scrutinising a particular small domain in great detail.
   • Deductive, positivistic studies, in general, tend to encourage the construction and analysis of larger samples. Often statistical approaches are applied to these samples and a certain size of sample is required for these techniques to be able to be used (see Hultsch, MacDonald, Hunter, Maitland and Dixon, 2002).

- Even if your work is, relatively speaking, using a large sample, remember that it might relate to a specific context only. For example, if you have examined human resource practices in a wide range of steel manufacturing companies, it may well be the case that lessons are available for human resource practices in other industrial sectors, for example, retail, or logistics. However, this cannot automatically be assumed to be the case.

In relation to reliability, validity and generalisability, it is often suggested that triangulation can play an important role in strengthening these aspects of research design (Cameron and Price, 2009: 216–218 provide a useful expanded view of triangulation). Triangulation is generally seen as the use of a number of research methods in a research design, for example, combining interviews, questionnaires and focus groups so that a range of data is collected in different ways. This is seen as deepening and enriching the data especially in positivistic approaches. Some researchers using interpretivism do not believe that triangulation is relevant or appropriate. This is because interpretivism espouses subjectivism as a central principle of its approach. Therefore, interpretivistic researchers ask the question – if data are subjectively and reflexively constructed by researcher and respondent interaction in the research setting and context, to what extent will a further method to gather additional data actually be in a position to further corroborate subjectively developed data set? The suggestion would be that a new method would work only to generate a further, albeit interesting, subjectively derived data set.

**Quantitative** The term 'quantitative' implies the use primarily of statistics or numerical data in a study. It is also used sometimes when people state they are 'doing a quantitative piece of work' meaning they are using numerical data and a methodology of positivism and deductivism (Donaldson, 1996, 2005; Ha, 2011; Kremelberg, 2011).

**Reductivism** Reductionism is a term used to points to the simplification of complex research phenomena and data into more readily identified variables. For positivistic approaches, reductionistic-style approaches are an inherent part of the research process. In other words, these methods focus on identifying and isolating variables so that the effect they might have on each other can be examined. On the other hand, interpretivistic approaches are reluctant to overly engage in reductionism on data because it is believed that it might distort or diminish the riches of the material and the research outcomes.

**Representationalism** We can think of representationalism as involving the act of 'bringing the world and its artefacts into existence' through the act of categorising and labelling them. When we label something or someone, this is a very powerful act. Labelling, or representing, is likely to invoke a range of assumptions and presumptions regarding the object of it.

## KEY POINTS

- *Be brave enough (but also wise enough) to go deeper and further* – In many research reports and dissertations students often make very limited and rather simplistic (one might say 'safe') statements about the research methodology they are employing. Almost invariably, whether at undergraduate or postgraduate level, this will usually involve a choice between positivism and interpretivism. Often phenomenology is used as a synonym for interpretivism but please read the cautionary note on this above.

  This is laudable but potentially rather limited and simplistic. Go a little further and clearly demonstrate how your adopted methodology infuses and lives through you and the entire work. Remember, your adopted methodology is a statement about how you see and feel about, and perceive, the world. Learn about the ontological and epistemological characteristics and political commitments of your chosen approach (and the ones that you have decided not to choose). Really work to understand why you chose this one and not another and then relay that in your written work. Your academic reader will appreciate your efforts and you will feel more in control and fulfilled.

- Also remember that there are many other philosophically underpinned approaches to conducting research. Illustrations, among the many possible options, could include: Critical Realism; Critical Theory; Deconstructionism; Postmodernism and Poststructuralism. These particular examples lean towards the inductive part of the epistemological spectrum, but there are many other possibilities. Look at papers that have embraced and employed these terms and see how they shape the research.

- Ensure that you recognise the common (although somewhat misguided) usage of the terms of 'qualitative' and 'quantitative' and that, in fact, you should be asking deeper questions about your adopted methodological approach.

- Recognise that the choice usually discussed in research methodology sections of dissertations and articles is between positivism and interpretivism. Recognise that a wide range of further choices are also available and worth investigation and consideration.
- Central to understanding methodology is the need to understand the concepts of epistemology and ontology and the role of subjectivity and objectivity in relation to these.
- Recognise the difference between research methodologies and research methods – methodologies are rooted in (often historically founded and developed) philosophical schools and positions; methods are more akin to tools and techniques (for example, interviews and questionnaires) which are used within methodologies.

## REVISION QUESTIONS

Think about situations where individuals hold different opinions about issues, topics and situations. Why is this the case? Why do you hold the opinions you believe in? (Clue – for example, think about the ideas surrounding social constructionism and sensemaking (Berger and Luckmann, 1966; Weick, 1995)). How does this connect and interface with methodology?

What do you feel about the validity of the statement: 'X is an objective and scientifically proven fact'? (Clue – think about the issues in the question above and the constant tension between objectivity and subjectivity).

## FURTHER STUDY

1. Easterby-Smith, M., Thorpe, R. and Jackson, P. (2012) *Management Research*, London: Sage Publications.

   *Chapters 2 and 3 cover the philosophy of management research and the design of management research. These presentations present very useful and cogent insights into the historical and comparative aspects of research design. In particular, a number of useful tables are offered.*

2. Bryman, A. and Bell B. (2007) *Business Research Methods*, Oxford: Oxford University Press.

   *Chapters 1 and 2 provide a useful and in-depth consideration of epistemological and ontological research methodological issues and dimensions. This is a complex and detailed text; however, the writing is lucid and there is a range of tables and diagrams that elaborate important aspects of the topic.*

3. Eriksson, P. and Kovalainen, A. (2008) *Qualitative Methods in Business Research*, London: Sage Publication.

   *This is a rich and intelligently worked text. There are useful expositions of philosophical approaches such as positivism, post-positivism, critical realism, post-structuralism and postmodernism.*

4. Cameron, R. and Molina-Azorin, J.F. (2014) 'The acceptance of mixed methods in business and management', *International Journal of Organisational Analysis*, 22 (1), pp. 14–29.

# 4

# RESEARCH METHODS AND DATA GATHERING

## OBJECTIVES

*Successful completion of this chapter provides guidance on:*
- How to understand the difference between methods and methodology;
- How to appreciate the strengths, weaknesses and issues surrounding specific methods;
- How to select appropriate methods as part of your research design;
- How to use a range of research methods competently in order to gather data.

## INTRODUCTION

Research methods and data gathering require planning, but they might be considered very much at the 'doing' or implementation stage of the research process. There are a number of choices, complexities and processes in relation to methods and data gathering that have to be taken into account. Vitally, it is important to understand the interaction of methods in relation to methodology.

## CONSIDERATIONS AND CHOICES IN RELATION TO METHODS AND METHODOLOGY

### What is the relationship between methods and methodology?

It is a common oversight to confuse research methods and research methodology. This possibly occurs for a number of reasons. On the one hand, research methods

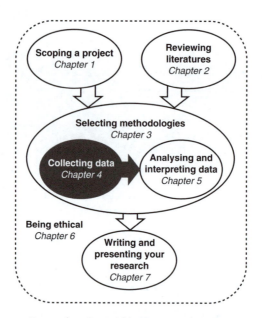

Current location within the research process

and research methodology share the same words in whole or in part – research and method. However, it is important to remember some basic facts regarding these areas:

- *Research methodology* is about the conceptual and philosophical framework of your work. In other words, it maps out the epistemological and ontological character, commitments and design of your investigation (you will remember these technical terms from Chapter 3).
- Alternatively, the area of *research methods* is about the *specific tools and techniques* that you will be employing *within your specific research methodology*.

*IMPORTANT: Your choice of method will always be guided and influenced by the overall and over-arching methodology you have chosen (and not the methodology being influenced by the method).*

For example, if you chose interviews as a research method then you will view and conduct the process of carrying out those interviews and the analysis of the data you glean from them very differently if you are using, for example, a positivistic methodology than if you are using, for instance, an interpretive methodology. To elaborate this illustration further, in a positivistically framed interview, you will be aiming to ensure that the data collection and analysis is conducted with evident objectivity in mind. All possible influences of the researcher will be excluded as far as possible. In order to achieve this you will need to frame the data collection in a well-bounded and controlled manner (using structured or possible semi-structured interviews), so that it will be possible to analyse them by employing, for example, statistical analytical techniques (Saunders, Lewis and Thornhill, 2012). Alternatively, if you are using interviews within an interpretive framework, your approach is likely to engage with the idea that the researcher's thoughts are likely to play a role in

**Table 4.1** Diagrammatic illustration linking probable alignments of exemplar research methods and research methodologies

| Research Methodology | Likely Research Methods | Guiding Principles |
|---|---|---|
| Positivism | Structured Interviews Questionnaires | Substantial efforts made to ensure *objectivity* in research. Distancing of the researcher from the respondent. |
| | | *Reductionism* – categorisation of the data. |
| | | Causality – the seeking of *cause-and-effect* interactions between variables. |
| | | Research experiment and environment may be likely to be subjected to control and structure (for example, a laboratory or interview/meeting room – in part to ensure the desired objectivity and rigor of the process). |
| Interpretivism | Unstructured/ Semi-structured | Recognition of *subjectivity* at play. |
| | | Acknowledgement that research respondents exercise own *sense-making in the creation of meaning in their settings and contexts*. |
| | | Data emerges from a *rich and complex environment in its own natural setting* (as opposed to setting up formal interviews/ observations). |

shaping the research and the interpretation of the data in conjunction with the sense-making taking place among respondents and the research context and setting. You are likely to use a style of interview that will suit this, namely, semi-structured or unstructured interview which will allow respondents to express themselves fully in their own terms (Bryman and Bell, 2007). It is possible to attempt to portray these broad dispositions in the form of a diagram (see Table 4.1).

The ideas and contents of the above table are indicative rather than constituting a directive. However, the main purpose of laying out these opening thoughts on methods and methodology is to provide an example that will point up some of the possible linkages between the two interconnected domains.

### What might be some useful questions to help you choose a method for your research design and marry methodology and method?

As indicated in the previous section, it is always important to choose a research method that will fit with your overall research design or methodology. If there are points regarding which you are still not clear on research methodology, then it may be useful to revise Chapter 3. A key issue to bear in mind during this process is to ask yourself the following types of question and consider what your answers reveal. Based on your answers you will know which methodology-method combination might work best for you:

#### In what ways, patterns and types of environments do I like to work?

Am I a sociable, interactive person who finds making contact with people easy or not? If you are, then an interactive process such as an interview or semi-structured questionnaire may feel comfortable for you. If you are a more self-deprecating or quiet person then you may feel more at ease by having some distance between you and the respondents – remote observation, postal questionnaire, for example, may work better for you. This is a common issue and challenge, for example, for many undergraduate students who sometimes feel that, as yet, they lack life experience and confidence to try to conduct lengthy interviews with senior and highly experienced managers in various forms of business and organisations. This is of course completely understandable and a skill that needs to be developed over time.

#### What are the potential complexities in relation to the methods and methodologies I am aiming to employ and the questions I am seeking to answer?

If your aims and objectives require a rich range of in-depth views from multiple perspectives, then imposing too much structure on your methods may not be helpful or conducive to this purpose. An illustration of such a case might be an attempt to talk with senior managers and directors regarding their views on the challenges and difficulties of work-life balance. This could involve gathering fairly categorical data on hours worked; however, you may also wish to gather data based on managers' views, feelings and impressions about their quality of life, the demands of their role and their career ambitions (Saunders, Lewis and Thornhill, 2012). Therefore, you will need a methodology that will provide the possibility of accessing the 'softer' style data as well as the 'hard' data number of hours worked.

However, by way of an alternative example, if you need to gather data that are aiming to gauge the scale and scope of a given phenomenon, then a more numerical approach that allows responses to be proportioned and scaled might need to be undertaken (Walsham, 2006). Again, in this case, a research method (structured interview, questionnaire or survey) that allows data to be quantified in some way may be helpful. An illustration here might be an investigation into types of marketing employed by organisations (the relative percentages they are employed – for example, social media, print materials, television and radio).

Clearly, the two examples above are merely a brief illustration, and the potential range of studies is extensive and varied. The key to being able to approach and make judgements of the kind made above is to try to develop a good and sound understanding of, to begin with, inductive and deductive approaches. When you have done this, it will begin to become a relatively well-rehearsed and straightforward task of seeing how particular methods will operate or function under inductive and deductive commitments and principles.

### How do you see, perceive and make sense of the world around yourself?
This question draws the discussion back to you and your personality and identity:

- Who are you?
- What do you stand for?
- What are your general views as to the epistemological and ontological nature of events you witness on a daily and yearly basis?

These are of course very major and significant questions to ask of yourself (Schön, 1987). You may think that you are just doing a dissertation or a piece of research rather than undertaking what is a voyage of self-discovery. To a large degree you may well be correct in thinking this. However, to not see that an understanding of methodology, with its underpinning paradigms and philosophies, is not also an opportunity to see how you typically make sense of the world is a potential missed aspect in relation to the experience.

You have to choose a research method that fits and responds to this question as was illustrated in the table above. Moreover, this almost inevitably links to the question of 'which research methodology shall I use'? As mentioned above, you need to choose a research methodology that will suit the way you think it is best to make sense of the world, the activities that happen within it and your research question. The two subsequent sections attempt to assist in reiterating and contextualising these ideas in relation to some of the materials that were introduced in Chapter 3.

### Linking the above questions to methods and methodological paradigms in relation to:

### What are Positivism and Empiricism?

If you are convinced by, for example, everyday notions and statements such as 'facts are facts' (i.e. for you they seem self-evident and unequivocal) and you seem to take events at face value, then you are displaying a way of thinking that is kindred with empiricism (Bryman and Bell, 2007; Tadajewski, 2009).

Empiricism uses the five senses to observe and experience stimuli outside of your own body and physicality. In other words you 'see' a world fixed and formed 'out there' and operating independently to you and your physical being. In order to investigate that 'world' you are likely to want to use methods that will 'discover answers' about this world that 'already exists' (as opposed to, for example, being in some process formation or under construction).

In essence, this is one of the principles at the core of the scientific experimentationalist methodological approach to research which underpins positivism. In seeking to find your 'truth(s)' you are likely to construct *hypotheses* about what is probably true or not true and then attempt to prove or disprove them. Reductionism, causality, objectivity, linearity and representationalism also are all characteristics of such an approach (please see the outlines of these terms at the end of Chapter 3). You are also likely to choose methods that allow you to ensure that these features and their boundaries can be maintained and ensured – for example, structured interviews, closed questionnaires and surveys.

### What are Interpretivism and Constructivism?

However, if you feel that quite often you have the impression that people come to the view of what constitute 'facts' through discussion and interaction with others in a range of contexts, situations and experiences, then you are thinking more like an interpretivist. In general terms, for an interpretivist the world is not fixed but rather is 'produced' through language, behaviour, perception and discourse. These interact and crystallise to form individual and collective, that is, group sense-making – if you want to conjure up a very rapid example of this in operation, think about brands and how they operate and influence discursively and semiotically in relation to human/consumer behaviour (Weick, 1995). On a more everyday level think about how your family or you and your friends 'create' a 'world', or 'worlds', of meaning, identity and symbolism that has resonance only with you. For example, a particular place is associated with a particular mood and shared events.

Many interpretivists lean towards theories of social constructivisim in order to attempt to explain and account for how meaning and sense-making are formed in the above processes and situations (Berger and Luckmann, 1966; Al-Amoudi and Willmott, 2011). Essentially, social constructivism suggests that through constant reiteration and exchange, shared ideas and notions gradually emerge and are reinforced and operationalised as 'facts' in people's minds. An example of this might be how a group comes to form an opinion about an issue or another person. This might be based on some discernible events or 'facts', but these events and facts will indeed have been the product of interpretations of individuals that have fed into the socially constructive common sense-making process. For example, in most disagreements, it is common to have differing and sometimes conflicting sets of views and opinions on what occurred. If this is the way you see and approach research work, then embracing subjectivity and reflexivity are likely to be two key aspects of your overall approach. Consequently, you may use methods that can respond to, and reflect, these values. Such approaches might involve unstructured or semi-structured interviews, participant observation and/or focus groups – essentially any method that will allow a free-flow of respondent perceptions and data in a natural (rather than artificial, for example, a laboratory or an interview room) setting (see an illustration in Shinkle and Spencer, 2012).

## A note of caution in relation to the number of methods employed

Early researchers and students often tend to be tempted to use too many research methods. Unless there is a very good reason, be wary of using more than three methods to gather your data. The design of too many methods in your study creates a tremendous amount of work for you in relation to gathering the data and then to undertake analyses of it. Implementation of one or two methods, properly executed, will allow you to gather quality data and still achieve appropriate processes such as *validity, reliability* and *triangulation* (Myers, 2013).

*Illustrations of a range of approaches/methods within methodologies*

The above discussion has made a number of developmental comments in relation to fitting research methods with research methodologies. In the examples above, the discussion has made use of interviews by way of illustration. Therefore, it will be useful to elaborate how other commonly used methods might be operated within particular methodological approaches.

## What is case study method?

Case studies are often favoured by many students and researchers (Rohlfing, 2012). They frequently go hand-in-hand with interviews and questionnaires as something of an automatic choice for the elected research method. You may recognise this and it may be explained because many students have worked through a large number of cases in course materials as the use of case studies in business and management teaching and learning is a frequent occurrence on undergraduate and postgraduate programmes.

A case study can provide a usefully delimited and focused sphere of study. For example, if you have to go into only one organisation or one setting to collect data, it can reduce travel time and costs and also simplify access negotiation processes. It also allows you potentially to build up an in-depth data and knowledge bank on the organisation.

It is important to realise that when preparing a case study it is very difficult to generalise too extensively from the basis of a single case study, or indeed, several case studies. A case study cannot be referred to as a sample because a sample would more likely be a range of cases drawn from a particular population (See Bryman and Bell, 2007; Quinton and Smallbone, 2006: 133 and also see the comments on sampling below).

Typically, case studies are often seen as offering holistic knowledge (Tellis, 1997) or thick description (Geertz, 1973). Equally, they are seen as providing a device that develops 'real-life' data. When you are collecting data for a case study typically there are a number of ways that you might think about organising these data. Usually these will be either:

- time-or chronologically based (more technically termed 'temporal' constructs)
  Or
- based on a particular theme or dimension (more technically termed 'spatial').

As indicated above, the arrangement of your case study in time/chronological order is often a normative part of laying out a case study. In other words, it is usual to provide a historical backdrop leading up to the contemporary period and then focusing on a particular immediate issue. Related ideas on ordering of text were discussed in Chapter 2 concerning literature reviews.

Complementing this, it is sometimes more common to focus on a spatial approach, that is, themes and constructs. For example, in a case study of behaviour among customer service staff in an airport it is possible that recurrent themes of, for instance, dedication, 'going the extra mile', camaraderie, may emerge in parallel with issues of boredom and disillusionment with management initiatives and resistance to change. The case may be constructed more around these issues rather than a temporal approach. However, within these constructs, it is equally possible that there may be chronological presentation. To take an example: the case data may have generated a theme of 'dedication'. This theme will have many traits and characteristics within the case context. However, in addition to this it might be possible to chart the development over time of this phenomenon within the airport where potentially dedication was present, grew and then was damaged and diminished by other factors within an alternative emerging and colliding theme of disillusionment.

## How do case studies relate to deductive methodologies?

In relation to using case study methods in inductive or deductive approaches, there are a number of points to consider. A case study is an approach that has its own literature which discusses it both as a methodological approach and as a research method. Therefore, there seems to be a rather confusing set of commentaries and views on the approach. However, it might be useful to think of a case study as an approach having it a typical format. It will have an introduction and this will be followed by an initial background history to the case. Having laid down the historical context a brief narrative outlining key events and critical incidents leading up to the contemporary setting will be outlined. Then the case will turn its attention on the focal issue(s). This will be evaluated and the discussion will move towards a range of proposed solutions (Yin, 2002, 2011).

All of this can be conducted within an overall inductive or a deductive methodological framework. If you are developing a case study, and following the above outlined structure and process, within an overall deductive approach, then you will tend to be mindful of all the constructs and principles that operate within deductivisim (see Chapter 3). Most importantly these will include the observance of objectivity as far as possible and beliefs and practices of reductionism, causality and representation. In this methodological spirit, the case study will provide a clear boundary and framework that allows you to establish categories, aspects and issues to be examined in an empirical manner. At the end of the case analysis and discussion it will be anticipated that you provide 'answers' and 'solutions'. You will recall from the discussion in Chapter 3 that the adherence to the belief in deductivism and positivism that a world 'out there' can be 'found' and commented on is a central tenet.

## How do case studies relate to inductive methodologies?

When using a case study approach within an overall inductive methodological approach, it is important to ensure that you are respecting the principles and characteristics of inductivism. These include beliefs that, within the data gathering, analysis and production of the case:

- differing perspectives and subjectivity of perspectives form and make sense of the 'facts' of a shared situation;
- the possibility that multiple causes of a given event or phenomenon are likely to play a central role in the various stages of study design;
- there is unlikely to be one 'answer' or 'solution' to the examined issue of the case. Rather, the case used within an inductive approach will aim to elaborate, fully describe and provide rounded and in-depth understanding pertaining to the issues (Yin, 2011).

In summary, a case study within an inductive methodology provides a space in, or a stage on, which a set of issues might be better examined. Rather than providing boundaries the case tends to provide a context and an arena in which the actors and issues can be considered.

## What is ethnography?

Ethnography is a technical term and approach reasonably widely employed in research methodology (Fetterman, 2010). In fact, it is a very straightforward and an engaging and often varied and enjoyable research methodology and methods.
Ethnography –

- Is about the study of people and groups or communities of people;
- Uses what it sees as 'natural' and 'live' or 'real' settings in which to gather data;
- Examples of 'natural' settings are many and varied and might include a street, house, building, office, park, school, factory and so on and so forth;
- Does not, for example, rely on research in artificially constructed or recreated environments or laboratories;

- As a research approach is best considered an 'array of techniques' (Van Maanen, 1988);
- Is generally an inductive research methodological approach;
- Typically, uses research methods such as unstructured interviews and participant observation;
- Values authenticity of action and language of research respondents;
- Attempts to relate and portray the natural and original flow of action and dynamics;
- Is generally concerned with ideas and data that revolve around emotion, lived experience, sense-making and subjectivities (Weick, 1995; Alvesson and Deetz, 2000; Alvesson and Sköldberg, 2009).

In summary, ethnography means that you plan your research to go and spend time in a given setting, typically using participant observation and interviews in order to collect data. What you are trying to achieve is to develop a rich and in-depth understanding of a particular research setting and the issues that operate and play out therein. This is likely to involve you making a number of visits to one or more physical sites. To accomplish this, you will need to make contact and negotiate access and permission to conduct your study. When on site, you will need to decide how you are going to record observations and interviews and whether you are going to try to do it at the time i.e. as it happens or make notes very soon after events and conversations.

### How does ethnography relate to inductive and deductive methodologies?

It is pertinent to consider inductive and deductive methodological approaches in relation to ethnography because the position is reasonably categorical. Ethnography is almost without exception viewed as a methodological approach that inherently employs inductive approaches. As discussed above, ethnography very much involves considering and seeking to understand how research participants and respondents make sense of, perceive and construct their experiences and the environments in which they take place. Evidently, this invites a wide range of subjectivity (or multiple 'subjectivies') to be at play. For this reason, inductivism is well placed as an approach to try to take account of these issues. In terms of research methods, an ethnographic, inductive approach is prone to using methods that will afford respondents opportunities to express and relate their own understandings of issues.

In the light of the above, it can be seen that the principles to which deductivism adheres are less well suited to an ethnographic approach. In particular, it is virtually impossible to secure the requisite 'objectivity' for a positivistic style study. This is for the simple reason that ethnography operates on the basis that multiple views on 'truths' and 'facts' may be in operation. Similarly, ethnography might, but is unlikely to, engage with hypothesis construction, reductionism and linear causality which have all been discussed in some depth in earlier sections of the text. The reason for this is that they are susceptible to over-simplifying the rich and complex subjectivities of the respondent accounts in a manner that inductivism does not invite (see a background illustration in Power's (1991) comments in relation to accountant training).

## What is Critical Incident Method?

Critical Incident Method (CIM) is a research method that aims to identify and describe key and significant moments in respondents' experiences (see by way of example Trönnberg and Hemlin, 2013).

In order to secure its data CIM tends to use approaches like, for example, interviews, participant observation and questionnaires. Typical questions you might use include:

- 'What led up to the event?';
- 'Who did and said what to whom?';
- 'What happened next?';
- 'What were you thinking and feeling at that moment?'
- 'What was the outcome?' (Paraphrased from Bryman and Bell, 2007: 288).

As a researcher you will sometimes realise that the people you are meeting and talking with may not realise that what they are experiencing might be characterised as critical incidents. To them it might be what happened in a normal day within their working lives. Critical incident approaches have been widely employed in a range of practitioner research settings. For example, it has been used to try to better understand experiences in health service provision contexts for varying stakeholders (Tripp, 1993; Ghaye and Lillyman, 2008). Butterfield, Borgen, Amundsen and Maglio (2005), in their article 'Fifty years of the critical incident technique: 1954–2004 and beyond', provide a very valuable review of the approach.

## How does critical incident method relate to inductive and deductive methodologies?

CIM could potentially be employed within either an inductive or a deductive approach. If CIM were employed as part of a deductivistic or positivistic study, then the boundaries and delineations of what constituted the 'incident' would be clearly determined. You as researcher would be important in determining which 'incidents' would be identified as the critical moments. Moreover, you might designate and measure a number of pre-determined metrics or key indicators that would assist you in identifying these points. Around this you would be keen to construct variables and hypotheses that could be tested in relation to data collected within the incidents.

Alternatively, if you were to use CIM within an inductive framework you would probably enter the research environment or setting and allow the respondents responses and actions to signal what constituted the critical incidents. In other words, it would be the data from the research respondents that would signal the salient and important issues and features of their experience. The aim of inductive approaches within CIM would be to provide a rich and complex description and analysis of the incidents and, in particular, the context(s) in which they occurred (see examples of the above approaches in Tuuli and Rowlinson (2010) and Kraaijenbrink (2012)).

## What are interviews?

Interviews are a commonly selected method that students chose to use for their research methods (Gubrium, Holstein, Marvasti and McKinney, 2012). An interview might seem relatively straightforward, after all, it is in one sense simply a situation wherein one person is talking to another. There are, however, a number of important considerations to take into account.

### Why use an Interview?

Interviews are generally used in order to:

- Gain data which is rich in descriptive and emotional colour and character;
- Allow interviewee respondents to elaborate orally at length and in their own terms;
- Allow the interviewer to be able to see, hear and generally sense the interaction with the interviewee.

### Types of interview

Interviews can be used either as part of deductive approaches (e.g. with positivism using extensive quantitative techniques and data) or, and in fact more frequently, as part of inductive approaches (e.g. with interpretivism and employing qualitative techniques and data) (King and Horrocks, 2010).

Interviews are conducted by **interviewers** and the people being interviewed are called **interviewees**. Interviews can include **open and/or closed questions**. Closed questions are questions phrased in a way that invites a 'yes' or 'no' answer. Examples of closed questions include:

- Which one of the following colours is your favourite one: green, red, blue or none of these colours?
- Which political party would you vote for: Conservative, Liberal, Labour, Green or None of these?

These sorts of questions are easy to count and conduct numerical or statistical analysis on.

Open questions invite a personal and varied response from the interviewee. They generally seek opinions and views and provide an opportunity for the interviewee to elaborate and expand their comments. Examples of open questions include:

- How would you describe your favourite colour?
- Who might you vote for and why?

The questions to be asked in an interview are generally drawn up into **an interview schedule**. This is essentially a list of questions looked at and used by the interviewer. Sometimes, the questions will have prompts next to them or supplementary/lead on questions from the principal question (Bryman and Bell, 2007: 217–218).

There are a range of **types of interview** and they can be used to suit particular circumstances and achieve certain desired effects. Interviews can be conducted in a number of *modes*, for example:

- Face-to-face
- Via telephone
- Via internet (for example, Skype)
- In a focus group whereby a few or several people are present at the interview discussion

The face-to-face mode is the most common means of doing interviews. This way allows the interviewee to witness expression, tone and body language more directly. All of these can be very useful contextual signals and clues in the interview setting.

In terms of actual *forms* of interview the usual forms employed are:

• Structured
• Semi-structured
• Unstructured

## Structured Interview

In a structured interview, the questions to be asked to the respondent are all mapped and written out very clearly. The interviewer then straightforwardly asks the interviewee the questions without varying from this question schedule. This can be frustrating for the interviewee. On occasion, inexperienced researchers use a structured interview with closed-style questions thinking that this will provide them with all the details they will need in order to be able to write up their research. However, unfortunately, they end up with a series of answers that are rather truncated and limited. Structured interviews are more frequently used in deductive and positivistic-style research. Therefore, it is more common in scientific-orientated research than business and management which more often than not tends to employ semi-structured and unstructured approaches (see an illustration in Stel, H., Staal, I., Hermanns, M. and Schrijvers, A., 2012).

## Unstructured Interview

An unstructured interview is very much the opposite of a structured interview. In an unstructured interview there will be a number of questions that relate to a particular item or topic. These will serve to open the interview conversation and then it is anticipated that the interviewer and interviewee will engage in what is essentially a conversation. The interview schedule will contain further prompt or steering questions which can be used to steer or re-energise the conversation (Blumberg, Kelly, Olmstead and Youmans, 2013).

## Semi-structured Interview

This style of interview is a combination of the structured and the unstructured interviews. Essentially, there will be a number of fixed questions. Indeed, some of them may even be closed questions interspersed with more open-style questions. This structure of approach allows flexibility in questioning approach and also allows specific and systematic data to be secured (see an illustration in Aarikka-Stenroos and Jaakkola, 2012).

## Issues and procedures in conducting interviews

There are a few thoughts that might be useful to reflect on when you are thinking of conducting interviews. Firstly, it is sometimes helpful to conduct some trial interviews as part of a pilot study rather than waiting until the principal study. A pilot study will be undertaken with respondent interviewees who are not the individuals who will be the main target of the study. This means that you will not make mistakes and waste time using a weak or inappropriate interview approach on the people you genuinely want to interview for your study. Remember that if you conduct a poor interview and the interviewee has a poor experience, you are unlikely to be able to return with a more polished version. A pilot study therefore allows the interviewer to see how well the questions and the interview approach work.

Your interview questions will be shaped by the following factors that have already been discussed above:

- Research aims;
- Objectives;
- Research questions;
- Sampling issues and choices;
- Identifying members of the sample;
- Gaining access and making appointments.

In terms of interview logistics and personalities; your interview choices must match the interviewees you are engaging. This includes the process of gaining access to interviewees and the process of completing and exiting the interview. (For further valuable insights and background in relation to interviews, see Fisher, 2010: 167–172; Kvale, 2007 and King and Horrocks, 2010).

Generally, it is a valuable idea to record interviews. To do this, ensure that you have a high-quality recording device and that practicalities such as leads, batteries and mode of operation have been worked through before the interview. One of the authors once attended an interview using audio centre equipment from an institution which had been guaranteed as ready and operational. Due to pre-allocation elsewhere, the equipment was available only a short time prior to travelling to the interview. On the way to the interview, the equipment was verified by a co-researcher and it transpired that the specification had changed from that requested and also the batteries were flat. This produced a hurried rush in the rain around a set of small stores located near the interview venue in an attempt to find batteries and a rapid familiarisation re-briefing session on the equipment operation in the car prior to starting the interview. If we had proceeded as planned the author would have arrived at the interview, opened the 'guaranteed operational' equipment only to find it non-functioning. It can be seen that preparation and checking are always vital.

From experience, many interviewees do not mind being interviewed. Indeed, although some respondents are cautious at the beginning and mindful of the recorder, it is common for the interviewee to forget very quickly that it is present and engage in a more relaxed mode.

Following the completion of the research it is, in some cases, generally considered good ethical practice to return the recording, if possible, to the interviewee. Or, alternatively, to delete and destroy it when the research has been completed and written up. Whatever your decision, you should inform each of your participants about your approach before the research starts.

## How do interviews relate to inductive and deductive methodologies?

Interviews can be, and are, used extensively within both inductivistic and deductivistic research. In deductive and positivistic research interviews are carried out as a means of gathering data. Typically, deductive approaches use structured or semi-structured interviews. As indicated above, these allow you as the researcher to structure and pre-determine the direction of the interview and the area of data that you wish to collect. In deductive research you are collecting data that will be analysed with a view to responding to, and answering, your research questions and hypotheses. Your analysis will most likely employ some form of coding, grid or similar structure (Saldaña, 2012). It is also possible that it may include some statistical and quantitative analytical elements. This might be part of a mixed (quantitative and qualitative) approach or not. This will allow for the implementation of categorisation, reductionism and the establishment of causality between the variable(s) around which you have established the questions, structured and conducted the interviews and then analysed the interviews in relation to the coding you have established.

Within inductive research, it is common to use semi-structured and unstructured interview formats. Inductive research seeks to allow respondents an opportunity to discuss and reveal experience, as much as possible, in their own terms and through their own perspectives in an in-depth manner. The data from the interviews are generally analysed through various forms of intensive reading and re-reading. This will produce themes that emerge from the data; however, this emergence will, for the most part, be driven by respondent responses (Silverman, 2010a, 2010b). Importantly, unlike deductive approaches, inductive approaches will also take account, through reflexivity, of the subjective interactions between the researcher and the data and the researcher and the research participants.

## What is participant observation?

Participant observation is a long-standing research method that essentially involves watching and engaging with people in order to be able to develop data about their behaviour and the events and environments in which they operate (Hammersley, 1993).

This approach involves using means to record actions, behaviours, speech, expressions, body language, situations, settings and contexts (DeWalt and DeWalt, 2002). It should be noted that participant observation is usually employed in order to collect qualitative data. These data would be records of the events and features described above. However, it can also be used to collect quantitative data which might be frequency counts. An example here would be the number of people entering or leaving a shop or another establishment. It might also be the number of times a term or expression is employed by an individual or in a group.

As an approach, participant observation draws on a number of classic sources. One of these, Junker (1960), provides useful a typology of the approach:

1. the *complete participant*, who operates covertly, concealing any intention to observe the setting;
2. the *participant-as-observer*, who forms relationships and participates in activities but makes no secret of an intention to observe events;
3. the *observer-as-participant*, who maintains only superficial contacts with the people being studied (for example, asking them occasional questions);
4. the *complete observer*, who merely stands back and eavesdrops on the proceedings.

Although well known, this typology remains an indicative one, and clearly, it might be possible for you or other researchers to modify or develop this typology to include further states. For example, in the virtual era, it is reasonable to suggest that, on occasion, observation could be carried out remotely through, for example, closed circuit television or video link (Marschan-Piekkari and Welch, 2004: 247)

Though it cannot be stated categorically, in general, the mode 1 and 2 of the typology would generally lend themselves to inductive styles of research. These modes allow you to immerse yourself completely in the research environment in order to draw out rich data and description. This will involve recognition of reflexivity and subjectivity between you as researcher and the people you are researching and this will have to be reflected in the way you analyse the data and write up your research.

On the other hand, the modes 3 and 4 invite a more deductive type of approach. Here, it can be seen that, distance and remoteness offer a possibility of objectivity that aims to address deductivistic approach principles.

Moreover, Spradley (1980) provides a classic, well-cited and useful typology of aspects of the research field in relation to which data can be gathered. These aspects or dimensions are paraphrased below:

- **Space** – The researcher can describe the physical space in which he or she is operating – what does it look like, smell like and feel like?
- **Actors** – Who is the researcher observing? What are their age profiles and personalities? What relationships exist between the various actors?
- **Activities** – What is taking place in the setting? Who is doing what with whom?
- **Objects** – What objects or 'things' are present in the research setting and what role do they play in relation to the actors?
- **Motivation and Goals** – What are the actors moving towards? What is driving them?
- **Feelings** – What emotions are at play? How do actors behave? What is their mood – happy, sad, depressed, elated and so on and so forth.

Observation is a commonly employed method within ethnographic research. One of the reasons for this is that it enables the observer to collect data in naturalistic settings (i.e. as opposed to an artificial environment, like an interview room, specially constructed for the research). For example, a researcher might want to observe how people interact in particular work environments. Being able to locate yourself in those settings and quietly observe situations can be a useful way to see the rich and full context of what is taking place:

> Ethnographers engage in participant observation in order to gain insight into cultural practices and phenomena. These insights develop over time and in relation to the social relationships in the field as well as through repeated analysis of many aspects of our field sites. To facilitate this process ethnographers must learn how to interact with the people in the field and how to take useful and reliable notes regarding the details of what happens in their research contexts. (Erikson and Kovalainen, 2008: 141)

Participant observation can be overt or covert. Overt observation means that the people being observed know that the researcher is indeed a researcher and is in the act of observing them. In other words it is open and candid about its act and intentions. Overt observation is the most common form of observation.

However, on occasion, you might decide that for the purposes of the research it is necessary to conduct observation in secret. In this event, you would be carrying out covert observation. This means that the people being observed do not know that the researcher is in fact a researcher undertaking a research study on them. Clearly, covert research can be highly contentious for all concerned, and many researchers do not believe it is appropriate or ethical in under any circumstances. However, some researchers decide that it is the only way that the data they seek can possibly be collected.

### How does participant observation relate to inductive and deductive methodologies?

Participant observation is used in connection with both deductive and inductive methodologies. When it is used with deductive approaches it is most probably going to adopt a form of observation that is relatively distant or remote from the situations observed. This echoes the more distant modes of Junker (1960) types 1 and 2. This will be linked to a desire to maintain a sense of objectivity which is important to the deductive paradigm.

On the other hand, participant observation is a central technique used within inductive approaches and, therein, it would be most probable that, as the observer, you would wish to be as close to, and embedded in, the situations as they are being experienced by the research respondents. For this reason, it is most likely that you would be inclined to employ modes 3 or 4 of Junker's (*ibid*) typology. As indicated above, these modes are the observer-as-participant and complete observer forms of engagement. These modes mean that you work and live, for significant periods of time, almost in the same manner as a participant would do so. Almost inevitably, this will mean that you get close to the research subjects and it will be extremely difficult, if not impossible, to claim any sense of subjectivity. Indeed, as an inductive researcher you would tend to embrace and acknowledge the operation of subjectivity within these modes and take account of it through the concept of reflexivity in your analysis and writing up.

### What are questionnaires?

In its most basic form, a questionnaire is a list of questions the purpose of which is to secure data on a given topic or research subject (Gillham, 2008). When people first set out on a piece of research they often immediately think of using a questionnaire. Perhaps one of the reasons for this is that it is a research instrument they are most likely to have experienced in some form or other in everyday life. However, there are two *caveats* to keep in mind. Firstly, a questionnaire may not suit the research question or the approach you intend to adopt. Secondly, it is dangerous to make the assumption, as some people do, that research questionnaires are relatively easy to design and conduct. Questionnaires require considerable thought, design and testing in order to ensure that they will deliver the data and ultimately the information that is required.

Generally, questionnaires tend to be designed in order to produce precise responses and resultant data. They are not generally used for lengthy, descriptive answers – something to which interviews are more suited (Quinlan, 2011: 326). Whatever form of questionnaire you choose to draft and employ, the questions need to be shaped by your title, aims, objectives and research questions. This will ensure that the questionnaire is aimed at the appropriate target audience and will ultimately deliver valuable and useful data.

Questionnaires usually contain *open questions* or *closed questions*. The comments made above in discussing interviews apply here also. There are a range of forms that a questionnaire might take. An illustration (among the many possibilities) of a questionnaire is provided in Vignette 4.1. This questionnaire could be used to some greater or less extent in relation to the approaches to questionnaires discussed below.

---

### An example of a questionnaire

Below is one example of a questionnaire. It is by no means the only style or format that might be possible. However, it provides indicative ideas on what a questionnaire might contain.

**London *SME Needs Analysis Questionnaire**
**(*SME – Small- to Medium-Sized Companies)**
**Contact Details:**
Name: ................................................................................................................
Organisation: ....................................................................................................
Address: ............................................................................................................
E-mail: ................................................. Telephone: ...................................

1. Type of business:
   ☐ Finance
   ☐ Property
   ☐ Manufacturing
   ☐ Retail
   ☐ Other (please specify) ................................................................
2. Would you describe your business as selling a service a product or both?
   ☐ Product     ☐ Service     ☐ Both

VIGNETTE 4.1

3. Where is the postal address of your business located?

☐ Central London    ☐ Berkshire    ☐ Essex    ☐ Other

4. How long have you been established?

☐ Pre-establishment phase    ☐ Less than 2 years    ☐ 2–5 years

☐ 6–10 years    ☐ 11–15 years    ☐ More than 15 years

5. What is the structure of your business?

☐ Sole Trader    ☐ Partnership    ☐ Limited Company

☐ Other (please specify) ...........................................................................

6. Do you employ any staff?    ☐ Yes ☐ No

If Yes, please state:    ☐ No of Part-Time    ☐ No of Full Time

7. What is the turnover of your business per annum?

☐ ‹£25k    ☐ £25–£55,999    ☐ £56k–£99,999

☐ £100k–£249,999    ☐ ›£250k

8. Business philosophy: Which of the following best describes your attitude to business growth?

☐ We are happy to grow our business to a stage where it supports our choice of lifestyle but would not wish to grow beyond this.

☐ We want to grow the business even if it means making lifestyle changes.

☐ Our decisions are made upon a commercial basis.

☐ Other (please specify) ...........................................................................

9. Have you ever used a business support service (bss)?    ☐ Yes ☐ No

If yes who did you use?.................................................................................

When did you last use a bss?    ☐ ‹2 years    ☐ 2–5 years    ☐ ›5 years?

10. Do you need to develop your product/service further?

☐ Yes ☐ No

*Level Rating:*    1    2    3    4    5    6    7    8    9    10

Are there particular areas of support that would benefit your business? ..

........................................................................................................................

11. How important is marketing and promotion to your product/service?

*Level Rating:*    1    2    3    4    5    6    7    8    9    10

12. What methods of marketing and promotion do you currently use?

13. Do you need any support with marketing and promotion?

☐ Yes ☐ No

*Level Rating:*    1    2    3    4    5    6    7    8    9    10

14. Do you use any of the following in the running of your business:

a)  IT    ☐ Yes ☐ No

Is this an area that you would like to develop further?    ☐ Yes   ☐ No
*Level Rating:*    1    2    3    4    5    6    7    8    9    10
b)   E commerce    ☐ Yes    ☐   No
Is this an area that you would like to develop further?    ☐ Yes   ☐ No
*Level Rating:*    1    2    3    4    5    6    7    8    9    10
c)   Social media    ☐ Yes    ☐   No
Is this an area that you would like to develop further?    ☐ Yes   ☐ No
*Level Rating:*    1    2    3    4    5    6    7    8    9    10

**15.** How do customers interact with your company?
   ☐ Online – Own website
   ☐ Online – Third-party website
   ☐ Direct – By telephone/e-mail
   ☐ Direct – In person
   ☐ Other (please specify) ...........................................................................

**16.** Would you be interested in joining a county-wide online booking system?
   ☐ Yes   ☐ No

**17.** If you employ staff, do you have personnel systems in place?
   ☐ Yes   ☐ No
   If yes, please specify what type of systems are used

**18.** Are there any identified training needs for you or your staff?

**19.** Do you have plans to employ anyone in the next 6–12 months?
   ☐ Yes   ☐ No

**20.** Would you consider employing someone through an apprenticeship?
   ☐ Yes   ☐ No
   *Level Rating:*    1    2    3    4    5    6    7    8    9    10

**21.** Do you need any support with staffing/recruitment/training issues?
   ☐ Yes   ☐ No
   *Level Rating:*    1    2    3    4    5    6    7    8    9    10

**21.** Other funding exists to support employers when recruiting staff, would
you like further information on this?
   ☐ Yes   ☐ No

**22.** Other funding exists to support employers when recruiting staff, would
you like further information on this?
   ☐ Yes   ☐ No

**23.** Does your business need any support with grants/finance?
   ☐ Yes   ☐ No
   *Level Rating:*    1    2    3    4    5    6    7    8    9    10

**24.** Do you need any support with legislative issues such as?
- ☐ Health & Safety
- ☐ Taxation
- ☐ Quality standards
- ☐ Licensing
- ☐ Environmental
- ☐ Equalities, discrimination or disability legislation

**25.** Does your business operate internationally?
- ☐ Yes  ☐ No

## Conducting face-face questionnaires

A face-to-face questionnaire is a questionnaire where the researcher goes through the questions on the document in the presence of the respondent.

Face-to-face questionnaires can be very good for personal interaction and creating a positive atmosphere with the respondent. In contrast, postal and online questionnaires are likely to be less successful in this regard as they are completed by the respondent remotely from the researcher who designed the questionnaire (Irvine, Drew, and Sainsbury, 2013). Generally, face-to-face questionnaire approaches tend to illicit a reasonably high response rate because it is possible to engage and encourage the interviewee to undertake it. These forms of questionnaire can, however, be time-consuming and mean that data collection is relatively slow. This is particularly the case where gaining access and undertaking travel have to be carried out in order to be able to administer the questionnaire. In addition, if, for example, as a researcher you feel that you are of a quiet or retiring personality then a face-to-face questionnaire may not be an ideal method for you. It will be better to collect data through a more remote method.

## Conducting postal questionnaires

A postal questionnaire uses land-based mail and postal services to deliver a questionnaire to the respondent. Using the post can be very expensive if large numbers of questionnaires are planned. One of the advantages of this form of questionnaire is that it potentially enables a large number of people to be contacted providing that the costs and administrative tasks can be supported. However, if contacting a wide range of people is one of the objectives of your research, then some email and social media approach may be preferable (Brace, 2013).

A major disadvantage with postal questionnaires is that usually the response rate is very poor. Response rates will of course depend on: the nature of the research, the questions asked and the nature of the target audience; however, generally response rates for this method can range from as low 5–20%. In addition, even when responses are forthcoming, respondents rarely want to write in great length to open-style questions and therefore the depth and quality of answers is limited.

### Conducting email and online questionnaires

Questionnaires can be relatively easy and cheap to distribute. This is especially the case since the advent of the internet. There are now free applications and websites that can assist researchers to write online questionnaires. Survey Monkey™ is one such example of an online survey and questionnaire (Buchanan and Hvizdak, 2009).

### How do questionnaires relate to inductive and deductive methodologies?

Although it is difficult to be overly categorical, deductive approaches will tend to employ forms of questionnaire that are going to provide data that will allow specific responses to specific questions. While these questions will not necessarily, or automatically, be of a closed nature, they are, nevertheless, unlikely to invite wide-ranging and lengthy responses. If the research methodology is deductive and it does seek data through semi-structured or unstructured approaches, then there will usually be a series of hypotheses that are being tested and also the data analytical framework will aim to distil key terms and themes in relation to the hypotheses through a pre-determined coding system. This may, or may not, involve the application of statistical testing techniques. Structuring and approaching the study this way works to provide the sense of objectivity which is valued and required for deductive methodologies.

In the case of inductive techniques, it is much more probable that semi-structured and unstructured interview approaches would be used from the outset. Here, the intention will be to allow respondents to respond at great length and depth in a free-ranging manner (within, of course, the scope of the question posed). Subsequently, these data will be inductively analysed which will involve multiple and varying forms of reading and re-reading in order to identify emergent salient themes and aspects of the data. This process will recognise the role of subjectivity through reflexivity between you as the researcher-reader of the data and the respondent-participant who produced and delivered the data (David and Sutton, 2011).

## Narrative research

We can think of narrative as being similar to storytelling. Storytelling techniques are now a relatively widely employed technique in relation to research methods. Key commentators and works in this field include Josselson and Lieblich (1993), Boje (2001), Czarniawska (1998, 2002, 2003, 2004) and Gabriel (2000). Storytelling is generally associated with inductive and interpretivistic methodological approaches.

The data are usually collected through methods such as participant observation and interview. Other devices such as reflective and autobiographical diaries, logbooks and techniques are also employed.

### How does narrative research relate to inductive and deductive methodologies?

Narrative research approaches are, for the most part, engaged within an inductive approach. Narrative approaches have a very rich tradition and invite respondents to recount stories. As they do so they are joining together and relating pieces of their experience or their impressions of events. This is clearly from their perspective and therefore involves individual opinions, viewpoints and subjectivity. Inductive approaches embrace this variety as a central value and worth of what they are able to contribute to research.

This is not, however, to marginalise narrative completely from deductive approaches. It is possible to gather data, in a similar manner to semi-structured interviews or questionnaires and then subject the data to analysis (coding and/or statistical) into order to respond to, and answer, pre-determined hypotheses.

## Statistical analysis

Statistical analysis is a complex area which contains many techniques and approaches. It is generally used within deductive types of study because the numerical basis of the approach allows a sense of objectivity through the already described concepts of reductionism and causality. It is common to use some form of software such as SPSS in order to organise data and conduct analyses (Landau and Everitt, 2004).

It is quite feasible to use statistical analysis as part of a mixed method approach. This means that the research will employ both quantitative and qualitative approaches. For example, a piece of research may conduct a (qualitative-style) research interview with a group of managers in order to gauge their leadership styles. Alongside, it might be possible to carry out a statistical analysis on the performance indicators of the firm (e.g. profit level, staff turnover, etc.). This could then potentially allow some form of correlation to be assessed to see if, and to what extent, the indicators married with certain styles and approaches of leadership (see Stein and Foster, 2011, for further illustrations).

Statistical analyses are more often than not techniques that work with, and on, quantitative data. However, it would be an over-simplification as statistical approaches are also accompanied by, and require, a narrative to run alongside the numerical aspects of the approach.

### How do statistical analyses relate to inductive or deductive methodologies?

In general, statistical approaches are a central part of deductive approaches and form a key part of the typically underpinning positivistic methodologies. As indicated above, this is not to say that a statistical technique cannot play an important part in a mixed methods approach. You will note the important and careful phrasing here.

We talk of *mixed methods* but it is best to be cautious of employing the term *mixed methodologies* and the issue around statistical approaches points this up well. While it is possible to use *different methods* (i.e. interviews, questionnaire, etc.) within the same study, it is considerably more challenging (not to say contradictory or incommensurate) to use *different methodologies* in the same study. This was a point raised and addressed at some length in Chapter 3. The reason resides in the complete contrast of characteristics and principles between inductive and deductive methodological approaches. Therefore, if you use a statistical approach in your research you will need to ask yourself the question – Am I looking at these statistics with an inductive or a deductive eye and mind-set? If you are in a deductive mode then the use of statistics, employing all the usual and pertinent tests for statistical significance and accuracy of findings, will deliver 'answers' and 'proofs' for the hypotheses you have already most likely mapped out. You will not be questioning the validity of the techniques themselves and the nature of the data they are producing (Bryman and Bell, 2007; Marsh and Elliott, 2008).

However, if you are using an inductive approach, you will potentially want to challenge some of the deductivistic assumptions that are underpinning the statistics you are using. These will usually be statistics from a third-party source that you are using. Because of the conflict between inductive and deductive approaches it would be very unusual to actively engage a deliberate statistical element in an inductive piece of research. Overall, in relation to mixing qualitative-based (inductively linked) and quantitative-based (deductive-linked) approaches you might consider qualitative methods as allowing you to undertake a process of: of 'going 'deeper into something' and quantitative methods showing 'how broad or wide' a research problem is' (Cassell et al., 2005: 30).

## SAMPLES, POPULATIONS AND SAMPLING PROCESSES

### What is a population and a sample?

When research involves gathering primary data it will nearly always involve some form of target audience or *population* on which it is focusing. In research methodology, the word 'population' is used in a technical sense rather than an everyday sense. A population means the entire sphere or group in which you are interested. This does not at all mean that you are looking at, or actually examining, that whole group; rather it is the group from which you are going to choose the smaller group that you are intending to study (Thompson, 2012). For example, if you were interviewing a sample of employees from the company about team-working practices, then the population would be the entire company workforce. From this overall population of the entire workforce you would choose a smaller selection of people in relation to whom you would actually conduct the research. However, alternatively, if you were investigating this issue with selected individuals in a given department, then the 'population' would be 'the department' and you would select a sub-section or sample of people from the department, and on this sample you would apply your research methods within your chosen research methodological framework.

### How ambitious should you be in establishing your sample?

Early researchers and students are often very ambitious in relation to conducting research with all or a large portion of the population in their studies. It is not uncommon to read early drafts of research proposals that aim to access an unrealistic population. For example, one student once produced an outline proposal to examine certain consumer behaviour issues across a range of supermarkets. The plan was to talk to board-level management in all the major supermarket stores in the UK. It can be imagined that the cost, time and logistics involved in this would be immense and it would clearly be a task for a large and experienced team. Equally critically, gaining access to such a sample of senior and busy managers would be challenging if not near impossible. The risk of over-ambition is a particular risk when you are conducting research on a personal or hobby-related area of interest. For example, another student wanted to conduct research in relation to Premiership football management. His intention was to contact and interview all the well-known names of English football management at the time including Sir Alex Ferguson, Arsene Wenger and so on and so forth. As will perhaps be appreciated, there is an immense number of people in various professional capacities who are seeking an audience with these high-profile individuals, and access would be all but impossible. Leading on from these brief examples and the illustrative lessons they indicate, it is often best to identify a sample that is realistic, accessible and achievable in terms of the study.

### What role does a sampling frame play in the study and what are the considerations that you need to keep in mind?

In order to select a sample, it is quite common to develop a sampling frame. This is a listing of all the categories or types that reside within the population. The sample is then methodically selected from the frame. The aim of this selection process is an attempt to achieve a representative sample that will broadly reflect the composition characteristics of the entire population.

For deductive, positivistic processes, sampling commonly needs to adhere to strict procedures and techniques that must suit the requirements of the statistical technique being employed. Although these vary considerably common ranges of sample sizes in positivistic studies might range from 30 to 50 respondents and above. These types of sample will usually aim to be *purposive* in some way. In other words, the researcher has set out to deliberately construct the sample in a particular way (see the data collected and the discussion by Cassell et al., 2005: 28–29).

For inductive, interpretivistic approaches, samples tend to be smaller in size and more localised to a particular setting. For example, researchers might select a sample of a number of managers from different departments in a firm. Alternatively, the researcher might choose to interview a number of managers from a given department. In inductive and interpretivistic research, samples are often not achieved purposively but, in contrast, are often *convenience samples*. This means that the researcher accesses sites to which he or she has ready access, and the respondents in the sample emerge and become available rather than being deliberately sought out (Teddlie and Fen, 2007).

In sampling, a key question is 'to what degree do wish to be able to *generalise* your research findings?' If your sample is representative of the population then generalisation from your data will potentially be more feasible (Hultsch, MacDonald, Hunter, Maitland and Dixon, 2002). However, if you have a small sample and it is not representative then you are able only to draw conclusions on the sample you are looking at. It will be impossible or unwise to generalise any further as the sample is not representative of the population.

The above issues and tensions are highlighted by the work conducted by Cassell et al (2005: 28) who interviewed expert researcher opinion in their ESRC study:

> I think we're a lot more lenient with the qualitative work because we will accept a convenience sample. In quantitative work, that would be just looked down upon. In qualitative we'll also permit snowball sampling, purposeful sampling and on the quantitative side we kind of obviously look down on that because you can't make any generalisations if you have a non-probability sample.

Moving on to consider different types of sample in a little more detail, there are a range of possibilities for determining a sampling frame. As already alluded to, a sampling frame is the domain and materials (and identified process of access to them) that is used to secure a sample of a given population. Sampling techniques can be divided up into *probability and non-probability sampling types* and these are detailed below:

## Probability sampling

*Simple random sample*    This type of sample means that in choosing who to sample you are as likely to choose any one of the population (White, 2009). An illustration here would be if you were to close your eyes and point randomly at a list, or choose names from a hat. If you were doing research on monitoring stock exchange shares you might pin the stock exchange data tables up on the wall, blindfold yourself and throw darts at the sheets. Whichever shares the darts hit will be the ones chosen. These data items would thus be randomly selected. For a sample to be truly random you need to ensure that you are selecting from all the possible population pertaining to that item.

*Systematic sample*    This is similar to random sampling; however, here you make a decision to use a form of system in the process (Lohr, 2011). For example, if you are planning to interview employees in a company (here the company = the population) you might make a decision to choose every 15th or 20th employee from a list of employees. However, to ensure the randomness of the sample you will need to ensure that the employee names are in random order (i.e. not in alphabetical order as is often the case on employee lists or in organisational telephone directories).

*Stratified random sample*    This form of sampling is useful where the population is not homogenous or uniform (Bryman, 2012: 183–207). Quite often within populations there will be clusters or subsets of various types within a population. Examples of this might be socio-economic groupings in populations of cities or a country.

There are many further possible examples, but an additional illustration might be age groupings – teenagers, 20–29, 30–39, etc. The objective of stratified random samples is to *ensure that each group is proportionally represented in relation to the overall population*. In other words, you want to make sure that you have covered all the variety in the sample of the population appropriately. Clearly, at the outset, this will mean that you will need to be able to identify the research setting or issue as involving a population that has a non-uniform nature and thus requires stratified random sampling.

*Multi-stage cluster sampling* This is often employed in order to overcome a *geographic* challenge in the data collection. Multi-stage cluster sampling (sometimes referred to as multi-stage sampling) creates a progressive series of sampling frames. For example, you may wish to study consumer behaviour with regard to a particular product or market in your country – a very large geographic area for you to cover. Clearly, if you are conducting the research on your own, or even if you are part of a small team, it will be impossible to have sufficient time and resources to conduct a survey or research across the entire population. It should be noted that carrying out a survey is often a potentially complex and labour-intensive approach (Fowler, 2008).

Multi-stage cluster sampling will help to determine a representative sample. A way forward might be to identify cluster areas in the overall population. In the example provided above, this might be, for example, counties (or comparable regional governmental administrative units) within the country. Then you can number the counties and make a random selection of a quantity of them that you are able to logistically realistically able to visit. This means that each person (consumer) you may end up eventually interviewing has an equal chance of being selected. However, counties still represent a large area to tackle, so it will be necessary to move to another stage of geographically narrowing down the sample. Thus, you could identify another level of geographic division. Examples here might be, for instance, electoral wards, parishes or other administrative boundaries. From this you move to the next stage and identify post codes of individual households. Through this process you will have ensured that you have done your best endeavours to ensure a probability based sample.

## Non-probability sampling

*Convenience sampling* In essence, this means that you choose a sample because you have access to the members or units of that given sample. Convenience might have some value as a way of conducting a pilot study as it is readily possible. For example, if we have to conduct interviews you might decide to try to identify respondents in your own organisation. Alternatively, you might decide to approach family and friends. For a number of students, this is a common approach especially when they are having difficulty gaining access to a group of people that they do not know (see Zhu, Sarkis and Geng, 2005, for an illustration).

*Snowball sampling*   This form of sampling involves gradually building up the sample through referrals and networks (Baltar and Brunet, 2012). It is common to use a convenience sample in order to start this process and then roll it into a snowball sample. You start out by contacting people who will be probably and likely to be relevant to your study. From these people, you will hopefully secure recommendations and referrals for the next round of research respondents. Often the referred individuals are open to being part of the research because you are approaching them on the recommendation of somebody that they know and trust. However, for that very reason of unpredictability, with a snowballing technique there is no knowing where the research journey might take you. This is not necessarily a problem but it does mean that your research data gathering will feel like an emergent and unfolding story.

*Quota sampling*   In this method you decide on the traits and characteristics that you want your sample to have. Then you gather members into the sample who qualify until you reach the amount, or quota, you wish to reach. In general terms, in relation to sampling, useful and more detailed presentations are available in Bryman and Bell (2007); Maylor and Blackmon (2005) or Saunders, Lewis and Thornhill (2012).

## INTERNET SOURCES FOR DATA

The internet has obviously transformed the manner in which information is transmitted and accessed. This has of course presented a range of challenges for researchers. In an earlier chapter, the issues and approaches surrounding, for example, Wikipedia™ sources were discussed. The following discussion and expert contribution responds to some of the issues in gathering data on-line.

### The difficulty of obtaining reliable internet statistics

(Written and contributed by Dr Jessica Lichy, IDRAC, France)
    The internet is a diverse medium that conforms to the notion of a *global village* and illustrates a feature of post-modernity, manifested in the popularity of social media. As the online population increases, it follows that greater interactivity generates a

greater diversity of ideas, content and internet user behaviour. At the time of writing (early 2013) over 2.5 billion people use the internet globally. Researchers are beginning to understand what people do online, and the impact being online has on consumer behaviour and interpersonal relationships.

However, knowledge of internet user behaviour is limited. Methods of gathering data on internet usage are often ambiguous and this means that there is a gap in both knowledge and methodology. The various ways of collecting data on internet use are extremely fallible and can be challenged on several points. Measurements of technology usage fluctuate greatly depending on the choice and timing of survey methodology, sources of funding, the interpretation of the data and the purpose of doing research. Website statistics are not entirely accurate either. They cannot measure precisely how many users are using a website. Many statistical sites show referred traffic from a website as a visitor. While this does not affect total visitor numbers, it distorts the overall figures as the webmaster does not see the correct source of traffic to the website. Comparing international trends in internet usage is therefore particularly complex.

Secondary data give a very general view of how individuals use internet-based services; however, there are numerous reasons why published measurements of internet activity need to be used with caution. Six such reasons are discussed below.

First of all, internet statistics are often inaccurate because sales of computer hardware and software are used to gauge the number of internet users. Telecommunication companies report the uptake of triple-play offers (free national phone calls, digital TV and unlimited internet access). However, subscribing to such an offer does not guarantee that the consumer will (or can) access the internet. Some consumers in France, for example, who have purchased triple-play can only use the facility for free national phone calls and digital TV because their geographic location lacks the infrastructure for broadband internet access. But they are included in the statistics as internet users since they subscribe to an Internet Service Provider (ISP).

The second point concerns the practice of circular citation and replication of data among sites. Internet usage statistics are circulated worldwide across different languages and countries. The English-language *Internet World Stats* data are often drawn from Nielsen//NetRatings, the International Telecommunications Union (ITU), the Central Intelligence Agency (The CIA), local ISPs and 'other reliable sources'. The French-language Journal du Net website quotes internet data from Nielsen//NetRatings, ITU, the CIA, local ISPs and Internet World Stats. The Russian-language *Ассоциация Коммуникационных Агентств России* website quotes internet data from eMarketer. Moreover, each country has a different approach of gathering and analysing data on internet usage. Thus, the overall internet user trends consistent across many sites may simply be the cumulative effect of this tendency to use each other's figures – figures that strictly speaking are not comparable figures since there is no guarantee that rigour has been applied in gathering data.

Thirdly, a number of different survey methods and definitions of 'internet access' are used by analysts. Some companies begin counting internet users at the age of two, while others begin at sixteen or eighteen. Some studies include users who have accessed the internet only within the past month, while others include people who have access but do not use the internet (Lake, 1999). Definitions of 'active users' also vary from one market research firm to another. Certain companies count internet users over fifteen years old who surf the web at least once every two weeks for any amount of time; other companies count casual surfers, email browsers or even the number of customers who purchase computer hardware.

Fourthly, much research into internet use has been driven by the concerns of commercial interests seeking to understand the demographics of online audiences, in much the same way as research is done on other media. The intention is to gather sufficient data about an internet user in order to build a customer profile which can be sold on for marketing purposes. Measures of web page 'hits' (the number of times a page is viewed, regardless of whether it is the same person) and domain name growth give a rough indication of the internet's shape – but such measures say little about internet use. For example, measuring the number of domain names registered says nothing about the uses to which those domain names are put. Commercial internet users amass domain names and often do not use them. It is a form of trademarking; thus, McDonald's not only reserves mcdonalds.com but also hamburger. com, ronald.com and so on. Often if they do use all of these names, they all lead to the same web page (Jones, 1998). The web content of school and university domains is likely to be even greater than the web content of commercial domains, since most staff and students have the possibility of creating an educational blog. Tracking hits or domain name growth can at best give a snapshot of the number of internet users but not their user behaviour. Similarly, tracking search engine key-words can only partially reflect the evolution in internet user trends; it does not indicate the evolution of the internet itself. Users looking for a particular site via a search engine may follow several links before finding the site they want to look at (or they may lose the train of thought and end up on a completely different website). Typing errors mean that people sometimes call up a website that is then not consulted. Users without unlimited high-speed internet access may avoid looking at some sites that take too long to load. Moreover, certain servers block access to some sites.

Fifthly, there are weaknesses in the methods used to obtain data on internet traffic (MINTS, 2007); sites that make traffic statistics publicly available are not a representative sample of internet use. Data are often collected from publicly available sources such as 'routers' which forward data along networks. 'Log files' are collected from sites that make them available showing a history of activities performed by the server. Many sites cease updating their traffic records due to intermittent problems, maintenance or changes in network architecture. This can result in actual data being lost; or sometimes a site will record a huge but incorrect traffic volume as a result of some fault. According to Baekdal (2004), roughly 90% website statistics are directly misleading due to how they are calculated. This view is substantiated by Bubley (2009: 1) who draws attention to 'the shameless and unquestioning way that care- less, woolly figures get rolled out' to boost figures. To a certain extent, much of the problem stems from obscure definitions and semantics.

Sixthly, research funding can also skew results, especially when companies are looking for a return on investment. The bias manifests itself in the presentation of incomplete or, worse, inaccurate quantitative information slanted towards the perspective of the funding institution. Generally speaking, government statistics are published less frequently but are more accurate than commercially funded surveys. However, the problem with government data is that 'official statistics' are neither collected nor published in the same way. This means that direct comparisons between two or more countries can be limited. Different organisations gather data in different ways; for example, in the UK, the National Office of Statistics records data by government office region, OFCOM collects data at national level, the Chambers of Commerce collect data about regional or civic business use. In France, some city councils monitor internet penetration in certain areas and industries, as in Lyon,[1] but this is not mandatory. The *Forum des Droits sur l'Internet* publishes quali- tative data concerning ICT usage in France, whereas the government and marketing research companies publish statistics on internet adoption. In Russia, the *Russian Internet Forum* publishes internet data from the Russian Electronic Communications Association in partnership with the leading companies on the internet in Russia. No two countries gather data in the same way.

Thus, the internet presents a unique problem for undertaking a survey. As there is no central registry of all internet users, completing a census or attempting to contact every internet user is neither practical nor financially feasible. For this reason, many internet user surveys attempt to answer questions about all users by selecting a subset to participate in the survey, in other words *sampling*, and then extrapolate these data. Internet users are spread out all over the world and it is thus difficult to select users from the entire population at random. An alternative is to post a survey

---

[1] Le Programme Lyonnais pour la Société de l'Information (PLSI)

online, making it available to all internet users – but the respondents who make time and effort to complete the questions are self-selected and unlikely to reflect the whole population of internet users. Likewise, there is nothing stopping an internet user from completing the survey more than once.

It is, therefore, difficult to gather dependable data on internet use, in order to make reliable comparisons of international (or even national) trends. Over two decades ago, Williams, Rice and Rogers (1988: 15) suggested a possible approach to such a problem:

> Although we consider possible research methods for new media as mainly extensions of existing methods, we propose that the new media researcher should consider alternative methods, or even multiple methods, and to attempt a triangulation of methods.

Triangulation is of course the combination of two or more data sources, investigators, theoretical perspectives or analytical methods within the same study. It is always preferable to employ a variety of methods for collecting data on internet user behaviour to reduce the risk of bias. Methods include surveys, focus groups, customer visits and measurements of people's motivations, perceptions, attitudes and preferences. Secondary data can give a broad-brush outline of internet user behaviour but – in the light of the problems discussed so far – primary data are certainly needed to provide a realistic indication of what is happening in the online environment.

## GLOSSARY OF TERMS

**Case study**  A case study is a research method that involves looking in an in-depth way at a particular company, situation, issue or problem. A case study is bound by the limits of the case narrative and where the case is described as taking place. In other words, the case study is bounded by temporal and spatial limits. By this it is meant that it relates its facts in relation to a particular historical and/or contemporary time period. Equally, it is geographically linked to a particular place or places in relation to that time period. These boundaries mean that part of the case study methodological approach is that only what is written in the case is what the reader knows about the case situation. There may be other facts known outside the case, but if they are not mentioned in the case then these are not necessarily taken into account.

Within a case study, a range of methods such as, among others, interview, question-naire and critical incident method could be used to gather the data required for the research. The purpose of a case study is to identify solutions to situations and problems identified in the case study (see Vignette 4.2 below)

VIGNETTE 4.2

### In brief - What is a case study?

A case study is: Limited by prescribed and specific boundaries detailed in the case. These might be represented by the limits of, for example, a given industry, organisation, environment or individual.

Broadly, tend to follow and be comprised of a series of stages or sections. These generally comprise:

- an introduction;
- background history leading up to the contemporary period or moment;
- the current situation and the focal issues or problems that are to be considered;
- analysis of the issues;
- proposed solutions (Yin 2002, 2011).

Further points about cases studies:

- Generally examine real-life situations;
- Can employ qualitative or quantitative data or, indeed, a combination of the two;
- Can be used in interpretive (inductive) research or positivistic (deductive) research;
- In broad terms, where case studies are used in inductive research, the emphasis will be on elaborating and deepening understanding of various perspectives and subjectivities in relation to a given question or situation with a view to identifying ways forward;

- Generally, where case studies are used in deductive research, the emphasis will be on using objective, positivistic methodology in order to answer a pre-set hypothesis (Yin 2002, 2011);
- A case study has 'boundaries' that define and include what it is looking at and what it is not considering.

On case studies, 'One reason for the popularity of case study research is its ability to present complex and hard-to-grasp business issues in an accessible, vivid, personal and down-to-earth format' (Eriksson and Kovalainen, 2008).

**Critical incident method** As the name suggests Critical Incident Method (CIM) is a method that focuses on identifying, isolating and analysing salient and seminal moments and events in a research setting. Rather than treating all time and action as an even flow, eligible for equal analysis, this technique identifies cameos, vignettes and moment that, when examined in-depth, reveal wider significance for the overall research setting.

**Discourse** Discourse is a term that aims to represent an exchange, expression and communication of meaning, sense-making and identity. Its meaning goes much further than simply being a synonym for the term 'language'. The methodological approach called discourse analysis is a collection of approaches that aim to identify, analyse and understand the effects of communication and exchanges that are taking place in a given setting(s) or context(s). Discourse and discourse analysis will nearly always be dealt with and addressed through interpretive style methodological approaches.

**Ethnography** Ethnography is an over-arching term which points at a range of techniques and methods concerned with the study of groups of people. It is an interpretive, inductive methodological approach that aims to study and demonstrate how meaning, interaction and sense-making occur in groups and settings. Typical methods employed within this approach include unstructured interview and participant observation. Vignette 7.1 provides an extended example of an ethnographic study.

**Interview** An interview is a conversation using some form of structure in order to obtain data leading to information and knowledge. Interviews can use varying degrees of structure ranging between structured, semi-structured and unstructured.

**Narrative** The term 'narrative' is associated with story. It represents and relates a series of inter-linked events. Narrative is generally employed within an inductive framework and, among other objectives, its purpose is to portray interactions in a vivid and lived experience way from the respondent(s) perspective.

**Participant observation** Participant observation is an inductive, interpretive research method that collects data through the researcher spending time in the research setting and with research respondents. This method is commonly used in ethnographic-style studies. See Vignette 4.1.

**Questionnaire** A questionnaire is a list or stream of written questions on a particular topic. These can be asked by a researcher to a respondent and the answers recorded or noted down by the researcher. Or, alternatively, the respondent him or herself can complete the questionnaire. Questionnaires can included open or closed questions.

**Sampling** This is the method and process by which a selection of cases, units or people are made from an overall population (i.e. the whole set or entity). This selection can be made on a probability or non-probability basis.

**Semiotics** The area of semiotics involves the study of signs, symbols and logos in order to understand the meanings and actions that emerge and are created in relation to them.

**Social constructionism** Social constructionism is a concept that seeks to understand and explain the ways in which people employ, for example, discourse and semiotics in order to make sense and develop meaning around language and interaction in groups and wider social settings. Simply stated, these processes take place between individuals who, while believing that they are operating in an objective manner, are actually engaged in subjective sense-making and the building of meaning around the actions and environments that they are jointly engaged in (Berger and Luckmann, 1966; Weick, 1995).

**Statistical analysis** A statistical analysis is a quantitative approach rooted in deductivism which gathers numerical data in order to test and examine research questions and hypotheses. This approach uses precise mathematical techniques and processes linked to the field of statistics in order to identify features in data such as significance of a given finding, correlation and average occurrences.

**Survey** A survey is a research method that asks questions generally to a large number of people. This can be conducted via, for example, internet, telephone or paper.

## KEY POINTS

**1.** *Methodologies* (e.g interpretivism and positivism) can be thought of as background or over-arching philosophies that guide behaviour and perception, whereas *methods* are like tools (each with their own way of being used) that are used within an overall methodology.

2. It is unlikely, if not impossible, that a piece of research will attempt to use inductive and deductive approaches in a combined manner in a piece of research. This is because the processes they use to develop data are so contrasting (i.e. subjective versus objective commitments and characteristics).

3. Nevertheless, many methods, such as, by way of example, interviews, questionnaires, focus groups can be used in either inductive or deductive approaches. However, they will be used in line with the principles and philosophical characteristics and commitments of the over-arching, background inductivism or deductivism, that is, the data approach must either respectively embody objectivity or embrace subjectivity.

## REVISION QUESTIONS

- Think about your own inter-personal skills:
  - What are your strengths and weaknesses?
  - Which research method would be most comfortable and convenient for you based on your answer? For example, if you are generally a reserved person then organising and conducting one-to-one interviews is unlikely to be your preferred choice of method. If you are more out-going and extrovert then a more interactive method might suit you.
  - Students tend to choose research methods from a well-frequented repertoire. For example, interviews and questionnaires tend to be amongst the most common. What opportunities and risks might be involved by you trying a method a little less commonly employed? For example, you might consider focus groups or participant observation.

## FURTHER STUDY

1. Jakobsen, H. (2012) 'Focus groups and methodological rigour outside the minority world: Making the method work to its strengths in Tanzania', *Qualitative Research*, 12 (2): 111–130.

2. Brown, P. (2010) 'Qualitative method and compromise in applied social research', *Qualitative Research*, 10 (2): 229–248.

3. Bryman, A. (2007) 'Barriers to integrating quantitative and qualitative research', *Journal of Mixed Methods Research*, January, 1 (1): 8–22.

4. Cameron, R. and Molina-Azorin, J.F. (2014) 'The acceptance of mixed methods in business and management', *International Journal of Organisational Analysis*, 22 (1): 14–29.
5. Hardy, B. and Ford, L.R. (2014) 'It's not me, it's you: Miscomprehension in surveys', *Organisational Research Methods*, 17 (2): 138–162.
6. Luyt, R. (2012) 'A framework for mixing methods in quantitative measurement development, validation, and revision: A case study', *Journal of Mixed Methods Research*, October, 6 (4): 294–316.
7. Mills, D. and Ratcliffe, R. (2012) 'After method? Ethnography in the knowledge economy', *Qualitative Research*, April, 12 (2): 147–164.
8. Wiles, R., Crow, G. and Pain, H. (2011) 'Innovation in qualitative research methods: A narrative review', *Qualitative Research*, October, 11 (5): 587–604.

# 5
# DATA ANALYSIS AND INTERPRETATION

## OBJECTIVES

*Successful completion of this chapter provides guidance on:*
- How to understand the various issues involved in, and approaches to, data analysis;
- How to appreciate the strengths, weaknesses and issues surrounding particular data analysis approaches;
- How to develop and understand the relationship of reliability, viability and generalisability in relation to data analysis processes.

## INTRODUCTION

Having designed your study you then proceed into the field or research situation in order to gather the data that will be required to respond to your title, aims and objectives and research questions. Once the data are gathered, the next phase is to look at these data, process them and then attempt to come to some decisions about what the data might indicate and mean. The lengthy processes that these actions entail underline that it is important not to undervalue or waste all the effort that you have put into gathering the data. Therefore, it is vital and worthwhile taking time to think carefully about how you are going to approach the analysis phase of your research. The aim of this section is to assist you in this task.

## WHAT IS DATA ANALYSIS?

When the information, observations, recordings or statistics (i.e. the data) have been gathered for a piece of research, project or dissertation, it is subjected to

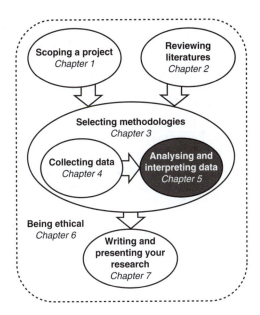

Current location within the research process

examination by the researcher (Bazeley, 2013). This involves carrying out identified and chosen processes on the data in order to, among other things, identify:

- patterns;
- salient features;
- relative size and importance of certain features in relation to various variables;
- meaning;
- significance;
- information, inferences and implications.

You may feel reasonably confident in the design and field aspects of your study. However, it is not uncommon to become rather uncertain about what to do with all the data once they have been gathered. The techniques outlined below are intended to assist you in responding to these matters.

## WHAT SHOULD YOU REMEMBER FROM YOUR RESEARCH DESIGN DURING THE DATA ANALYSIS STAGE OF YOUR WORK?

Following Fisher (2010), any map or grid that you employ in order to make sense of data will be influenced by the perspectives and philosophical commitments of your chosen methodology. The discussions in this chapter build on the work developed in the earlier chapters. With this in mind it is important to reiterate that inductive and deductive approaches each have their own philosophical commitments and principles and this, as you will have seen in earlier sections, have a practical impact on the shape of your study. It is vital that the data analysis phase of your work continues to take account of these commitments and that this stage of a piece of research *employs the same perspective and value system that has been cast over the research* during all the earlier phases of the work.

## QUANTITATIVE AND QUALITATIVE DATA ANALYSIS

### What is quantitative data analysis?

Quantitative data analysis frequently involves statistically based techniques. Some of these approaches can be understood rapidly and readily following a basic initiation and study. However, others can be very complex and require substantial study and training in order to be able to employ them effectively (Treiman, 2009). The following insights and recommendations are intended to direct you towards useful materials that will support you.

### What are the various types of quantitative data?

Saunders, Lewis and Thornhill (2012) (drawing on Morris, 1993) provide a useful overview of the various kinds of quantitative data which you might develop and analyse. This is useful because it assists in illustrating that all numerical data are not the same and may require differing treatments and processes (see Figure 5.1).

*Categorical data*, as the name indicates, are able to be placed in groupings or types with particular labels, that is, categories. This allows the types to be described and in so doing differentiated from each other. They may even be able to be judged to have particular qualities and characteristics that enable them to be placed *in some form of order* (i.e. ranked). An example here might be quality assessments of organisations including, for example, the 'best firm to work for' type league tables. University league tables will also involve forms of these data and in turn produce rankings – for

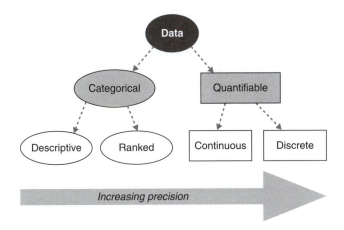

**Figure 5.1** Types of quantitative data

instance, see how the National Student Survey (www.thestudentsurvey.com, 2013) feeds into university league tables based on descriptive and individually subjective responses. These data offer a degree of precision but not to the same extent as quantifiable data.

*Quantifiable data* can be discussed in terms of being *continuous and discrete*. Continuous data tend to be data occurring (or spanning) over a period of time – for example, time spent on a task or served in a role. In other words, it is difficult to see how it might be broken up. Alternatively, *discrete data* can be readily counted. These data might be concerning individual products, people or other items. There is a clearly a measurable boundary and a 'beginning' and 'end' to the set of data. In general, it is common to place codes against quantifiable data. These might be code numbers or indicators which allow the piece or item of data to be uniquely identifiable (Streiner, 2013).

Many of these data will be termed as *variables*. A key aspect of positivistic, quantitative style analyses is to attempt to establish the relationship between variables and this is usually accomplished through the use of mathematical and statistical data analysis techniques. This will typically be undertaken through what is termed *bivariate* analysis which means that two variables are examined in order to discover what, if any, relationship may exist between them. If the analysis involves three or more variables then this is termed *multivariate* analysis (Hair, Black, Babin and Anderson, 2013). Statistical approaches are interested in a number of measures but most particularly in terms of correlation, linear regression and statistical significance. Correlation and linear regression look at the manner in which two variables relate to one another. Some variables change in a similar manner over time while others change in differentiating manners. In relation to statistical significance, this is a measure of the extent to which findings of a given quantitative analysis, conducted on a randomly selected sample, can be generalised in relation to the overall population from which the sample is taken.

## How should you approach quantitative analysis?

All of the work conducted through these above techniques will be seeking to establish if a given hypothesis or hypotheses are variously proven, partially proven or remain unproven. This objective is a central purpose of positivistic-type research approaches. Bryman and Bell (2007) and Maylor and Blackmon (2005) provide useful and more detailed presentations on quantitative data analysis processes and techniques. In addition, it is equally possible to secure a wide range of dedicated texts on the topic area many of which deal in great detail with specific aspects of quantitative approaches.

Quantitative data will often be gathered through the following methods and approaches, for example:

- structured interviews (often composed of a significant number of closed questions);
- archive research – organisational data sets such as company accounts or government statistics;
- participant observation involving frequency counts (an example of the latter approach might be the number and types of customer entering a particular outlet at varying times and times);
- structured questionnaires;
- surveys.

It is important to recall that quantitative data are usually gathered in connection with the use of positivistic methodological approaches. This means that you are likely to be employing numerical data of the categorical and quantifiable types indicated in Figure 5.1 above. This does not mean that quantitative data cannot be used in inductive or interpretevistic-type studies; however, where they are used, it will be in a different manner. For example, it might be in the form of tabular data in order to show trends in sales or profit figures. Equally, 'counting' or quantifying data forms part of inductive approaches such as content analysis. Within this research method, events, situations, language, words and phenomena are recorded and then analysed in order to look for emergent patterns and themes. An example of quantitative data being used in this way might be an analysis of television advertising campaigns for particular products. For example, a study might examine how food or toys are advertised to children and consider the time slots, frequency of adverts, types of adverts, number of appearances of particular figures (mother, father, etc.), the number of times certain words or language are used (see Morgan, 2007).

A very important point to remember in relation to analysing quantitative data is the need to relate it to the principles of the overall methodological framework you are using. Usually, although by no means, not always, use of quantitative data is associated with positivistic-style methodologies. These approaches tend to value discrete or categorical measurement and, above all, the need for you as researcher to maintain distance and objectivity in relation to the study and data collection and analysis. This means that the logic and rationale underpinning the judgements you make on the data must be completely separate from any subjective opinion interference (see Denzin's (2012) comments on this). There are a substantial range of resources available in relation to the analysis of quantitative data.

## What specific quantitative and statistical techniques are available for you to use?

Many of the statistical techniques applied to these data gathering approaches are supported by software packages which can facilitate the data analysis. One example of such a package is SPSS which is capable of analysing both quantitative and qualitative data and will provide a range on results and potential information (see Acton, Miller, Maltby and Fullerton, 2009; Pallant, 2013). Nevertheless, it will be useful to consider some of the techniques for analysing quantitative data in closer detail.

An early question in relation to quantitative data is how much data you will need in order to be able to employ a statistical or mathematical measure or technique. The answer is that a surprisingly small sample of data, say a range of 30 to 50 discrete pieces of data, may be enough to conduct the analysis. For example, this might be an analysis of trends in operating profit figures from 50 different firms in relation to another variable (e.g. expenditure on research and development) or, alternatively, it might constitute an analysis of labour turnover data in relation to months of the year. Even a small data sample allows a significant and meaningful comment to be made on the phenomenon for the sample under examination. A key issue to remember concerns the scope for generalisation. The smaller the sample generally the harder it is to make broad generalisations regarding the population (a range of useful general discussions are available on this including: Liu, 2013).

## STANDARD DEVIATION, THE MEAN, MEDIAN AND THE MODE

For a set of quantitative data, it is possible to calculate a series of measures that will help you assess the scope, breadth, concentration and significance of the values and numbers in your data set. A series of features can be established from a set of quantitative data one of which is a set of measures relating to what is termed the *normal distribution* (Stein and Foster, 2011; Steinberg, 2010). The normal distribution is derived from the probability domain of mathematics and it is based on the theoretical assertion that a given set of data will be spread evenly around a given value or number. Therefore, if the data were spread out in a *normal* distribution pattern, then 50 per cent of the data would be situated on one side of the given value and the other 50 per cent would be situated to the other side of the given value. Diagramatically, this tends to produce the image of the data in the shape of a bell curve (see Figure 5.2). The dome of the bell curve indicates the predominant occurrence of the values in the data set. The two thinner spreads either side of the dome indicate value or number occurrences, but there are fewer of them (i.e. to reiterate – the majority of items in the values in the data set fall in the area of the dome).

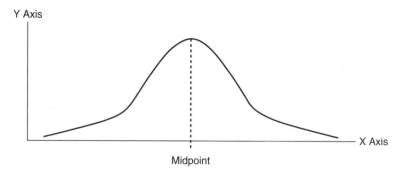

**Figure 5.2** Normal distribution of data (the bell curve)

So, to provide an example of this, you might be regarding the quality levels of a range of products produced in a factory. The majority of products will have a level of quality within an acceptable range. This will be represented by the area covered by the dome. The thinner bands at each end of the dome represent the (fewer in number – as one would expect) products made whose quality falls outside of the acceptable range.

On occasion, the data set will not follow a normal distribution pattern. It is possible that the majority of the values or recordings in the data set may fall closer towards the y axis, or alternatively, further along the x axis. In other words, the dome containing most of the values finds itself shifted more to the left or the right of the chart, respectively. When this happens the data are said to be exhibiting *skew* features. This means that the data values are not laid out in a normal distribution pattern but in an alternative pattern that sees the main body data recordings located in one area of the possible span of values (Freedman, Pisani and Purves, 2013).

In association with the normal distribution curve it is possible to calculate and assess measures such as the *standard deviation*, the *mean*, *median* and the *mode*. Quantitative and statistical measures such as averages and standard deviations are generally employed (although not exclusively) in research using deductive and positivistic types of research methodology. As mentioned in the earlier chapters on methodology, deductive forms of research are based on scientifically orientated principles such as objectivity, reductionism and causality, and therefore, quantitative techniques and methods are often seen as being better positioned to be able to adhere to and underpin results in line with these principles (Ha, 2011; Steinberg, 2010).

The mean is a technical term representing a way of measuring averages in statistics. The mean is often discussed in connection with two other technical measures – the mode and the median. When people discuss averages the mean is the average that enters the popular imagination. The mean is the result you obtain when you add up all the values of a data set and then you divide that number by the quantity of pieces of data. For instance, you might be interested in collecting data on the number of staff attending training courses each month in a large company. In order to accomplish this you obtain the data from the human resources department of people who attended a course in January, February, March, etc. The next step is to add up the number for each month in order to secure a total for the overall year. Then divide by 12 (the number of units, periods, or categories – in this case that happens to be 'months'). This then will tell you the mean. This process is illustrated numerically below:

Training courses attended by staff per month:

J-4 , F-6, M-7, A-2, M-8, J-9, J-7, A-4, S-3, O-6, N-6, D-2

Total training courses =
4+6+7+2+8+9+7+4+3+6+6+2 = 64 in the year

Mean average number of training courses attended per month = 64/12 = 5.3 training courses.

The median is a further measure of average used in statistics and is often employed alongside the mean. The median constitutes the 'middle' value in a set of data. Alternatively expressed, if you were to organise the data in order of their size then what you would notice is that, more or less, there should be an equivalent quantity of pieces of data either side of the median value. Taking the training courses example used above:

Training courses attended by staff per month:

J-4, F-6, M-7, A-2, M-8, J-9, J-7, A-4, S-3, O-6, N-6, D-2

Re-organising these data in median order
D-2, A-2, S-3, J-4, A-4, F-6, O-6, N-6, M-7, M-8, J-7, J-9.

Median average number training courses attended by staff per month = 6 training courses per month.

The comments made in the entry for the mean regarding the tendency to use statistical averages (see statistics) also apply for the median.

The mode is a further measure which signifies, in absolute terms, the most commonly occurrence in the data. For example:

Training courses per month:

J-4, F-6, M-7, A-2, M-8, J-9, J-7, A-4, S-3, O-6, N-6, D-2

Re-arranging these in clusters of months having the same number of sales:

D-2, A-2
S-3
J-4, A-4
F-6, O-6, N-6
M-7
M-8
J-9
J-7.

The mode, or modal value (i.e. the most commonly occurring) is 6. In this example, the mode is the same as the median; however there is no guarantee that this will always be the case.

In summary, the mean, the median and the mode can be derived by analysing a body of data and, thereby, allow you to identify significant numerical patterns and trends in the data. More often than not these measures can be calculated readily using software packages (Davis and Pecar, 2013). In turn, this permits you to signal implications and inferences in relation to the research questions you are employing and pursuing. By identifying the average measures and spread of the data, you will be able to better analyse and comment on your data in a more focused and specific manner.

### Frequency tables

A further approach for analysing quantitative data that you can develop is that of *frequency tables*. A *frequency* means the number of times or occurrences that you recorded a piece of data, for example, the number of days sickness for a sample of employees. Further examples could be the number of products produced on a given series of days or, alternatively, the footfall of a store – a technical retail management term meaning the number of customers entering the retail premises at various times (see Table 5.1).

### Times/day

From the data gathered and put within the frequency table it is possible to indicate a range of patterns. For instance, of the three days Monday is clearly the busiest day in terms of footfall (i.e. people entering the store). Equally, the busiest time slot is 11–1 on all of the days – does this suggest that people use their lunch breaks to do their shopping? On the other hand, the quietest time on any of the days is 9–11 on

**Table 5.1**  Frequency table for footfall in store 'X' 30th September–2nd October 2013

| TIME → | 9–11 | 11–1 | 1–3 | 3–5 | | % Frequency – Days |
|---|---|---|---|---|---|---|
| DAYS ↓ | | | | | | |
| Monday | 42 | 89 | 27 | 56 | 214 | 35.7 |
| Tuesday | 24 | 78 | 33 | 60 | 195 | 32.5 |
| Wednesday | 25 | 90 | 24 | 52 | 191 | 31.8 |
| | 91 | 257 | 84 | 168 | | |
| % Frequency: | 15.2 | 42.8 | 14.0 | 28.0 | | |

a Tuesday and 1–3 on a Wednesday. Overall, in order to be able to know the reasons behind *why* these data are as they are you would also need to be able to gather data from the individuals regarding the nature of their visit and this would probably require some form of brief questionnaire or short closed question interview.

## What further tests and measures can you use on quantitative data?

The discussion thus far has provided insights into how you might summarise data. In addition, there are a range of tests of significance and comparison that are available to apply to quantitative data sets. In a brief overview of the nature provided here, there is not sufficient space to be able to outline them at space; however, it is important to provide a useful indication.

### t-test

A well-known test is the t-test. The t-test is used in the comparison with the mean averages between two sets of data. The test allows you to measure and see differences between the two data sets. For example, you could compare the production levels between two work sites and make inferences regarding the average outputs at particular times (see an example in Jane, 2013).

### ANOVA (F-statistic)

This is a test that can be applied to data when you have more than two data sets and it is not possible to employ the t-test. (An illustration in an organisational context is provided by Vilmos, Misangyi, LePine, Algina and Goeddeke, 2013). As with the t-test much of this work can be done through software packages.

## How can you use graphs and charts to represent and present quantitative data?

Quantitative data lend themselves to be presented visually and diagramatically. There are a range of approaches that can be used including, for example, graphs, bar charts, histograms and pie-charts (Landau and Everitt, 2004).

### How do you construct bar charts?

A bar chart is a diagram which visually employs columns in order to represent the size or magnitude of a set or sub-set of data (Jobman, 1998). It is quite possible to use vertical or horizontal columns. There are two axes on a bar chart, one axis is vertical and one is horizontal. For instance, along the vertical axis the chart could have 'profit in pounds (£ millions)'. On the horizontal axis, different companies could be listed. By looking at intersections between the two axes, it will be possible to read off the relative profit levels of the various companies for various year quarters. This is illustrated in Figure 5.3 below.

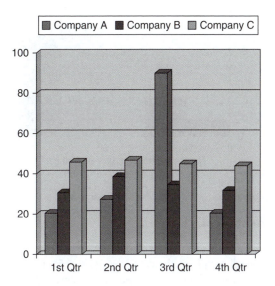

**Figure 5.3** Profit in millions of pounds (£)

### How do you construct histograms?

A histogram is a type of diagram (see Figure 5.4). The key feature of a histogram is that mathematical surface area of the bars in the chart represents the actual value of the data. In other words, the size (sic: area) represented by the bar or column is proportional to the magnitude or size of the data. This means that, unlike a bar chart, there are never any spaces between the bars of a histogram because all the area has to be continuously covered without a break (Woods, 2007).

A bar chart is often confused with a histogram. This is an important mistake to avoid. Each bar on a bar chart is stand alone and separate. In contrast, in a histogram the bars have to flow on one from another.

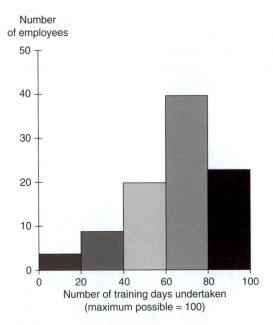

**Figure 5.4** Histogram

*How do you construct pie charts?*

A pie chart is a diagram that is represented in the form of a circle. The entire circle represents the overall sample of the data (see Figure 5.5). The various categories, groups, sections or areas of the data sample can be shown as different wedges of the circle. The wedges are drawn relatively to represent the size of the sub-sets or categories of the sample (Ha, 2011; Payne 2011).

In summary to the discussion on assessing quantitative data, the approaches and techniques indicated above will assist you in developing particular insights to your data (Kremelberg, 2011). Moreover, quite often it is common to accompany quantitative data analyses with qualitative data commentaries and assessments in the form of a mixed methodology approach.

## What is qualitative data analysis?

Qualitative data tend to be based on *inter alia* words, pictures, signs, symbols, films and images. Numbers can also be considered in a qualitative manner. For example, it is possible to look at the issues, differing interpretations and situations that lie behind

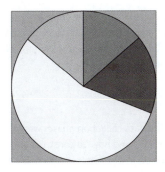

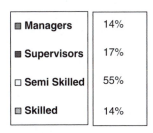

| ■ Managers | 14% |
| ■ Supervisors | 17% |
| □ Semi Skilled | 55% |
| ▨ Skilled | 14% |

**Figure 5.5** Relative size of employee type at ZXY organization

the *prima facie* picture painted by a set of figures. Where some form of numerical presentation or statistical analysis is used alongside a qualitative study, this is often with the purpose of illustrating the scope or physical dimensions of a given phenomenon. This is what is generally referred to as the use of *mixed methodological* approaches.

Typically, qualitative data tend to be developed through inductive and interpretivistic-style methodological approaches. A key reason for this is that such approaches to research value detailed and in-depth descriptive analytical elaboration and understanding of contexts and settings and qualitative data are generally well suited to accomplishing this. While qualitative analysis employs a range of techniques and frameworks, in their ESRC report *Benchmarking Good Practice in Qualitative Management Research*, Cassell et al. (2005: 5) nevertheless observed:

> Assessing qualitative management research appeared to be more of an intuitive decision-making process than an application of known and agreed criteria. Judgements in these areas vary according to the beliefs and commitments of the individual.

Following the design of the study, qualitative analysis will usually involve the following stages:

- *Data collection* – this will be through research methods such as, for example, semi-structured or unstructured interviews, questionnaires, focus groups or participant observation;

- *Reading and re-reading the data* – often this will use some form of approach or methodology for coding the data. The intent here is to be able to generate themes, types, categories, tropes, etc. In other words the large and complex mass of data is sub-divided by this identified and implemented framework;
- *Interpreting findings*;
- *Writing up the report*.

Each phase will present its own challenges. The data collection phases were discussed within Chapter 4 – dealing with research methods and how to construct and operate them. The 'Writing up the report' is addressed in the latter chapters of this text. In the light of the topic of the current chapter, it will be useful, in the subsequent paragraphs, to reflect on the stages or 'reading and re-reading the data and interpreting the findings'. Easterby-Smith, Thorpe and Lowe (2006) propose a range of stages through which the processes of reading, analysing and interpreting might pass. These involve:

- *Familiarisation* – This, in essence, is about you becoming completely familiar with the data secured from the research respondents;
- *Reflection* – Here, the crux issues surround whether or not the data are going to produce something of value – will the data support or challenge existing knowledge bases – what is the same, new or different?;
- *Conceptualisation* – This is the process whereby important themes and reiterations raised by respondents start to connect with themes in the literature. Thus, they begin to produce the concerns, structure and framework of the research;
- *Cataloguing concepts* – When the emergent structure mentioned under conceptualisation above is felt to start to become sufficiently solid, then, it is important to begin to formalise the coding and the categories through the various coding approaches discussed in this chapter;
- *Re-coding* – When the cataloguing and conceptualisation architecture of your study appears to be crystallising then there is an opportunity to return to the original data transcripts and see if more data can be mined and aligned with the now established framework. This will serve two key purposes: firstly, it will familiarise you with the data yet further; secondly, it will enable you to ensure that you have now overlooked any key concepts in relation to the original coding from the data sets;
- *Linking* – Relate the data more and more closely with the extant and evolving literature. This will involve a form of compare and contrast exercises moving between the data sets and the literature;

- *Re-evaluation* – Look for potential criticisms, imbalances, exaggerations and oversights in your work.

Within the analysis phase of the research process Quinlan (2011: 365–366) suggests that the process of analysis might also be thought of as comprising four stages:

- description of the data;
- interpretation of the data;
- conclusions relating to the data, leading ultimately to theorisation;
- the generation of concepts and theoretical frameworks emerging from this overall process.

Quinlan indictcates that this might be thought of as a cyclical process whereby the theories feed into the data once more. In this way you are constantly testing the theory in relation to fresh and emergent data sets.

## CODING DATA

In the reading and re-reading stage of qualitative data, as indicated, there is always some attempt to classify and codify the data. In relation to coding there is a range of ways in which this might be approached.

Much of the groundwork in relation to codifying and classifying qualitative research has been laid by a range of classic writings undertaken by widely cited authors, including Ritchie and Spencer (1994), Bryman and Burgess (1994); Cresswell (1997), Denzin and Lincoln (1998), Feldman (1995), Miles and Huberman (1994) and Silverman (1993). It is worthwhile reading these writers in conjunction with more contemporary readings as they constitute the basis on which much qualitative analysis has evolved (see by way of more contemporary indicative readings, Bazeley and Jackson (2013), Bazeley (2013), Saldaña (2012) and Grbich (2012).

Attride-Stirling (2001: 388–389) provides an illustration of one approach to coding that you might adopt. This is elaborate in an extended quotation below:

Thematic networks systematize the extraction of: (i) lowest-order premises evident in the text (Basic Themes); (ii) categories of basic themes grouped together to summarize more abstract principles (Organizing Themes); and (iii) super-ordinate themes encapsulating the principal metaphors in the text as a whole (Global Themes). These are then represented as web-like maps depicting the salient themes at each of the three levels, and illustrating the relationships between them ... This is a widely used procedure in qualitative analysis and parallels are easily found, for example, in Grounded Theory (see Corbin and Strauss, 1990). The procedure of thematic networks does not aim or pretend to discover the beginning of arguments or the end of rationalizations; it simply provides a technique for breaking up text, and finding within it explicit rationalizations and their implicit signification. The three classes of themes can be described as follows:

*Basic Theme*: This is the most basic or lowest-order theme that is derived from the textual data. It is like a backing in that it is a statement of belief anchored around a central notion (the warrant) and contributes toward the signification of a super-ordinate theme. Basic Themes are simple premises characteristic of the data, and on their own they say very little about the text or group of texts as a whole. In order for a Basic Theme to make sense beyond its immediate meaning it needs to be read within the context of other Basic Themes. Together, they represent an Organizing Theme.

*Organizing Theme*: This is a middle-order theme that organizes the Basic Themes into clusters of similar issues. They are clusters of signification that summarize the principal assumptions of a group of Basic Themes, so they are more abstract and more revealing of what is going on in the texts. However, their role is also to enhance the meaning and significance of a broader theme that unites several Organizing Themes. Like Toulmin's warrants, they are the principles on which a super-ordinate claim is based. Thus, Organizing Themes simultaneously group the main ideas proposed by several Basic Themes, and dissect the main assumptions underlying a broader theme that is especially significant in the texts as a whole. In this way, a group of Organizing Themes constitute a Global Theme.

*Global Theme*: Global Themes are super-ordinate themes that encompass the principal metaphors in the data as a whole. A Global Theme is like a claim in that it is a concluding or final tenet. As such, Global Themes group sets of Organizing Themes that together present an argument, or a position or an assertion about a given issue or reality. They are macro themes that summarize and make sense of clusters of lower-order themes abstracted from and supported by the data. Thus Global Themes tell us what the texts as a whole are about within the context of a given analysis. They are both a summary of the main themes and a revealing interpretation of the texts. Importantly, a set of texts may well yield more than one Global Theme, depending on the complexity of the data and the analytic aims; however, these will be much fewer in number than the Organizing and Basic Themes. Each Global Theme is the core of a thematic network; therefore, an analysis may result in more than one thematic network.

## GROUNDED THEORY

One of the most commonly invoked and discussed approaches is *Grounded Theory*. While this is only one such approach it has grown to considerable prominence. Grounded Theory is primarily associated with a number of authors. Central figures in this group include Glaser and Strauss (1967), Strauss and Corbin (1998) and subsequently Charmaz (2006). Goulding (2002) has also emerged as a useful commentator on the field. Among more contemporary texts, Cameron and Price (2009: 409–422) provide an accessible set of insights on the approach as do Eriksson and Kovalainen (2008: 154–172).

Grounded Theory uses inductive methodological processes and one of its principal contributions was to progress notions of the systematisation of coding. Grounded Theory employs terminology such as *open coding*, *axial coding* and *selective coding*.

### Open coding

This is the first stage of coding. The same name or label will be accorded to pieces of data that are the same or very similar. These are the *broad labels or categories*.

### Axial coding

The axial phase of coding follows the open coding phase. It involves looking for *relationships and interconnections between the categories* identified in stage one of open coding. In addition, it also involves looking for *hierarchical relationships between items*. In other words, making decisions about which items of data might reside within other items of data.

### Selective coding

Selective coding is a phase of coding that can be undertaken as the data collection and the coding progresses. As the coding moves forward, it is possible that *particular categories emerge as dominant* or more important in relation to other categories.

One category may emerge as the principal category around which other categories might be structured.

So, to reiterate, the central idea in coding is to commence with large groups, clusters or themes. These will self-evidently emerge or become apparent from the data because they are repeated and have high frequency counts (i.e. there a large number of items or occurrences in relation to a particular item or event). Subsequent phases of coding work then takes place in order to sub-categorise within these larger themes. Usually, the various levels of data coding fit other pieces of data into these broader themes – sub-groups and sub-classifications are developed within them. Quite often, numbering terms and creating itemised numbered items within them will take place. Examples of coding field data are provided below in the next section of the discussion.

It should be remembered that, although it frequently seems to feature in discussions on classifying qualitative data, there are concerns surrounding Grounded Theory:

> It is important to make a cautionary note in connection with Grounded Theory. Since its inception, Grounded Theory, has been widely used in research and critiqued and commented upon in literature. This extensive adoption is to be commended and its success should not be underplayed. However, like many situations where populist and common-place usage occurs, this has not always done a great service to the name of Grounded Theory. It is not uncommon to hear a student or paper author state that they are using Grounded Theory when in fact they are not. Rather than following the highly systematic coding approach of Grounded Theory these acts of partial adoption are, in fact, effectively just inductive and interpretive in nature. This is of course completely fine but it is important not to state that it is Grounded Theory that is being used. Overall, Grounded Theory has been employed to produce a wide range of research. Nevertheless, some commentators (of inductive and deductive persuasion alike) find it cumbersome, contrived, over-structured and artificial and ultimately a misleading approach in relation to the work involved and the messages the data might supply (Stokes, 2011).

## TEMPLATE ANALYSIS

Template Analysis (King, 2004b) is a coding approach that has caught the attention of a range of researchers in the last decade or so. The approach is one that attempts to organise qualitative data in terms of the themes that can be identified in the data. The forms of data that can be analysed cover a range of texts, including, for example, interview transcripts, unstructured and semi-structured questionnaires and focus-group recordings.

The central principles underlying template analysis involve developing a 'coding template' that organises themes you identify from the respondent data and these are subsequently structured in a hierarchy of terms and meanings. In more detail, this means:

1. Identify what are termed the *a priori* codes. *A priori* codes are the initial, broad themes that seem to immediately stand out of the data. You are likely to have a few to several in number. These are working ideas and they may change as the study develops and progresses.
2. When you have identified the *a priori* codes, you then start to look through all the data (i.e. transcripts, texts, documents, etc.) in detail.
3. At this stage you mark 'segments' of text which appear to offer some insight or information in relation to the research questions you have posed.
4. If the identified segments appear to relate directly to *a priori* codes then they are classified as such. However, if they seem different from the *a priori* codes then you need to classify them with a new code.
5. King (2004b) suggests that when you have read an initial number (for example, three or four) of the transcripts, texts or data collections you will start to achieve a sense of what the template might look like. This will provide you with your initial template.
6. All the data are then coded along the framework of this template. As you hone and develop your template analysis you may wish to adjust some of the data codes.

Template analysis has been used by a range of research papers and projects. Examples of template analysis usage include:

McDowall, A and Saunders, M (2010) 'UK managers conceptions of training and development', *Journal of European Industrial Training*, 34 (7): 609–630.
Raub, S. and von Wittich, D. (2004) 'Implementing knowledge management: Three strategies for effective CKOs, *European Management Journal*, 20 (6): 714–724.
Waring, T and Wainwright, D. (2008) 'Issues and challenges in the use of template analysis: Two comparative case studies from the field', *The Electronic Journal of Business Research Methods*, 6 (1): 85–94.

## MIND-MAPPING AND COGNITIVE MAPPING IN RELATION TO CODING

Mind-mapping or cognitive mapping is an approach that can be useful in trying to work out the patterns and structures in data sets (see Buzan, 2002; Buzan and Rustler, 2012; Ackerman, Eden and Brown, 2005). It is possible to use something as simple as Post-it™ sticky notes and write down one idea per note and then stick it on a large area of any wall surface. This effectively allows you to map the data in a flexible manner. Moreover, this facilitates you moving the paper and ideas around and building, and rebuilding, the emergent and crystallising pictures in the data. It is important to remember that, by doing this, you are reflecting your own thoughts in relation to the data. It is your eye, your beliefs, your perceptions and understandings that are making decisions in relation to the data. In this way, you are cognitively mapping the data. The respondents will also have played a central and key role in this process in the way they will have placed importance on events, the language they will have chosen to use and the actions, behaviours and emotion they will, or not, have displayed during the research situations and environments during data collection.

In summary, as a general point, it should be noted that all of the above techniques discussed thus far under the heading 'Qualitative Analysis' can be used for interview, questionnaire, focus group, survey or participant observation data.

## THREE EXAMPLES OF CODING

Three examples of coding within a qualitative research study are provided below (Smith, 2011). These examples all came from the same piece of research. Interestingly, early work and drafts of the research decided to espouse a Grounded Theory approach. As a consequence of various expert inputs and discussions, a decision was later taken within the research to move away from that approach and to engage in a more general approach to coding (not linked to any specific or particular coding methodological approach such as Grounded Theory). The primary reason for this decision having been taken in this particular case was because an external reviewer determined that Grounded Theory imposed too much structure and 'methodological architecture' over the work. Instead, the reviewer suggested that the data be coded in a much less rigid and less hierarchical manner. This sort of change, although not necessarily common, can occasionally occur during a piece of research as particular patterns begin to emerge in the data and varying views and inputs on how the data should be shaped are offered.

## BACKGROUND TO THE RESEARCH CODING EXAMPLE

It is important to set the examples provided below in their wider context. The piece of research considered the scheme *Investors in People* (IIP) in the UK which is a government-linked scheme intended to allow organisations to develop their training and development and competitiveness. A major part of the existing research work on IIP discusses the initiative in a positivistic and rationalistic manner. This tends to overlook the more human aspects and experiences of the initiative. The research examined the 'lived experiences' of individuals in six organisations engaging, or which had engaged, in IIP (see Table 5.2).

**Table 5.2**    Profiles of organisations involved in the study

| Organisation | Size | IIP status | Participants |
|---|---|---|---|
| High School | Large (less than 1000 employees) | Since 2002 | 3 senior managers (SM); 2 line managers (LM); 2 teachers; 3 support roles (exams officer; technician; support assistant) |
| University | Large (employee numbers in their 000's) | Since mid to late 1990s | 3 SMs; 2 LMs; 2 lecturers; 2 research roles; 1 support role |
| National Health Service (NHS) catering department | Large (employee numbers in their 000's, but the department has less than 200 employees) | Since 2003 | 1 SM; 1 LM; 4 front-line employees (chef; catering assistant; administration officer; learning and development advisor) |
| Transport company | Large (with less than 1000 employees) | Since 2004 | 1 SM; 2 LMs; 2 front-line employees (building role; body trade role) |
| Third sector organisation | Small (ten full-time employees) | Since 2007 | 2 SMs |
| Adult themed retailer | Small (forty staff within 14 outlets) | Since 2005 | 2 SMs |

Source: Table extracted from: Smith and Stokes 'The Investors in People Standard: Performance Claims, Dichotomies and Lived Experience', forthcoming, work in progress.

The data were generated from 35 interviews with employees of the organisations. In the end analysis and write-up, the research drew out three main findings in relation to the literature:

- the findings did not support an apparent relationship between organisational performance in the IIP training and development actions;
- the findings did not support a linkage between IIP and job satisfaction;
- the results showed weak employee awareness of, and commitment to, IIP.

Within the research example, the organisation types and the abbreviations used between them are:

**Sch** – High School
**Uni** – University
**Cat** – Catering Department within the National Health Service
**Def** – Defence Organisation
**Tran** – Transport Organisation

## 1. An Example of a General Approach to Coding (Grounded Theory not being employed here – extracted from Smith (2011: 132–139).

**Code:** *Why* – *relates to feelings on why IIP status was first achieved and is subsequently maintained*

**Summary:** Within the high school, the catering department, the defence organisation, the transport company, the third sector organisation and the adult-themed retailer, interviewees felt that IIP status was first achieved to represent standards of practice that had already been attained. Respondents within the university make reference to a shift towards IIP in the 1990s that coincides with the behaviour of Higher Education establishments at that time.

**Example quotation:** 'We actually got a gong for something we're already doing, rather than chasing a gong and having to put something in place to get the gong.' Defence respondent – senior manager.

**Code:** *Ease* – *relates to interviewees feelings on achieving IIP recognition with ease*

**Summary:** For the school, catering department, defence organisation, transport company, third-sector organisation and adult-themed retailer, it is felt that IIP recognition was easy to achieve because significant changes in practice had been made prior to the involvement/consideration of the standard. Respondents within the university were unsure of the original changes that were required for initial recognition, although they feel that IIP recognition is easy to maintain.

**Example quotation:** 'We used it [IIP] because of all the training we were doing and we thought we need to get some sort of recognition here.' Catering respondent – senior manager.

**Code: *Contribution*** – *relates to feelings on how much contribution IIP has had on training*

**Summary:** Feelings relating to the contribution of IIP on training are mixed – some respondents were even struggling to formalise an opinion. Some interviewees feel there must be a link or association, but others, especially those that understand IIP to a greater extent, suggest training and development quality has come, and remains, completely independent of IIP input.

**Example quotation:** 'We've always done training and always will do training, regardless of IIP.' Catering respondent – support role.

**Code: *Stopped*** – *relates to interviewees feelings within the defence organisation on why IIP accreditation was ceased*

**Summary:** Almost all interviewees strongly feel that their organisations can sustain quality without IIP involvement or recognition. Some respondents within the university remain unsure of any potential differences.

**Example quotation:** 'Effectively, we grew beyond it [IIP].' Defence respondent – senior manager.

**Code: *Knowledge*** – *relates to interviewees' knowledge of IIP*

**Summary:** Knowledge of IIP is generally found to be very limited throughout the cases studied, especially within front-line employees. The level of knowledge tends to improve with progression up the management hierarchy. Direct experience with IIP assessment does link to improved levels of knowledge, although this is inconsistently found.

**Example quotation:** 'The only thing I know about Investors In People is it's at the bottom of our headed paper.' University respondent – support role.

## 2. An Extract from a Grounded Theory Approach.

### Category table two

**Category two: IIP perceptions/ understandings**

**Code: *Knowledge*** – *relates to interviewees' knowledge of IIP*

**Summary:** Knowledge of IIP is generally found to be very limited throughout the cases studied, especially within front-line employees. The level of knowledge tends to improve with progression up the management hierarchy. Direct experience with IIP assessment does link to improved levels of knowledge, although this is inconsistently found.

(*continued*)

**Code: *Perception*** – *relates to the perception of IIP by interviewees*

**Summary:** Most interviewees express positive perceptions towards IIP, and training and development – however, interviewees struggle to distinguish between them (links to limited knowledge on the standard). Some respondents within the university and defence organisation suggest IIP has run its course.

**Code: *Interviewed*** – *relates to whether interviewees have been interviewed by an IIP assessor*

**Summary:** Of those asked, 15 had previously been interviewed by an IIP assessor, whilst 13 had not.

**Code: *Explain*** – *relates to how well an interviewee could explain IIP to somebody who had never heard of it*

**Summary:** Many of the interviewees admitted they would struggle to be able to explain IIP to others who had never heard of it. Those within higher management positions and/or with direct experience of the standard were clearly more confident in being able to explain what IIP is.

**Code: *Others*** – *relates to how the interviewees believe others within their organisations view IIP*

**Summary:** In four of the cases, it is agreed that the majority of staff within the workplace would generally have very little knowledge about IIP. The code is not discussed within the defence organisation. It is also thought that knowledge may improve when compared to direct experience with the standard.

**Code: *Clash-guide*** – *relates to any potential clashes between IIP and any other guidelines*

**Summary:** Interviewees suggest there appears to be no significant clashes between IIP and other external quality guidelines. However, these other guidelines usually take precedent and IIP must fit within the parameters of them. This code was not relevant to the transport company.

**Code: *Success*** – *relates to how much of a success interviewees believe IIP has been in their organisation*

**Summary:** Opinions on the success of IIP are mixed. Numerous positive comments are expressed in all of the organisations, but, at the same time, a number of interviewees refer to a limited impact. This includes the standard being more useful in its initial recognition stages, or simply acting as an external guideline/badge of recognition.

**Code: *Stopped*** – *relates to interviewees feelings on how well quality could be sustained without IIP*

**Summary:** Almost all interviewees strongly feel that their organisations can sustain quality without IIP involvement or recognition. Some respondents within the university remain unsure of any potential differences.

**Code: *Ease*** – *relates to interviewees feelings on achieving IIP recognition with ease*

**Summary:** For the school, catering department, defence organisation and transport company, it is felt that IIP recognition was easy to achieve because significant changes in practice had been made prior to the involvement/ consideration of the standard. Respondents within the university feel that IIP recognition is easy to maintain.

**Code: *Why*** – *relates to feelings on why IIP status was first achieved and is subsequently maintained*

**Summary:** Within all five organisations, interviewees feel that IIP status was first achieved to represent standards of practice that had already been attained. However, this is not representative of all respondents within the university. Others suggest it shows new staff they would be treated as assets, it provides external quality assurance, it aids recruitment, and it provides a different way of thinking about investment in staff. For the transport company in the future, having IIP may affect the attainment of contracts.

**Code: *Following*** – *relates to feelings on whether IIP is followed all the time*

**Summary:** For four of the organisations, it is felt that IIP is only really followed when initial assessment or reassessment is imminent. Within the catering department, it is suggested that all training is conducted with IIP in mind.

**Code: *Intrinsic*** – *relates to feelings of an intrinsic ability to deliver quality without IIP*

**Summary:** Interviewees from four of the organisations feel strongly that good practice has existed and does exist outside of the IIP's influence. Only respondents within the transport company are split as to whether or not IIP has actually made an integral contribution.

**Code: *Importance*** – *relates to feelings as to the importance of the IIP logo/symbols*

**Summary:** The IIP logo/symbols are thought to be very important visual aspects of recognition in four of the organisations – the code is not discussed in the school, as the issue was later added to the questionnaire. In the defence organisation, however, the value of the IIP logo/symbols is thought to have significantly reduced since the nineties and since more small organisations have achieved status. The transport company also highlights that its industry is unconcerned with IIP, which reduces its value and significance.

*(continued)*

**Code: *Employment*** – *relates to feelings on whether IIP makes any difference to applying for jobs*

**Summary:** The majority of interviewees believe there is nominal difference made to themselves or others when applying for a job within an organisation with IIP status. Some respondents suggest it could possibly impact on those interested in the standard. The code is not discussed within the school, as the issue was later added to the questionnaire.

**Code: *Customer*** – *relates to feelings on whether the IIP logo/symbol makes any difference to customers' perceptions*

**Summary:** It is strongly felt by the majority of interviewees that the IIP logo/symbols makes little or no difference to customer perceptions – only two respondents within the catering department suggest a positive impact. The code is not discussed within the school, as the issue was later added to the questionnaire.

3. **This example is also linked to Grounded Theory (and provides an extension and reformatting of the data from Example 2)**

| Category | Code | Findings |
|---|---|---|
| **IIP perceptions/ understandings** | *Knowledge* | *This code relates to interviewees level of knowledge on IIP:* |
| | | **Sch** – Knowledge of IIP is found to be very limited within the majority of interviewees. Those with prior experience and those at the top of the hierarchy demonstrate greater knowledge. A lot of the management positions, however, still have large knowledge gaps, and even some of those previously interviewed by IIP assessors still have very limited knowledge. |
| | | **Uni** – Knowledge of IIP is found to be very limited within the majority of interviewees. Some interviewees' previous experiences with IIP in other organisations help a little with the knowledge deficit. Those interviewees found to be knowledgeable relate to upper hierarchical management positions whereby contact with IIP has been very direct. |
| | | **Cat** – Half the interviewees admit a very limited knowledge of IIP. Of the other half, they all relate to leadership positions with knowledge improving the further up the hierarchy you go. |
| | | **Def** – The three interviewed are extremely knowledgeable of IIP, which is reflected by their lengthy stays within the organisation. |

| Category | Code | Findings |
|----------|------|----------|
| | | **Tran** – The interviewees related to upper management demonstrated a greater breadth of knowledge of IIP. Knowledge becomes very scarce the further down the hierarchy you go. Staff without leadership responsibility and even lower ranked managers/supervisors has very little knowledge of IIP. |
| | *Perception* | *This code relates to the perception of IIP by interviewees:* |
| | | **Sch** – All but one of the interviewees express positive comments concerning IIP and the potential links to improved training and development. The one that did not only expresses their inability to answer the question because they know so little about IIP. One of the interviewees suggests that the reality of being able to measure training needs is questionable. |
| | | **Uni** – The majority of interviewees express positive comments that relate to investments made in staff. One interviewee expresses no opinion because they know so little about IIP. Another interviewee suggests that IIP has had its place in the organisation, and that the university's HR strategy now fills the gap potentially left by not having recognition. |
| | | **Cat** – Interviewees make a lot of connections to training and development within a positive context. Several mention IIP in terms of being a reward for input into training practices. |
| | | **Def** – Interviewees express usefulness of IIP as an external reward/gong. There are suggestions IIP has long since run its course in this organisation. |
| | | **Tran** – Interviewees express a number of positive comments relating to value and quality. One suggests IIP has more value than the Charter Mark because it is harder to achieve. |
| | *Interviewed* | *This code relates to whether interviewees have been interviewed by an IIP assessor:* |
| | | **Sch** – 5 yes, 5 no. |
| | | **Uni** – 3 yes, 6 no. |
| | | **Cat** – 3 yes, 2 no. |
| | | **Def** – 3 yes. |
| | | **Tran** – 1 yes. |
| | *Explain* | *This code relates to how well an interviewee could explain IIP to somebody who had never heard of it:* |
| | | **Sch** – Similar to the code *perception*, the majority of interviewees positively suggest how they would relate IIP to training and development when explaining the standard |

*(continued)*

| Category | Code | Findings |
|---|---|---|
| | | to others. Three interviewees admitted they would struggle to explain to others what IIP is. It is noted that two of these three interviewees have an opinion relating to training and development in the code *perception*. |
| | | **Uni** – Just over half the interviewees admit to lacking the knowledge of IIP, or providing misled guesses, to be able to explain to others what the standard is. The rest provide positively related connotations with training and development. |
| | | **Cat** – Those outside of the management hierarchy admit to not being able to provide explanations to others as to what IIP is. Explanations become better as we move up the hierarchy and experience dealing directly with the standard increases. |
| | | **Def** – All interviewees can provide clear explanations to others as to what IIP is. Their emphasis does not retain positive links throughout; they warn of the limitations using the standard. |
| | | **Tran** – Explanations to others about IIP improves as we move further up the hierarchy. The greater the knowledge and direct experience with IIP, the clearer the explanations become. |
| | Others | *This code relates to how the interviewees believe others within their organisations view IIP:* |
| | | **Sch** – Some interviewees say they do not discuss IIP in the workplace, therefore, they cannot speculate. Other interviewees suggest there is a mixed view of understanding. One suggests the more involved people are with assessment, the more knowledgeable they are. However, another interviewee suggests that during assessment lower down staff do not get a full explanation as to what IIP does. Some suggest there might be very little understanding of IIP amongst other staff. |
| | | **Uni** – Nearly all the interviewees suggest that an understanding of IIP within other staff members is probably generally very limited. One interviewee suggests that involvement in assessment may increase knowledge. Another suggests a need for re-education within the organisation as IIP has not been mentioned since their arrival within the organisation (less than a year ago). |
| | | **Cat** – All interviewees suggest there is probably a general lack of knowledge as to what IIP is throughout the department. Only one suggests the possibility of employees realistically knowing more. |

| Category | Code | Findings |
|----------|------|----------|
| | | **Def** – N/A. |
| | | **Tran** – The majority of interviewees suggest that employees generally know very little about IIP. One interviewee suggests that managers are torn between whether IIP is a good thing or a waste of time. Only one interviewee holds the opinion that most people know what it is about and recognise its value. |
| | *Clash-guide* | *This code relates to any potential clashes between IIP and any other guidelines:* |
| | | **Sch** – There does not appear to be any significant clashes with the OFSTED (a body that regulates and oversees quality in schools) requirements, but this is mainly due to OFSTED taking priority over IIP. This means IIP has to fit around the OFSTED requirements, although there are no particular differences worthy of noting. IIP could be potentially used as evidence for OFSTED. |
| | | **Uni** – Other quality related guidelines, including HEFCE (a body that regulates and oversees quality in universities and higher education more generally), exist and these take priority over IIP. However, there are no examples of particular differences worthy of noting. |
| | | **Cat** – Numerous quality related guidelines exist – health and safety, hygiene, etc – and these take priority over IIP. This means IIP has to fit into existing structures and requirements. The department is said to fit very well with IIP requirements. |
| | | **Def** – All interviewees speak of IIP acting as duplication for other, more valuable, quality guidelines. IIP cannot be applied to an international market. |
| | | **Tran** – N/A. |
| | *Success* | *This code relates to how much of a success interviewees believe IIP has been in their organisation:* |
| | | **Sch** – Just over half the interviewees express a number of positive comments relating to the success of IIP. However, two interviewees remark on how the school would achieve this success regardless of IIP recognition. Some interviewees could not express an opinion as to the success of IIP and one interviewee expresses that IIP has not touched their life. |
| | | **Uni** – Two interviewees express that IIP has been useful as an external mark, but that's the limit of its contribution. Two interviewees suggest IIP success is limited if people in the organisation do not even know what it is. Only one interviewee expresses positively beyond external recognition |

(continued)

| Category | Code | Findings |
|----------|------|----------|
|          |      | and another interviewee suggests that IIP had much more value when it was first introduced. Some interviewees could not express an opinion as to the success of IIP. |
|          |      | **Cat** – All interviewees reflect positively on IIP's success within the department. It is emphasised that training was good before recognition. |
|          |      | **Def** – All interviewees express that IIP had much more value at the beginning of recognition. One interviewee suggests that IIP assessment cannot deliver everything that is needed within the organisation. |
|          |      | **Tran** – Interviewees outside of top management could not express an opinion as to the success of IIP. Opinion within management is split: some believe the standard to be successful in terms of providing a clear focus and issues for improvement; but others question whether improvement would have occurred naturally without IIP and suggest that the new managing director may have actually had the main influence on recent success. |
|          | *Stopped* | *This code relates to interviewees feelings on how well quality could be sustained without IIP:* |
|          |      | **Sch** – All ten interviewees feel the levels of quality improvement developed by the school would continue regardless of IIP status. It is felt by the majority that IIP status just works as a 'pat on the back' for all the achievements thus far rather than a radical initiative leading the school to great strides in terms of quality improvements. |
|          |      | **Uni** – The majority of interviewees feels that quality improvement would be sustained or could continue to improve without IIP. Others are unsure of any potential differences. Several interviewees raise concerns over the sustainability of the standard. |
|          |      | **Cat** – All of the interviewees feel confident that quality improvement would be sustained or continue to improve without IIP. |
|          |      | **Def** – All interviewees are adamant that quality would not reduce without IIP. The organisation is considered to have grown beyond it. |
|          |      | **Tran** – All interviewees believe quality would continue, although one suggests an alternative and similar guideline would be required. There is an argument that changes would have occurred regardless of IIP recognition. |

From the illustrations provided above, it is possible to see how the coding is based around key themes that emerge from the research participants' responses. This takes place as individual respondents, in individual interviews, seem to return to similar concerns, feelings and issues. Then, you as researcher, following the processes outlined above in relation to analysing qualitative data, identify and nominate a label for particular patterns, groupings, themes and categories that you feel are apparent in the data. It is usual to illustrate the themes or coding by aligning them with illustrative quotations.

## Analysing case studies

There are number of issues to take into account when analysing a case study or case studies.

Generally, as in much qualitative research, there is a tendency to analyse the data as they are being collected. This is often the reality of working through a case rather than pretending that somehow the data collection and the data analysis are automatically separate phases. As you work with the people in your case study setting and/or organisation you will glean many insights and you are likely to engage in an on-going sense-making and 'working out what is taking place within the case' manner (see examples in Hoon, 2013; Ambrosini, Bowman, and Collier, 2010).

As was indicated above, during the development of your case study you are likely to have employed a chronological and/or thematic basis for collecting together your observations. When you are conducting your analysis it is important to respect that original structure and to show how the findings correlate and respond to particular themes over time.

A key question relates to what extent it might be possible to generalise from a case study (Quinton and Smallbone (2006: 133–138) and also see discussion on generalisability below). For example, if you have conducted a case study on human resources practices in a small- to medium-sized enterprise (SME), you may have found out that in this particular company the human resources manager actually has very little power and all the decisions are in fact taken by the managing director. This would be a valid statement in relation to this particular firm and case study, but it would not be appropriate or possible to suggest, or generalise, this finding to other manufacturing SMEs or indeed any SMEs. The reason for this is that you have gathered data from only one SME. How could you possibly know what happens in other SMEs? However, in conducting your analysis and exploring generalisability (see below), it might be feasible for you to allude to the possibility that what you have identified might be found into other firms. But this would be the role of a new or extended piece of research across a wider sample of firms and case studies. In order to generalise from case studies it is necessary to conduct a series of case studies. Moreover, this may also require a sampling frame to be developed and applied in order to ensure a degree of reliability (see below).

## RELIABILITY, VALIDITY AND GENERALISABILITY IN RELATION TO DATA ANALYSIS

Reliability, validity and generalisability are very important aspects that need to be established in a piece of research and these have already been raised in earlier chapters. These dimensions of research are important at every stage of the work, from the design of the aims, questions and objectives through to the choice of methodological paradigm, method and data gathering (Maylor and Blackmon, 2005). However, it is perhaps in the analysis and the writing-up phases that the consequences of those choices and decisions begin to crystallise and, for that reason, the decision has been made to include a discussion on validity, reliability and generalisability at this point of the text.

Reliability, validity and generalisability are as equally important for inductive, interpretivistic (social science) approaches to research as they are for deductive, positivistic-style (natural science) research. The important thing to note is that they are viewed, discussed and considered in varying ways depending on the methodological approach adopted.

### Reliability

Reliability concerns questions and issues about the degree to which the methods and approaches employed in the research can be considered dependable. In other words, reliability asks and responds to the question: 'if the research project under consideration were to be replicated by the same or, perhaps more importantly, different researchers using the same questions, methodology, methods, data analysis to what extent can it be assured that the same results would have been obtained?' Maylor and Blackmon (2005: 157–159) supply a useful insight to many of the questions pertaining to these issues.

### Validity

Validity in research concerns assuring that the methods and instruments the research employs are likely to produce dependable and accurate answers and outcomes. In other words is the research likely to, or indeed has it, produced 'truth' (Silverman, 2010a)? Part of this is the question relating to the fact of whether or not the research might be considered 'accurate'. Another way of expressing this would be – 'did the research achieve the responses that it sets out to achieve in accordance with the research questions, methodology and all the other aspects of the given planned research project?'

Triangulation (Silverman, 2010a: 275–278; Cameron and Price, 2009: 216–218) is often cited as a means of pursuing or ensuring validity. Triangulation usually means using a number of different research methods in order to ensure that the findings are accurate and precise, that is, valid. However, in the case of inductive and interpretive research, triangulation offers an additional challenge because of the principles that underpin the inductive approach. Having the possibility of saying that something is completely accurate or indisputably truthful means that we can be *objectively* clear about this. You will recall from the discussion on research methodologies in Chapter 3 above that the concept of objectivity is a central and vital principle in deductive, natural scientific and positivistic approaches to research. Succinctly expressed, this is the notion that 'the truth is out there (as an objectively identifiable entity or artefact) and it will be found sooner or later through the construction and repetition of experiments'. This idea hinges on the very possibility of an objective view or piece of information existing being considered possible and probable.

The above deductive and positivistic view contrasts sharply with inductive and interpretivistic approaches. These approaches believe in the role of subjectivity operating at individual respondent (and researcher) level being in operation in the research realm. This means that the notion of being able to establish a clear and unequivocal truth is highly problematic for these methodological approaches. Turning all of this immediate discussion back on to the topic of triangulation, this means that triangulation becomes inherently tenuous. If the central thrust and intention of triangulation is to cross-authentic the findings identified by a parallel research method, then the researcher (believing in, and employing his or her inductive approach, if this is the case) will be no closer to establishing *the possibility* of a definitive truth. This is because, for the inductivist and interpretivist, all 'truths' have subjectivities and subjective aspects and dimensions aligned with them. In other words, it is highly unlikely that there will be a one-answer-covers-all form of finding or conclusion because various individuals, and research participants will potentially have contrasting or conflicting views and perspectives.

In contrast, for deductivist and positivistic approaches, this situation does not arise because they adhere to the principle that an objective truth is possible to determine and identify. Alternatively, expressed, categorical answers are possible and sought.

In inductive, interpretivistic style research validity has been a concern from some quarters, and receive charges of, partialism or anecdotalism. These concerns are based on the frequent use in research of, for example, very small sample sizes. Silverman (2010a: 278–286) offers one of the most convincing accounts of techniques with which to take this issue when handling qualitative data. He suggests:

- *The refutability principle* – this involves the difficult challenge of putting aside our initial assumptions about the data. Then, having cleared our mind as much as possible we look with fresh eyes and if relationships emerge in a striking manner, then we can suggest that there is a significant event that we should be taking account of. Silverman (*ibid*) suggests that this approach to analysing and validating qualitative data resembles what Popper (1959) termed 'critical rationalism'.
- *The constant comparative method* – this involves seeking to compare your data set and emerging analyses to other data sets and cases. Usually, for most researchers, these will constitute already published data sets in the public domain. Alternatively, it might be the case that you have another case available. Furthermore, we should not overlook the possibility of what can be referred to here as *internal* comparison. It may well be reasonable and possible for you to compare different parts of your data set. For instance, in the data set illustration indicated above, there may well be scope to make useful comparisons between the various cases in the study.
- *Comprehensive data treatment* – due to the relatively small data sample sizes it is often possible to look over the data repeatedly and in great detail. This, in turn, produces its own validity effects and consequences as Silverman (2010a: 280–281) indicates:

> This comprehensiveness arises because, in qualitative research, "all cases of data … [are] incorporated in the analysis [Mehan, 1979: 21]" … Such comprehensiveness goes beyond what is normally demanded in many quantitative methods. For instance, in survey research one is usually satisfied by achieving significant, non-spurious, correlations. So, if nearly all your data support your hypothesis, your job is largely done … By contrast, in qualitative research, working with smaller datasets open to repeated inspection, one should not be satisfied until one's generalization is able to apply to every single gobbet of relevant data you have collected.

- *Deviant case analysis* – It is always important to ask the question of your data:
  - 'how well does your data and evolving analytical framework explain and account for cases that seem to be outside that framework?' In other words, if

you find an instance that is difficult to fit into the data, to what extent can your analysis account for that?;
• *Using appropriate tabulations* – These are presentations of the data in table form that often use numerical representations of data. These offer an alternative presentation of the data to the usual prose based texts and arguments.

## Generalisability

The concept of generalisability involves the degree to which the concepts and conclusions developed in the research might be relevant and pertinent to other settings and similar contexts.

In general, deductivistic- and positivistic-style studies often seek relatively large samples and data sets as part of a design to achieve generalisability. Through use of various quantitative and statistical techniques, deductive approach seeks to establish answers that may be relevant for a wider sphere than the sample (see Hultsch, MacDonald, Hunter, Maitland and Dixon, 2002).

In contrast, inductivistic- and interpretivistic-style studies tend to employ small-scale and localised samples and, therefore, do not intend or plan to generalise much beyond, for example, the limits of a small number of interviews, questionnaires or cases.

## GLOSSARY OF TERMS

**Analysis** The term 'analysis' means the process of studying and organising data and information in order to be better able to understand it. Often, it involves developing frameworks, models, categorisations and typologies in order to be able to grasp, explain and illustrate complexities. The act of analysis is inextricably intertwined with underpinning conceptualisations and assumptions about how knowledge is formed (see epistemology).

**Content analysis** Content analysis involves studying the texts in documents and formats such as, for example, advertisements, television programmes, radio, posters, newspapers, films, speeches, company annual reports and pictures to see if any recurrent patterns or themes can be identified. Equally, it might be a question of, for instance, counting the number of occurrences of an event of language in a given media.

**Grounded Theory and coding** Grounded Theory is a specific interpretive methodological approach. It gathers data and then involves the development of coded categories for different types of pattern identified in the data. These patterns become apparent to the researcher during the process of conducting the analysis. Typically, illustrations of these coded categories might be based on expressions or sentiments that respondents repeatedly use in the workplace. Usual forms of coding employed are: *open coding, axial coding and selective coding*.

**Quantitative data analysis** Quantitative data analyses typically involves use of numerical or statistical approaches and techniques in the analysis of data. The underpinning methodologies used and applied tend to be deductivist and positivistic.

**Qualitative data analysis** Qualitative data analyses typically means the use and interpretation of words, images, symbols and so on and so forth in order to develop understanding and information about a given topic, case or phenomenon. The methodological approaches usually associated with qualitative analysis are inductive and interpretivistic approaches.

## KEY POINTS

1. The analysis stage of the research is often one of the weaker parts of the final written document in many undergraduate and postgraduate studies. There could be a number of reasons for this. One possible reason is that students find it difficult to develop ideas in relation to their own results. We have provided tips on this above so it is best to avoid these types of problem by making use of these approaches.

   A further, less commonly recognised issue is that people are often 'running out of steam' by the time they arrive at the writing of these latter stages of the write-up of their work. Try to remain mindful of this effect. If you find that this is occurring, sit down and, with a fresh mind, focus only on your analysis section. Imagine that you are looking at all the other sections through the lens or prism of your analysis:

   • What ideas and value can you draw from those other sections?
   • What aspects and themes have been mentioned elsewhere in the work that need to be resurfaced and recontextualised in relation to your data?

2. Remember also that your analysis and discussion are very much a fusion of your literature review and your data. Think of it as a conversation that will show and strengthen the arguments you wish to make.

3. Remember that it is you the researcher who is driving the analysis. In subjectivity embracing inductive approaches, this is particularly the case; however, even in the interpretation of deductive quantitative approaches it may play a role.

4. Analysis is inextricably linked with your overall inductive or deductive methodological stance.

5. The analysis stage of your research should be thought about and planned at the very outset of your research rather than treated as an afterthought.

## REVISION QUESTIONS

1. How do you like to make sense of the world – through numbers or words? The answer to this question may well assist you in choosing your research method that you will have to analyse through words and/or numbers subsequently.
2. You have a lot of interview recordings and completes questionnaires – what do you do next? (Prompt – read the section above on coding.)
3. What is the purpose and end objective of an approach to research using a positivistic approach with primarily quantitative data? (Prompt – hypothesis – answers, 'truths' proven or disproven?)
4. What is the purpose and end objective of an approach to research using an interpretivistic approach with largely qualitative data? (Prompt – question exploration and description, deeper understanding?)

## FURTHER STUDY

1. DeCuir-Gunby, J., Marshall, P. and McCulloch, A. (2012) 'Using mixed methods to analyze video data: A mathematics teacher professional development example', *Journal of Mixed Methods Research*, July, 6 (3): 199–216.

   *This paper illustrates how the analysis of video may play a role in research and provides information on techniques and methods to conduct this.*

2. Dass, M. and Shropshire, C. (2012) 'Introducing functional data analysis to managerial science', *Organisational Research Methods*, October, 15 (4): 693–721.

   *This paper provides an insight into an innovative positivistic statistical approach. Both this paper and the previous one indicate the innovative directions in which research in its respective paradigms is being conducted.*

3. Aguinis, H., Pierce, C.A., Bosco, F.A. and Muslin, I.S. (2009) 'First decade of organisational research methods: Trends in design, measurement, and data-analysis topics', *Organisational Research Methods*, 12 (1): 69–112.

# 6

# ETHICS (GETTING APPROVAL AND DOING THE RIGHT THINGS)

## OBJECTIVES

*Successful completion of this chapter provides guidance on:*
- How to understand the various issues involved in, and approaches to, establishing ethical approval for your research;
- How to develop a sensitivity about critical incident moments in-the-field in relation to ethics and also being able to develop judgement to deal with these;
- How to deal with ethical situations in the latter stages and in the exiting the field stages of the study.

## INTRODUCTION

Ensuring that there is an ethical framework present in a piece of research has always been important but has become increasingly imperative and, indeed, obligatory in recent decades (Farrimond, 2013). In certain areas of the natural sciences the need to secure ethical approval has been the case for a substantial number of years. This is primarily because the natural sciences which embrace biology and medicine frequently involve physically or psychologically invasive medical interventions and procedures on people. However, even in wider areas of medicine, ethical approval for many aspects of public health and sociological types of intervention was not required until more recent decades (Oliver, 2010).

In the case of the social sciences which encompass business, organisation and management (as well as, for example, history, geography and English), ethical approval as a systematic, structured and procedural process is relatively novel. Nevertheless, it is now mandatory for most studies. In large part, this is a consequence of not only the growing awareness and sensitivity of the potential impacts of research

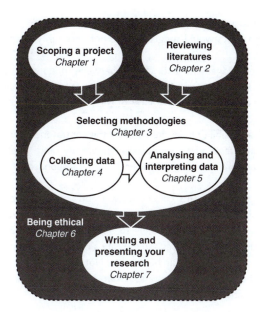

Current location within the research process

on the people involved but also an increasing caution with regard to possible litigation. Ethics in relation to research in the contemporary era is indeed about protecting respondents and researchers alike from potential harm; however, a well-thought-out ethical framework for a study is also likely to make it a more effective and robust piece of research. No matter what form or level of research you are undertaking – undergraduate dissertation or project, postgraduate dissertation or project – ethical approval and permissions to conduct the study will be deemed essential (Comstock, 2013).

## UNDERPINNING SYSTEMS OF ETHICS, VALUES AND BELIEFS

Many discussions on ethics in relation to research, surprisingly, do not tend to discuss the various underpinning ethical philosophical frameworks and principles that underscore ethical decisions. There appears to be an assumption in some discussions on ethics that it is simply about doing the right and good thing as if this were an unproblematic and unchallenging matter. However, as a wide range of historical commentaries on ethics would suggest, this is not necessarily as apparent as might first seem the case.

Ethics involves judgement and choice between notions of good and bad (DesJardins, 2011). The researcher(s) will always be faced with choices about what will be the right way to proceed. Instances of this might be, for example:

- when there is a possibility to secure data but this contravenes agreed protocols;
- when a research respondent supposedly 'innocently' and 'in-passing' asks the researcher to reveal a confidence regarding another respondent.

These are examples where the 'correct' answer and appropriate action may seem obvious. There are many more possible examples of such difficult moments. Ethical codes are useful but they are still likely to need interpretation. Bryman and Bell (2007) provide an exception to this and indicate a number of 'stances' and points of which researchers could and should be mindful. Not all of them are of course acceptable; however, they aim to map out a spectrum of potential behaviours in research settings. These positions include:

- Universalism;
- Situation ethics;
- Ethical transgression;
- (And certainly more contentiously …) Anything goes (more or less).

## Universalism

Universalism follows the idea that codes and guides on ethics should not be broken. Bryman and Bell (2007) discuss in particular how covert research (i.e. where the researcher does not reveal to the research respondent that he or she is conducting research more or less secretly without telling the researched person or people) may raise issues.

Although Bryman and Bell (2007) do not invoke the term, there is an allusion here to the ethics of *deontology*. Deontological ethical approaches are commonly associated with the German philosopher Immanuel Kant (1724–1804). His thinking indicated that the *categorical imperative* should always guide an individual's thinking. This imperative comprised the principle that only rules should be established that would seem reasonable for all to follow. Once established these rules should not be broken under any circumstances. It can be seen how this echoes Bryman and

Bell's discussion on universalism – the categorical imperative embraces a number of operational principles, one of which is *universality*. An example of a universal deontological code would be the Ten Commandments within the Judeo-Christian religious tradition. This contains directions such as 'do not kill' and 'do not steal'. And, indeed, many other religions possess comparable or kindred codes and edicts. Therefore, universalism or deontology does not necessarily take account of consequences in following the rules or code. They indicate that rules are there to be followed no matter what the circumstances or consequences. In relation to this, it can be seen that this approach does not try to balance out what might be 'good outcomes' in the decision. In contrast, it aims to make 'good' rules in the first place (Wood, 2008).

Unlike other approaches to ethics (for example, utilitarianism – which bases decisions on *the consequences* of decisions and the greatest good for the greatest number), deontology is not a *consequentialist* approach. This can lead to tensions and ethical dilemmas.

### Ethical dilemma – universalism and deontology?

For example, imagine that you have said to research participants that you will not conceal information from them and that you will be open about the data you are gathering. However, during the course of the research you inadvertently discover a managerial and organisational plan that involves possible redundancies among the people you are researching. If you are following a deontological approach to the ethics of your study should you tell the research respondents about what you have discovered or do you have an obligation to the organisational management? Such dilemmas are an implicit aspect of research activities and of course life in general (Campbell and Groundwater-Smith, 2007). See Vignette 6.1 for an example.

---

**Example – ethical dilemma in outdoor management development research**

In this example, research was being conducted into training and development programmes and operators that use outdoor activities and outdoor settings in order to train managers in large corporations. In the study, the researcher operated as a participant-as-observer i.e. heavily and covertly implanted in the manager teams undertaking the training

VIGNETTE 6.1

(Waddington, 2004: 154–164). He was asked by the outdoor training providing organisation to introduce himself as a participant on the course who had come to "self-develop" but who, by the way, happened to have a (research) interest in this type of training. The researcher was never doubted or questioned further by any participant. However, importantly, his position was nearly compromised on two occasions. On one of these occasions an outdoor training providing organisation had provided free accommodation on-site whereas the other course participants were accommodated in a nearby town in a hotel more fitting for business executives. This caused brief, but uncomfortable, discussions as to why the researcher was separated from the rest of the group. The reason was linked to a further issue, namely cost. As a result of the research negotiations, the outdoor training organisation charged the researcher only a small, notional cost instead of the full fee that the other delegates had paid. Obviously, it was cheaper to keep 'the researcher', on his tight budget, in an on-site cabin chalet (albeit very comfortable) rather than the hotel. This was, nevertheless, a tricky situation which had to be explained away by his referring to logistical issues and comments like 'Oh well, I'm settled in now'. He had to make a point of walking the two miles, in the pitch black, to and from the local town most evenings to spend time with the group both to be party to the casual, away from the facilitator, discussions and also to allay suspicions of the group regarding his research identity. In relation to these points Hammersley and Atkinson consider that reflexively:

> "We are part of the social world we study … This is not a matter of methodological commitment, it is an existential fact. There is no way in which we can escape the social order to study it; nor fortunately, is that necessary. We cannot avoid relying on 'common-sense' knowledge nor, often, can we avoid having an effect on social phenomena we study". (Hammersley and Atkinson, 1983: 15)

- If this arrangement had not been adopted the research access would have been prevented by the outdoor training organisation. However, this raises an important set of ethical questions. For example:
  - Should the researcher have accepted these terms and conditions for access?

- The outdoor training provider was a major body in the industry and access to the organisation was a significant element of the research. Did this justify misrepresenting himself to the respondents?
- Some researchers would see this as the only way in which the data might be secured (a utilitarianist and situationist ethical stance). Other researchers might decline on the grounds and in the belief that it would never be appropriate to misrepresent or operate covertly (constituting more of a deontological position).

### Possible response from universalism and deontology?

As a deontologist you are likely to tell the respondents what you have found out. This is because you have effectively 'promised' not to conceal information from the research participants.

However, clearly the situation is more complex. You have been allowed access into the organisation by management and this has been granted on the basis that you will not cause harm or damage to its activities or business. Also, the revelation to the research participants/employees is likely to cause many problems between the management and employees of the firm. The realities of the situation are far from stratightforward (Darwell, 2002).

The discussion now turns to consider the next stance in relation to Situation Ethics.

### Situation Ethics

Bryman and Bell (2007) suggest that when confronted with choices regarding difficult, questionable or deceptive actions, a situation ethics approach would point you towards considering matters in a case-by-case approach.

Bryman and Bell's (2007) term Situation Ethics is resonant of a more widely commented branch of ethics termed 'utilitarian ethics'. Utilitarianism suggests that you should take decisions based on the likely consequences linked to each decision option. In making this decision, utilitarianism is often simply summarised as trying to achieve 'the greatest good for the greatest number' (Baron, 2013). This means that you will need to judge what you might assess as:

- 'What' would constitute the 'good' events, people, items, situations that could take place?;

- And which of these would be the 'best' or preferable 'good'?
- Connected to this you are also assessing who (or what) might constitute the 'greatest number'?
- In other words, to whom or to what should this 'good' be directed towards?

## A possible response from situation ethics and utilitarianism?

If you consider utilitarianism in the light of the company research example outlined Above, with respect to becoming aware of redundancies, then the notion of the greatest good and the greatest number needs to be evaluated:

- What would you consider the greatest 'good'?;
- Would it be the protection of the confidentiality of the impending redundancies for company management that you would prioritise?;
- Alternatively, having indicated to the employee respondents that you would be open and candid with them, would telling them about the impending redundancy constitute the appropriate greatest 'good'?;
- Moreover, who might you consider as being the 'greatest number'?
  - Is it the entirety of the non-managerial employee grouping or, in contrast, the managerial collective?
  - As a further development of this, is it sections or particular individuals within these groups?
  - Sometimes 'the greatest number' is not simply a matter of quantity; it might also be an instance of standing, identity, importance, power or quality.

When following this discussion you may feel you have no choice but to take a compromising and questionable action. One key guide within this approach will be the idea of the 'means justifying the ends'. If a particular consequence is seen as desirable or 'good' then perhaps you will decide to lean towards that option. However, there is no guarantee that everyone will share your analysis and conclusion. The reason for this is that utilitarianism is often rooted in a matter of perspective or viewpoint of the individual (Labukt, 2009).

In conclusion, it will be seen that universalism and deontology contrast substantially from the discussion above on situation ethics and deontology. Having provided challenging illustrations and examples of these two key approaches to ethics, it is possible to see how ethical dilemmas might arise in research settings. The section now moves on to consider ethical transgression.

## Ethical transgression

Bryman and Bell (2007) indicate that ethical transgression is common and they draw on a number of sources which seem to suggest, but not condone, that not being completely honest is, in many instances, 'usual' or 'normal' in fieldwork. However, they rightly indicate that ethical transgressions in order to seek data or opportunities in the research field are often pervasive – one little 'wrong' can lead to bigger 'wrongs' as sensitivity barriers and impediments become lowered. This can be argued as leading to the completely unacceptable situation of 'Anything goes (more or less)' and that ethics is flaunted to achieve research aims. This approach is never condonable and it is important not to start small actions that could readily lead into such a transgression. It is mentioned here as an end of a spectrum of potential (though not recommended) behaviour and a signal and warning that this is not a route to pursue.

In concert with these above considerations, Stokes and Harris (2012) point at the potential role of, and value in, considering micro-moments in relation to research actions. A heightened awareness of this notion can, and perhaps should (if we were to adhere to a deontologically influenced stance), guide actions. Stokes and Harris discuss organisational life in the widest stance, but the observations of the paper offer reflections for researchers:

> ... the term micro-moments is employed to mean the many and varied interactions and minute events of the everyday life. These crystallise into the macro-situations that go towards forming ideas of culture, situations and atmospheres. Micro-moments consist of the dialectics and dualities of individual dubious and honourable conduct embracing a potent cocktail of *inter alia* Machiavellian-style gossip, lies, naivety, deceit, political manoeuvring jostling with aspirations of hope integrity, honesty, directness, reputation and wisdom – often simultaneously in any given moment or incident (Machiavelli, 1532/2008; Harris, Lock and Rees 2000; Kessler, 2007). Within these often fleeting incidental moments, how managers and employees respond to issues of choice and responsibility is paramount. This is not simply a base question of organizational politics or micro-political survival in the organizational 'jungle' or what Stokes and Gabriel (2010 drawing on its originator Levi 1986/1988: 25–26) remind us is the 'Grey Zone' of ambivalent human behaviour. Rather it is driven by a desire for notions of satisfaction, happiness – the Aristotelian *eudemonia* – well-being and to

live and co-habit in an environment that exudes a sense, albeit often highly subjective, of being decent, honourable, meaningful and worthwhile. This then would constitute an approach towards a notional *ideal* of a responsible and sustainable organization ...

Moreover . . . it is apparent that 'choice', and the taking of responsibility, is a key aspect of the micro-moment. It is sometimes the case, and this was borne out by the data, that people believe that they do not have a choice – an idea roundly rejected as false by, for example, the Sartrean [i.e. derived from the work of the existentialist writer and philosopher Jean-Paul Sartre] notion of 'mauvaise foi' (bad faith) and elaborated in his work *Being and Nothingness* (1943/2003). Choice is a key catalytic aspect of the micro-moment on the 'journey' to building a sustainable work environment. Only when appropriate integrity and a recognition of the need to take responsibility in the micro-moment are acknowledged are 'good' consequences reinforced and 'bad' choices avoided assisting the organization on a sustainable trajectory.

Micro-moments remind the researcher that choice, whether deontological or utilitarianism, is always in the hand of you – the researcher. Even if the choices sometimes seem very hard, then values and codes (ethical, institutional or other) will assist in guiding the researcher. Almost never, in operational research terms, will the (questionable) means justify the ends in itself and 'Anything goes (more or less)' is simply not acceptable.

### What should you ask yourself before you embark on and as you engage with your study?

Collis and Hussey (2009: 39 citing Kervin 1992: 38) remind researchers of an interesting set of questions that act as prompts in relation to many of the above issues. Their approach of putting the issues into question form is a useful one:

1. Will the research harm participants or those about whom information is gathered (indirect participants)?
2. Are the findings of this research likely to cause harm to others not involved in the research?
3. Are you violating accepted research practice in conducting the research and data analysis, and drawing conclusions?
4. Are you violating community standards of conduct?

## Example – unethical behaviour in the organisational context of an enthusiasts' club

A researcher was an enthusiast of model boating and wished to conduct ethnographic research into the organisational culture and atmospheres of model boat club gatherings round the boating pond. This involved the researcher (who was a member of the club) being present at boating meetings, discussing, working with, and sailing the model boats with his fellow enthusiasts. However, the researcher decided to use a recording device placed on a strap around his neck and concealed under his clothes in order to gather data. This was a covert and undisclosed piece of research. The researcher felt that the research needed to be conducted in this manner as he believed that it would be impossible to gather reliable and unfiltered data by openly declaring his intention to conduct research. He feared something of a Hawthorne Effect (Roethlisberger and Dickson (1939)), whereby respondents would modify their behaviour and responses if they were aware that they might form part of a research study.

During one of the instances when the researcher was conducting the research, the device fell out from under his clothing and became visible. Enthusiasts present at the meeting immediately asked what he had around his neck and why. He had little other option than to confess what he was trying to do and apologise. It is possible to imagine the embarrassment, and the uncomfortable and unpleasant atmosphere that ensued. His relationship and engagement with the club was never really the same. Substantial trust and reputation had been lost.

Questions on the case:

- Was covert observation really the only approach possible?
- What other approaches to research might the researcher have considered adopting?
- In the light of the presentations on ethical frameworks elaborated in the discussions above, how might the various ethical stances (situation ethics, universalism, etc.) assist in preventing situations like the one outlined in the case?

## ETHICS CODES, PROCESSES AND COMMITTEES

Many, if not most, organisations will be informed and guided by some form of code or body of principles. Occasionally, this will be a code established by discussion and conjecture within the organisation. Quite often, it is more likely to be a code advocated by a representative or governing body covering an area of economic, business or professional conduct and practice.

When you are planning a piece of research it is vital that you seek and find out what procedures and policies might be in place (Sieber and Tolich, 2012). For example, if you were conducting a piece of research for your dissertation whilst studying in higher education and your research involved talking to health care professionals, then you may very well have a series of ethical codes to observe. On the one hand, the higher education institution will have an ethics committee and you will need to comply with its requirements. On the other hand, the controlling body of the health care professionals, for example a hospital trust, will also have ethical and consent procedures that need to be taken account of and respected.

The key mechanism for all of the above is the 'ethics committee'. This will be a body that has been established in an institution in order to ensure that the research is conducted in an ethical and appropriate manner and that various rules and procedures are complied with. The membership of this body will include a range of people including senior figures in the organisation. Juritzen, Grimen and Heggen (2011) provide an interesting critical perspective on the work of ethics committees.

As an obvious example it will be useful to look at the code of ethical guidelines for the conduct of members of the British Academy of Management which is one of the key representative bodies for academics in the United Kingdom. The ethical code provisions below will be echoed by many similar associations and bodies worldwide. While the code is not expressly or uniquely focused on direct research activities, its message and impacts on those activities are very clear (see Box 6.1).

---

### Box 6.1 The British Academy of Management's Code of Ethics and Best Practice Policy

*'The principles outlined in the document are described in a statement of values, reflecting the fundamental beliefs that should guide the ethical reasoning, decision-making and behaviour of all BAM members. All members are expected to act in accordance with the principles outlined in*

the document. Although the code of the British Academy of Management does not explicitly state a focus on research, it covers all behaviour relating to research and the spirit of the code should be noted. The code is based on seven key principles outlined below.

- *Responsibility and Accountability:* All members are aware of their ethical, legal and professional responsibilities incumbent to the specific communities in which they work and also to BAM. All individuals should avoid any misconduct that might bring BAM or the reputation of the profession into disrepute.
- *Integrity and Honesty:* All members should endeavour to demonstrate accuracy, truthfulness, openness and transparency within their professional conduct with others.
- *Respect and Fairness:* All members will not discriminate against others on the basis of: ethnicity, gender, age, religion, disability, sexual orientation, social background, political beliefs, personal history or any other aspects of personal identity. All members should promote equal opportunity, celebrate diversity and encourage an environment free of discrimination.
- *Privacy and Confidentiality:* All members respect the individual and collective rights to privacy and maintain confidentiality in compliance with UK and International law and regulations.
- *Avoidance of Personal Gain:* All members should neither offer nor accept bribes or inducements either on a personal basis or on behalf of BAM.
- *Conflict of Interest:* All members should declare any competing professional or personal interests that may be pertinent to their activities within BAM. Any activities undertaken in BAM's interest must be consistent with BAM's vision, mission, strategic objectives and the principles outlined in this guide. Any competing interests can make it difficult to fulfil the duties impartially and steps should be taken to eliminate any potential conflicts of interest that may arise. If a conflict of interest does arise, the individual must inform the BAM Executive and Academy Manager immediately and following the consultation must undertake any of the below or any other actions deemed necessary:
  - *abstain from certain actions;*
  - *return the given task to a fellow colleague or*
  - *give up their role.*

*Failure to do so, may lead to the imposition of sanctions, including termination of their BAM membership.*

- *Collegiality: Collaboration between other societies and organisations should be encouraged in order to develop guidance relevant to the creation of management knowledge through research and help disseminate learning and good practice. This will help to further strengthen the integrity of the Business and Management Academic Community.*

### Summary

The Code of Ethics and Best Practice Policy has established the principles for all BAM members to adhere to, and uphold the highest standards of professional conduct. However this guide does not aim to provide the answer to every issue that may arise for individuals.

The Code of Ethics and Best Practice Policy encourages trust and respect from its members and non-members. Furthermore, through this guide, BAM will continue to have a strong reputation for integrity, openness, fairness and transparency within the Business and Management Academic Community.'

https://www.bam.ac.uk (2013)

You will also find it useful to examine the codes for institutions such as, for example, the British Sociological Association and the British Psychological Society. For example, the document 'The Statement of Ethical Practice for the British Sociological Association' covers some 61 statements and provisions to which it asks its members to consider and adhere. These provisions are categorised under headings including:

- Professional integrity …
- Relations with and responsibilities towards research participants …
- Relationships with research participants …
- Covert research …
- Anonymity, privacy and confidentiality …
- Relations with and responsibilities towards sponsors and/or funders …
- Clarifying obligations, roles and rights …
- Pre-empting outcomes and negotiations about research …
- Obligations to sponsors and/or funders during the research process.

Following on from these provisions, the British Sociological Association website (www.britsoc.co.uk, 2013) provides a very extensive range of web addresses of additional associations, organisations and government departments and documents that provide guidance and advice on ethical issues and protocols. This richness of resource in relation to ethics is not uncommon among professional and learned associations and societies.

All of the ideas and concepts that play a role in informing these frameworks are drawn from a longstanding and ongoing academic and philosophical debate across a variety of various national and international associations. Moreover, the wider realm of ethics is vast in extent. Clearly, various theories play a role in relation to developing the theoretical approaches that inform and construct the ethical codes and procedures in operations in myriad organisations. The ethical stances outlined above are intended to provide an insight and overview for your study. There will be considerable value for you to conduct further research of your own.

## What about laws and legal provisions you need to observe and respect?

In addition to codes and guidelines you must also be mindful to observe the laws of the country and national context in which you are operating. In the case of, for example, the United Kingdom this means that there will be a range of laws relating sex equality, equal opportunity and disability. Moreover, recent decades have also witnessed the advent of a range of legal acts relating to information and data. One such act is the Data Protection Act (1998). This indicates the reasons, method and duration of the rights organisations have in relation to keeping data on individuals. The comments above and those that follow are not meant to be a legal statement. It is crucial that this legal disclaimer is clearly made at this point. **If you are interested in looking up further details on this act or any other act then you will need to locate and investigate the appropriate government or legal website.** Jankowicz (2005: 66) provides a useful overview of the provisions:

### The Principles of Data Protection
If you are processing personal data, you have to comply with the following eight principles. Data must be:

- Fairly and lawfully processed;
- Processed for limited purposes;
- Adequate, relevant and not excessive;
- Accurate;

- Not kept longer than necessary;
- Processed in accordance with the data subject's rights;
- Secure;
- Not transferred to countries without adequate protection.

By and large, an individual about whom data are held and processed has the right to know the nature of the data, and to see a copy. When the data are used for research, then, so long as the research does not support decisions about particular individuals, it is not incompatible with the original reasons for gathering the data, and is processed in a way that doesn't cause damage or distress to those individuals:

- The data can be kept indefinitely.
- The individual's right to see the data is qualified, so long as the results of the research or any resulting statistics are not made available in a form which identifies any of the individuals concerned.

## TYPICAL AND USUAL ETHICAL CONSIDERATIONS IN RELATION TO CONDUCTING RESEARCH

In an attempt to clarify and elaborate further the discussion thus far, Bulmer (2001) indicates a number of central ethical considerations that should be taken into account when undertaking research:

- Ensuring and safeguarding confidentiality and anonymity of data and respondents
- Securing informed consent in research
- Avoiding deceit and lying during research
- If covert observation is employed – ensure it is justified
- Think carefully regarding what is reasonable and appropriate to put in surveys interviews and questionnaires
- Always have respect for privacy
- Attending to the consequences of publication (Paraphrased from Bulmer (2001) in Gilbert (2008))

It will be useful to expand and discuss a number of these ideas.

### Informed consent

When conducting research it always important to secure clear, signed and documented informed consent. For example, if you are interviewing people it is best to have a drafted consent form that they can read and sign if they wish to proceed with the research. An illustration of such a letter is provided below. On occasion, if you are linked to a university or college you may have a standard form that they encourage employees to use (see Israel and Hay, 2006: 60–76)

In addition, you may need to gain agreement and consent on behalf of a company or organisation in order to conduct research. Not always, but quite often, this is likely to come through the office of the human resources manager or director. He or she may also liaise with you and the manager(s) of the areas you wish to access.

Signed and completed forms should then be stored in a safe place for a number of years following the study. In some cases, a decision might be taken to keep the forms from a given piece of research for a number of years in the event of later claims and repercussions stemming from either the original research or the publication and dissemination of the findings.

An additional important aspect of obtaining consent is the idea of autonomy (Sales and Folkman, 2000). This is the idea that, within research, a person should be able to act as an autonomous agent in deciding whether or not to engage in your research. Autonomy, as a principle, encourages the researcher to create opportunities for the subject to 'say no' to being involved in the research at any stage of it – whether it be at the start (when you recruit subjects to the research), during the research (for example, when you are collecting interview data) or at the end (when data has been collected and analysed).

The American Psychological Association (2014) points out that participants should also be informed of 'reasonably foreseeable factors' that might influence their willingness to participate. Though this issue of obtaining consent can apply in all research, it becomes particularly prevalent in 'insider research' where members of staff are conducting the research within the organisation. The vignette below provides a real case example (Vignette 6.3 below).

### Example – Getting (real) consent from staff?

Within this case, the researcher was an 'insider-researcher', or a researcher who was employed as a full-time member of staff within the organisation in which he was researching. He was a manager of a department in a large retail business, and wanted to understand why there was a high turnover

VIGNETTE 6.3

of staff in his department compared to other departments within the store. All of the staff within the department were female and of a Muslim faith. For the manager, he believed it was sufficient to get the permission of the husbands of the wives and that the wives should, and will, therefore, give consent to participate in the research.

Methodologically, he decided to hold interviews with the staff in his department; from his perspective, he believed that this was an ethical and valid approach to get the views and opinions of his staff. He believed it was ethical because he had permission from the husbands of his female staff, and of course permission from the staff directly. It was a valid approach, he thought, because interviews are a valid way to obtain the views and opinions of his staff. The latter of these points is often the case, but this case raises a number of questions about consent and how it is achieved.

Questions on the case:

- To what extent did the staff in this case have the possibility to 'say no' to participate in the research or not?

- What specific power relations were at play to shape the outcome?

- What were the main ethical issues faced by the 'insider-researcher'?

- How might these be different to the 'outsider-researcher' in this case?

- What other methods might the insider-researcher have used to find out the reasons why people were leaving?

- What might be the ethical consequences of each of these alternative options?

### Avoiding harm to research participants

The notion of avoiding harm to participants may be self-evident. However, the researcher should be mindful that harm can *potentially* be done in myriad ways and the researcher should always be aware of this. So it is not just important to design your research to avoid harm but to also plan for what might happen and have contingencies (Vignette 6.4 below).

## Example – (un)expected emotional harm?

In this case, a researcher wanted to find out about the experiences of tourists when they visited very popular tourist destinations in Berlin, Germany. The researcher specifically chose to investigate the personal experiences of visitors to The Holocaust Monument (the Memorial to the Murdered Jews of Europe) in Berlin. From his perspective, this would not only be an interesting research topic to him personally, but would also potentially enable tourist and destination management organisations to enhance their marketing efforts for other destinations.

The researcher decided to use a random sample of older people who were at the destination, and conduct semi-structured interviews with them just after they had visited the site. He had only a short list of questions to prompt his participants about their experiences of visiting the Monument and their thinking about what emotions the experience generated for them during their experience.

The researcher was shocked and ill-prepared by how much pain and upset his participants talked about and did not really know what to do when people started to cry in front of him. He realised not only had he conjured up painful memories of older family members and some terrible stories of torture but that it was his questions that worsened an already painful state for some – and that he did not have the skill to manage the situation.

Questions on the case:

- What are the key ethical issues in this research?
- Who might be benefiting from the research, and who might be being harmed through the process?
- What might the researcher have done beforehand to have managed the situation better?

For example, harm could be done by:

- Asking subjects to relive emotionally disturbing or traumatic events, whether this is the planned focus of the research or not (in other words, the issue emerges through data collection or analysis);

- Mis-representing what a research respondent has said to you;
- Breaking a confidence to a third party that a research participant has made to you – for instance relaying it to the research respondent's boss or a colleague;
- Being careless with interview materials and allowing them to be left in places where third parties could access them or see them;
- Gossiping about things you have learned during the course of your research;
- Replying or forwarding emails that contain confidential information in the attached earlier streams or flows of emails;
- Doing things that go beyond the boundaries of the original consent agreement with an organisation in order to secure access to other data or some advantage.

### Ensuring confidentiality

In many ways, ensuring confidentiality is intrinsically linked with issues of avoiding harm and integrity. Evidently, all the data needs to be kept confidential in terms of storage. However, and perhaps even more important, when it comes to the time to write, produce, publish and disseminate your work to third parties, it is imperative to ensure that no statement or forms of words are likely to compromise the participants (Israel and Hay, 2006: 77–94).

On occasion, research findings might show a completely unfavourable view of certain individuals or organisations. In these instances, it is vital and essential to change and camouflage the name of the organisation. Most simply put, this might mean putting the organisation as 'Company X' or 'Institution X'. Often changing the name is not enough to ensure confidentiality. It might also be necessary to modify details about position in an industry, business or professional sector. Equally, geographic location details might be very revealing. It is especially important to remember that whilst the general public and readers may not be able to deduce who the organisations or individuals are, those people who work in the industry or business context are likely to be able to discern who and what the research is about with a very minimal number of clues. Therefore, it is important to think carefully about what might jeopardise the anonymity and confidentiality of your work.

### Integrity

Integrity refers to the need to be honest and straight, and observe the highest levels of probity (Storr, 2004). As individuals we develop our attitudes, characteristics and personality in relation to the earliest years of our life. It would be a wishful ideal to think that everyone grows into adulthood with a high positive sense of integrity;

however, sadly there are myriad examples of theft, fraud, lies, deceit and duplicity in everyday private and professional life to suggest that this may not always be the case. Clearly, there is, to use the colloquialism, no 'silver bullet' solution. In other words, there is no simple answer to ensure that integrity prevails. Nevertheless, a deeper understanding of ethics and related fields will go some distance in ameliorating the situation and ensuring that the research work in which you engage will have strong ethical values.

### Transparency, validity and plagiarism

It is always imperative to credit sources and materials to the authors or designers who produced them. Sometimes it might seem easy to overlook this, for example, when a general diagram seems to be used by everyone in an organisational setting. However, it should be recognised that the diagram belongs to someone and was produced by someone. If that individual cannot be traced then the diagram should at least be ascribed to the organisation from which it was derived.

In terms of copying work from academic sources without crediting the authors, this is a very unwise, foolish and dishonest practice generally termed as plagiarism. There are a number of forms of plagiarism (see Luke and Kearins (2012) for an interesting debate). For example, it is even possible to self-plagiarise by copying and reproducing work that has already been completed and used elsewhere for a subsequent piece of work. In terms of academic work many institutions now use software such as 'Turn it in' in order to be able to detect plagiarism, and there is a very high rate of detection with the attendant consequences for the perpetrator.

## CONCLUDING THOUGHTS ON ETHICAL ISSUES

Ethics is a vitally important aspect of your study. The essential thrust of most ethical concerns is that you should not cause harm or damage to any individual, group or entity. Ethical codes of institutions and organisations are helpful in guiding your actions. It is imperative that these are not contravened in either letter or 'spirit of the law'.

The background philosophical perspectives on ethics, for example, situation ethics/utilitarian and universalism/deontology, can be very helpful in providing frameworks and deeper understanding of the systems of ethical approach. It is worthwhile taking some time to explore these ideas as it offers the possibility of improving your overall work.

## GLOSSARY OF TERMS

**Autonomy** This is the ethical principle that participants must be able to act as autonomous agents within your research processes. This means they have the right to 'say no' at the start of your research, during it and once they have engaged within it.

**Anonymity** This means that, if they so desire, you should always conceal the real identity of your research participants and respondents. This may mean that you need to hide or change names of research respondents and organisations in your research writing up phase.

**Confidentiality** When gathering data it is imperative that a researcher respects the fact that data should not be passed on, or shown, to third parties. This also means protecting the data in a secure location even when the research has been completed. This is based on a need to respect the individual and also the ethical codes and/or any contract you may have signed. Equally, you could also be in contravention of legal stipulations through the provisions of laws such as, for example, The Data Protection Act (1998). This invokes a range of legal obligations particularly in relation to the handling and storage of data relating to individuals, and you and other people involved in the research need to be aware of it.

**Consent** An essential element of conducting research is the process of gaining access to the field, the researched organisation and the individuals within it. In order to do this it is important to secure the *written* permission from representatives of the organisation and/or the individuals involved. Taking only verbal consent is never very advisable. During a research study, unforeseen and unplanned events can occur and situations can change. If you have been given only oral confirmation of your access, then this can be changed or modified by third parties and there will be no record of it. Consent must be freely given, and must not be forced through coercion.

**Ethics** In it most simple expression, ethics is the process whereby you make choices between 'good' and 'bad'. Clearly, what could be meant or understood by notions of 'choice', 'good' and 'bad' in a range of contexts is a rich and complex domain, and this has given rise to wide conjuncture and discussion over the course of human history.

**Harm** This is a key principle within any ethical framework. All research should plan and conduct studies so that there is no risk at all that it will do harm to any of the respondents in any way whatsoever, be that physical, psychological and reputational.

**Informed consent** When this term is used it means that the research participant has the capacity and ability to fully comprehend what the research will involve. In addition, based on this understanding it means that they are happy and willing to sign a consent form in order to provide their permission to participate in the research.

**Negative consent** The term 'negative consent' is a form of consent that works whereby the respondent is deemed to be willing to participate in the research unless they expressly sign to say that they do not wish to. Clearly, this is a form of process fraught with potential difficulties and misunderstandings. This form of consent is generally avoided nowadays.

**Positive consent** Positive consent is the opposite of negative consent. Here research participants are considered as being involved in the research only if they expressly sign to give their consent. This is the form of consent that is usually employed in research work.

**Privacy** The notion and principle of privacy is closely aligned with anonymity and confidentiality. It concerns the need to respect an individual's right, within the bounds of the law, to keep certain matters confidential to herself or himself. The researcher too needs to respect these boundaries.

## KEY POINTS

- Always check with your employing or host institution that you are complying with their approval procedures for conducting research either within the institution or in an external institution/organisation.
- Always be mindful to not do, or say, anything that might possibly cause harm or offence to your research respondents. Ethics is generally one of the shorter sections in most students' work. While word counts are often an aspect of a report or dissertation that have to be managed, it may be useful to dedicate some extra space to elaborating the ethical aspects of your research. Rather than simply reiterating the basic points of, for example, confidentiality, harm and privacy, you may also find an opportunity to show how your ethical framework and conduct played a role in shaping your overall work. You might, for example, even provide an instance where an ethical dilemma or issue was addressed and resolved. This provides genuine context to your study and brings your section on ethics alive.
- Treat your research respondents with the utmost respect at all times.
- Remember to exit the field in a manner that is as orderly and courteous as possible to ensure that respondents feel happy, satisfied and comfortable with the research experience.

## REVISION QUESTIONS

- Have you ever found yourself in an ethical dilemma? What happened and what did you do?
  - Write down a few facts about what happened and work out various scenarios about how you might have addressed it alternatively. What lessons can be learnt for your research activities?
  - Do you think you tend to see the world and the situations it presents to you as a deontologist or as a utilitarian? What do you think are the implications for any research you undertake?

## FURTHER STUDY

1. Willis, R. (2010) 'Advice for Supervising PhD Students during the Ethical Approval *Process*: A Research Student's Perspective', *Research Ethics Review*, June 6 (2): 53–55.
2. Lomborg, S. (2013) 'Personal Internet Archives and Ethics', *Research Ethics*, March 2013; 9 (1): pp. 20–31
3. Gelling, L and Munn-Giddings, C. (2011) 'Ethical Review of Action Research: The Challenges for Researchers and Research Ethics Committees', *Research Ethics*, September, 7 (3): 100–106.
4. Angell, E and Dixon-Woods, M. (2008) 'Style Matters: An Analysis of 100 Research Ethics Committee Decision Letters', *Research Ethics Review*, September, 4 (3) 101–105.
5. Stevenson Thorpe, A. (2014) Doing the Right Thing or Doing the Thing Right: Implications of Participant Withdrawal, *Organizational Research Methods*, doi: 10.1177/1094428114524828. Available online at http://orm.sagepub.com/content/early/2014/03/17/1094428114524828.abstract, accessed 11 May 2014.

# 7

# WRITING, PRESENTATION AND DISSEMINATION

## OBJECTIVES

*Successful completion of this chapter provides guidance on:*
- How to understand what is involved in the processes of writing up;
- How to develop the ability to craft, articulate and produce research write-ups that are useful and valuable accounts of your data and research;
- How to understand the various formats, styles and conventions that may be required for particular research approaches, methods and methodologies;
- How to plan to disseminate your work more widely;
- How to manage your confidence and motivation during the writing up stage.

## INTRODUCTION

Having completed your research, you may find the act of writing up the research very challenging indeed. Just a few of the typical issues that may confront you at this stage are:

- Where to start?;
- What to do first?;
- When will I know what I have written is appropriate and satisfactory?;
- How do I overcome moments when my confidence or motivation is low?

These are indeed, difficult and testing questions and, in many ways, being able to address them will be a function of practice and experience. The ideas discussed below are an attempt to help you on your way.

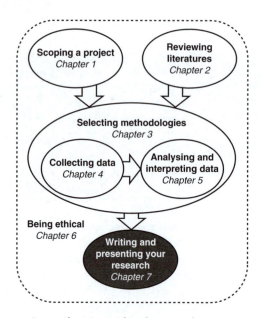

Current location within the research process

## APPROACHING WRITING YOUR RESEARCH

There are a number of key points to recall in relation to approaching the write up of your research:

- Always start writing early – writing and correcting often seems to take more time than you think it will. And, in particular, remember that polishing and fine-tuning a piece of work is as important as the first draft.
- Remember and respect the research methodology that you are using and make sure that this runs through and influences the way you write your work (Murray, 2011). The following sections discuss this in great detail.
- Be aware of the word count parameters of your write up, and always stay clear. This includes the expected word count of the entire written elements of your research, and also the different sections or chapters of your write up. This can also help you plan the number of paragraphs a section has, and therefore the number of key points you can realistically expect to cover and explain well (assuming a

well-developed paragraph is approximately 200–250 words). For example, if a section is of 1,000 words, this might have 4 or 5 main paragraphs and associated main points.

- Check that what you have written flows logically and reasonably from one sentence to another and from one paragraph to another. It is very easy to become lost in, and too close to, your text. Remember to stand back from the text occasionally during the writing process in order to see if it will make sense to your reader(s) (Hart, 2001; Ridley, 2012).

## What are the conventions and choices in writing up qualitative data and quantitative data?

When asked about their dissertation, many students typically reply that they are doing a 'qualitative' or a 'quantitative' piece of work. This is a usual way of talking about writing; however, it can be misleading. As mentioned in earlier chapters, it is probably more appropriate and useful to think about there being qualitative and quantitative *data* which are developed through particular methods and methodologies that you have employed. In perhaps over-simplified, but nevertheless helpful, terms for the purposes of illustration, quantitative and qualitative data usually refer in a prosaic sense to data composed, respectively, of either *words* or *numbers*. As indicated above, this is not to suggest that these two forms of data are mutually exclusive and, indeed, any piece of research and writing might easily contain both forms of data. Moreover, in relation to the data and methods, what truly characterises your study and research are the methodological principles to which you are adhering, such as positivism or interpretivism (Silverman, 2010a).

Nevertheless, in relation to writing up qualitative and quantitative data and field research, it is equally important not to adopt an overly myopic view of the paradigms in which they normally reside. For instance, in papers employing a predominantly quantitative approach – that is analyses rooted in statistics and numerical computations – it is common to see these data also accompanied by a written narrative (see Donaldson, 1996). However, all too often, the narrative is very limited and does not fully elaborate the findings of the research. It is almost as if some authors anticipate that the numbers should do all the arguing of the points that the research is trying to make. This is a significant oversight and omission on the part of the author(s). When conducting quantitative analyses and research, it is important to elaborate as fully as possible the written account of the findings. Equally, when working with more qualitative data, you should not be reluctant to employ statistical or numerical data alongside the prose argument (Davis and Pecar, 2013; Ha, 2011). Often, a body of numerical data, perhaps presented in a chart or other form of diagram, can be very helpful in illustrating a point or phenomenon that might take many words in order to make it clear. To coin (and modify) the well-known saying: 'a (quantitative or qualitative data) picture paints a thousand words'.

## What should you remember and respect in your research design in the write up?

All research is underpinned by methodological approaches and assumptions. Usually, it is normal to state the methodology you have adopted explicitly in a section on methodology in the written document. This will contain a statement to the effect that you are using, for example, a positivistic, deductive, interpretivistic, inductive, critical realist, Critical Theory, poststructuralist – the possible list is extensive – approach (Al-Amoudi and Willmott, 2011; Alvesson, et al., 2011; Dereli and Stokes, 2008; Stokes, 2011; Parkes, 2012).

All methodological and philosophical stances have particular views and attitudes in relation to epistemological and ontological issues (see Chapters 3 and 4). Usually this revolves around how these philosophies view matters such as subjectivity and objectivity on the part of the researcher in relation to the field and research respondents. When writing up your research it is vitally important to keep the nature and philosophical commitments of your chosen methodology and paradigm in mind. For instance, a common misunderstanding and oversight occurs in the use of interpretivistic approaches. As discussed in the earlier chapters, interpretivism acknowledges and embraces the role of subjectivity in the research domain. This means that the data generated emerge through processes of mutual interpretation and perspectives between the researcher and the research respondents. In essence they acknowledge and are grounded in subjectivity. However, in contrast, positivistic approaches embrace objectivity as being centrally important principle to maintain during the research (Wilson, 2010).

## How should you write up case studies?

There are a number of points particularly worth remembering in relation to writing up a case study. At the outset, if, for example, your case study has involved going into a number of organisations, it is a good idea to keep comprehensive notes of what has happened and what you did in the field in relation to the interactions you have. The reason for this is simply because it is a good way of capturing and recording the variety and richness of events, dialogue and overall data that you experience. If you do not do this, when you come to the writing up phase, you will not be able to remember all the fleeting yet interesting and revealing details about the case(s). This, of course, should be a standard procedure if you are adopting a research method such as a case study. However, all too often, it is easy to get too busy or too tired to make in-depth notes (Hammersley and Atkinson, 2007). This is unfortunate because when it comes to the writing up phase quite often it is very difficult to recall all the details which made an impression on you a while ago. Keeping good notes will improve the account of the case(s) you are able to produce in your final write up. Once the data and notes have been properly collected, it is important to remember that a case study, more or less, follows a usual format (Yin, 2003, 2011).

It is important to underline that when you are conducting your case study, or case studies, a central aim is generally the production an in-depth view of a particular company, situation or issue. The writing up of your case will have boundaries. These boundaries will be the organisational context, or the part of the organisation you were examining. While you may relate or discuss other aspects that may seem pertinent to the case, it is important to remember that you should focus on the case context on which you gathered data. You should avoid moving away from the focal area of the case and drifting on to connected but irrelevant areas.

The case writing format will usually include (although not exclusively to variations and alternatives):

- Introduction to the case study;
- Background context to the case issue;
- Examination of the focal issue;
- Proposal of solutions and recommendations;
- Conclusion.

A case study contains a range of methods including interview, questionnaire, focus groups, participant observation and critical incident method (Butterfield, et al., 2005; DeWalt and DeWalt, 2002; Gubrium et al., 2012). It is important to write about the use, and role, of these methods within the case context. Equally, and in parallel, you will have approached the case study through a particular methodological paradigm. The objectivity or subjectivity characteristics and values over-arching your chosen methodological approach need to be reflected throughout the case write-up.

## How should you write up ethnographic studies?

Much of what has been said above in relation to case study write-ups can also be applied to ethnography but perhaps more so. As indicated in earlier chapters, research using ethnography draws on a range of data detailing events, episodes, behaviours, emotions, actions and reactions (see, for example, Mills and Ratcliffe, 2012). This means that, typically, ethnographic approaches result in lengthy and detailed descriptive bodies of text. It is, in fact, the rich pictures portrayed by write-up of the data that allow the reader to produce vivid images in their own mind of what the research setting and actions were like when the researcher experienced them.

Ethnography, therefore, seeks to bring the research very much alive. Some commentators may argue that this may be in stark contrast to research conducted from a positivistic stance which seeks to portray events objectively through statistical or numerical data and representations. Ethnography is a vibrant and varied research form. (A useful resource illustrative of this, in addition to the many available texts, is the Annual Liverpool Symposium on Current Developments in Ethnographic Research in the Social and Management Sciences. This Symposium is held in association with *the Journal of Organizational Ethnography*).

As a consequence, when ethnographic data are written up they will almost certainly include quotations from respondents and participants encountered and interviewed in the research setting. Equally, your findings may be written up in the form of a story or narrative form (and is discussed in the next section). These materials might, for example, take the form of the illustration provided in Vignette 7.1.

### An example of writing-up ethnographic research

The text example below is extracted from Stokes and Oiry (2012) An Evaluation of the Use of Competencies in Human Resource Development – A Historical and Contemporary Reconcontextualisation, *EuroMed Journal of Business* 7(1): 4–23.

This provides an illustration of an ethnographic-style study write-up. In particular, it will be useful to note the manner in which the background and context are presented in the form of an overview of the context in which the study was set accompanied by a focus on the daily routines of the actors and respondents. In addition, it is helpful to look at the way in which a range of themes are identified in the data and explored through a range of arguments that use vibrant quotations to portray the lived experience of the study participants.

***Caveat:*** It is important to say that the account below is a naturalistic account and therefore includes illustrations of the raw language used by

VIGNETTE 7.1

these particular shop-floor operatives. This is an authentic representation of the research setting and it would be an interference with the data to edit out the bad language. As a compromise, it is useful, on occasion, to use some degree of allusion (although not always by any measure) rather than blatant statement of controversial expression.

## Abstract

### Purpose

Competencies have come to play a central role in a wide range of settings in United Kingdom public and private sector contexts. This phenomenon is usually analysed but rarely recontextualised. The purpose of this paper is to identify the epistemological and ontological paradigms on which these approaches are couched in a British historical socio-cultural context.

### Design/methodology/approach

To put into light what this alternative perspective on competencies could add to reflection and practice, we realise an in-depth two-year ethnographic study (employing participant-observer methods) of a consultancy delivered training programme for customer service competency based vocational qualification in a water utilities company based in the north of England.

### Findings

Based on a wide literature review on competencies, the first main result of this paper is to show that many competencies approaches are underpinned by an empirical, pragmatic and ultimately modernistic, positivistic predilection. In an attempt to reappraise this rigid and highly structured representation of competencies, the paper draws on the resources of Critical Management approaches and notions of 'lived experience'. The main empirical result is that competencies in practice are richer than competency frameworks (especially NVQs) usually suppose it and that critical perspectives are valuable in seeking to address these lacunae.

### Originality/value

The paper offers an innovative insight to alternative dimensions of the experience of working with competency frameworks. Overall, a further value of this paper is to provide an assessment and a critique of the experience of competencies and vocational training in the United Kingdom. This recontextualisation underlines that competencies are weak at capturing and portraying the rich panoply of multifarious emotions and social interactions that take place in the workplace and everyday job life.

**Key Words**: Competencies, Lived Experience, Paradigms, Positivism.
**Paper Type**
Research Paper/Case Study

## Introduction

Competencies have come to play a central role in a wide range of settings in United Kingdom public and private sector contexts (Bouzdine-Chameeva, 2006; Cappelan and Janssens, 2008; Barthe et *al.*, 2007; CIPD, 2010; Tilestone, 2011). In many regards, these developments reflect wider international and global discussions and movements concerned with competency and how to assess, nurture and develop it (Boyatzis, 1982; 2008). The paper provides a historical contextualisation of competencies in the United Kingdom. In particular, it outlines a brief history of the evolution of competencies in this context, underlining the recent and rapid emergence and implementation of competencies in a wide range of organisational and human resource development situations. The discussion examines the nature of competencies and the epistemological and ontological paradigms on which these approaches are frequently couched in a British historical socio-cultural setting. In an attempt to reappraise competencies, the paper draws on the resources of Critical Management approaches and perspectives and, in particular, embraces notions of 'lived experience'. In so doing, it combines with the small number of marginal revisionist voices in the mainstream competencies literature. This is supported by an in-depth two-year ethnographic study (employing participant-observer methods) of a consultancy delivered training programme for customer service competency based vocational qualification in a water utilities company. Overall, the paper provides an assessment and a critique of the experience of competencies and vocational training in the UK.

## Methodological Approach

The study used an ethnographic approach (Van Maanen, 1978, Bryman and Bell, 2007, pp.439-470, Eriksson and Kovalainen, 2008, pp.137–153).

Ethnography enables the researcher to use an array of qualitative techniques to examine a community in action in its natural, usual and everyday environment. In relation to Gold's (1958) well-cited classification of observer roles which indicate towards one end of the continuum 'complete participant', 'participant as observer' to, at the opposing end of the spectrum 'observer as participant' and 'complete observer', one of the authors and researchers worked as a participant observer. This meant that he was totally implanted in the milieu of the organisational operatives. Ethnography, as a methodological approach was ideally suited to the study. The participant observer also permitted unstructured and semi-structured interviews to be conducted (Maylor and Blackmon, 2005, pp.225-233). All data were recorded in the form of notes. It was deemed an unnatural intrusion to try to use recording devices because the respondents were not used to such an experience. Also recording would not have been easy in the day-to-day client calls. Moreover, many respondents would be worried what would happen to the tapes and feared they risked ending up in the hands of senior management.

In a study such as this it is important to underline the role of reflexivity of the researcher towards the individuals and groups researched and reciprocally by the people researched to the researcher (Alvesson and Sköldberg, 2009). The researcher spent many hours in the company of individual company employees, travelling many miles, visiting many clients over many months. This provided an opportunity to socialise and get to know each other reasonably well on a personal level. The research embraced this subjectivity at the heart of the ethnographic approach of the research. Within the reflexive tradition of inductive research it is important to signal that for some respondents the researcher felt great empathy whereas with others no strong relationship developed. A couple of the employees become personal friends. Others were rude, unfriendly, aggressive or obnoxious towards the researcher and this did not abate during the two years. Some were not unfriendly but were guarded and remote. One of the more extreme instances involved one elderly male worker who insisted on urinating into a bucket in secluded locations rather than find a public toilet. Clearly, therefore, there was a gamut of behaviour and personalities. The accompanying researcher's background as someone with personal experience of a working class life and factory floor working meant that, while alarming at the moment of their occurrence, none of the experiences were necessarily shocking.

The data analysis followed an inductive crystallisation process whereby the data were constantly reviewed in the light of repeat data capture. This form of review allowed emergent themes in the data to be identified and analysed.

## Reflections on lived experience of competencies in the field

### The field research organisation

The field research was conducted in a large utilities company employing approximately 5000 people located in the north of the United Kingdom. One of the authors was part of a team of some ten assessors who were delivering a National Vocational Qualification (NVQ), which involves training at level 3 on the UK's national training framework. He gained his A1/A2 Assessor Award during the process. The programme was targeted at ninety three Customer Liaison Officers (CLOs) who interacted on a daily basis with customers in the field. Each assessor was responsible for assessing approximately fourteen CLOs. The CLO role was the result of a change management programme and restructuring in the company. This had seen the creation of the new CLO role and the counterpart to this the Network Controller (NC) role. It was intended that the NC would look after the technical aspects of the network and would not have contact with customers. On the other hand, the CLO would be entirely customer facing and would no longer be involved with any technical aspects of the water supply network. Prior to the change the CLO and the NC role had not existed and both roles had been carried out by each member of the field team. CLOs used company white vans to travel around their designated area. Because half the original staff were now undertaking NC roles this meant that the CLOs were covering a territory surface area that was double what they had previously had to cover. On occasion, due to the scheduling at the central headquarters this could mean that CLOs would leave a customer visit and have to travel fifty miles to another visit and then return back to the area where they were previously for the subsequent visit resulting in very long journeys. The issue of poor scheduling was a recurrent issue and, together with the changing job role, was a source of great discontent and tension. The company was concerned about improving its ratings on customer feedback. It was assumed, without any major research and more on management intuition that it would be necessary to improve customer interaction with the newly formed CLOs. Overall, the changes were far from popular and had witnessed considerable discussion with unions and some acrimony over what was considered by the front-line staff to be an the ill-thought plan by management.

### A day in the life of a CLO

Typically the study and work involved spending whole days with the CLO at a few weeks' interval. The day would be preceded by the researchers telephoning the CLO to arrange the visit arriving at the works depot or the CLOs home address to meet up and drive off together in the van. The day would comprise visiting customers' houses and premises and entering customers' homes to discuss water supply and quality problems. Lunch and breaks times would be spent with CLOs in 'greasy spoon' basic workers' cafes. As the researcher became more friendly with and trusted by CLOs he would find himself accompanying them on small shopping trips, visiting family and friends and doing little errands as the CLOs fitted these 'unofficial' personal and domestic jobs into their planned and prescribed work routine. As such, a wide breadth of rich experiences were witnessed and experienced with the CLOs.

### Findings and discussion

The experiences from assessing and journeying with the CLOs produced a wide range of data. It is intended and hoped that this will facilitate the reader to obtain an impression of the relationships between the competencies, the employee/student CLOs, the assessor and other organisational actors. Four themes are presented below centred around competencies and resistance, competency frameworks as bureaucracy and anti-intellectualism, competencies as a device in a battle between managerialist and craft cultures, and private and professional lives lived out in a competency framework.

### A theme of competencies and resistance

A key emergent theme was the issue of resistance by CLOs to undertaking the qualification in the first place. The lead assessor on the programme suggested that in her experience this was not however typical of vocational qualifications programmes. By way of illustration, on the first visit to a CLO the assessor got in the van and greeted the CLO. The CLO shouted:

> So what the f******g hell is all this NVQ competencies b******ks about!
>
> (CLO 'A', 2007)

The assessor gradually built up a very friendly relationship with CLO A however the cynicism never really went away completely.

Many assessors on the programme reported various obstruction tactics used by CLOs to impede and delay their visits. These tactics included cancelling appointments at the last minute, calling in sick on a given day. All of this was resonant of the forms 'organizational behaviour' characterised by Thompson and Ackroyd (1999). There was little doubt that the introduction of the competency framework was seen and used merely as a managerial device to categorise and evaluate the CLO job. This afforded the opportunity for managers to have greater apparent say and control over CLO operatives. To some extent this was indeed true since what the job should consist of had now been made very explicit. Nevertheless, on a wide range of occasions older more experienced CLOs devised ways and loopholes to counter-manage the new job constructions. This would involve unofficially exchanging jobs on work schedules with other CLOs to overcome the illogical allocation of jobs from the call centre. Equally many CLOs would go beyond the role of the CLO and assist clients, particularly elderly clients in ways that were not permitted by new company regulations. As an assessor the participant observer researcher was of course automatically complicit in these deviations – he was present at the time they occurred and had no power (or necessarily desire) to block them. In essence, both respondents and researcher were engaged in a process of creating *new sense* of the job role. The competency framework assessing the workers actually had very little relationship to this. Rather it was the case that opportunities were looked for to 'tick any boxes' possible. This was often a collaborative (indeed quasi-conspiratorial?) process between the researcher-assessor and the respondent-employee.

## A theme of competency frameworks as bureaucracy and anti- Intellectualism.

A further emergent issue concerned the paperwork involved in the competency assessment process for the NVQ award. Many of the CLOs did not like the assessment documentation and needed considerable assistance with it. This was not always helped by the labelling of the documentation. The main form was called the 'MAD' form which stood for Multiple Assessment Document. Naturally this caused many amusing and witty remarks. It was clear that in some of the cases of problems with documentation it was a matter of further resistance on the part of the CLO. However, in other instances, there seemed to be issues relating to levels of education. Nearly all of the CLOs were semi-skilled /skilled manual labour. The world of written qualifications was not a world in which they felt automatically comfortable. Three of the CLOs left the role and returned to Network Controller (NCs) roles on the technical side of the team because this group of employees were not at that time completing the NVQ. However, the manner in which these few employees baulked at and procrastinated over written tasks also alluded to a deeper problem of potential illiteracy or semi-illiteracy. These workers had thrived well in a world that valued the empirical, the pragmatic, indeed the much admired British saying 'the university of life'. The paper based assessment in competencies proved a serious challenge.

With regard to the issues of skills, many of the CLOs (and especially the older and longer serving ones who had a depth of technical knowledge and experience) felt, and often stated, that the NVQ and competency approach was actually part of a process of further *deskilling* of their role rather than skills enhancing. Already they believed that the restructuring of their role was problematic and the competency based assessment was yet a further part of that action. Moreover, they stated that the assessment was belittling and demeaning of their longstanding technical skills and craftsmanship.

> This NVQ is a load of cobblers isn't it, admit it, go on. All they want is a monkey to do this job – when the managers get that then they'll be happy.
>
> (CLO 'D', 2008)

The temporal retrospective aspect of the award was a further difficulty. Many CLOs felt that they were getting an award for something that they already knew how to do and were doing. The sentiment of many was 'what is the point?' As the process went on what became increasingly important and informative was the interaction and exchanges between the participant observer as assessor and the CLOs. In many cases friendships struck up and it was in the more wide-ranging discussions over mugs of tea in 'greasy spoon' cafes they raised some of the lessons to be learned. These discussions were not couched in the dry language of NVQs but rather in an everyday vernacular drawing on common wisdoms.

## A theme of competencies in a conflict between managerialist and craftmanship cultures.

It is important also to draw attention to the wider context of the organisation and the CLOs managers. There were many managers and a great number of 'special task forces' of contingent manager groupings. There was very little respect between CLOs and any of the managers. In truth, there was not a great deal of respect in reality for the managers by the assessor team. The assessor team had met the managers before and during the initiative in a range of meetings. The corporate culture typically produced highly political 'yes' (wo)men behaviour. Managers were regularly moved between roles every two to three years. Therefore, no manager would take a risk of making a mistake so as not to jeopardise his or her chances of a promotion in the long-term. As one CLO put it succinctly:

They're all f*****g greasy pole climbers and arse lickers – no f*****g use at all.

(CLO 'G', 2007)

Concerning longer-term impacts and effects of the programme, it is difficult to determine sustainable consequences. For the organisation, senior management was able to state in corporate reports that 93 of their CLO operatives have attained NVQ level 3 in Customer Service. This had considerable political capital in national competitor league tables. For the CLOs the consequence was varied. Older CLOs were often not interested in the vocational qualification process at all. A substantial number were concerned more by opportunities for well-paid redundancy and retirement. Unfortunately, and perhaps linked to the socio-cultural characteristics of the group to some extent, many had experienced divorces which had resulted in their pension being reduced and given to the divorced partner. This was a major topic of conversation for some of the CLOs.

The younger CLOs were very different. These were typically not technically very experienced (the long apprenticeship routes of many technical jobs were simply no longer available in the contemporary structures of the organisation or indeed the wider economy) and so the NVQ in Customer Experience 'legitimised' them in the light of the new company ethos. The younger CLOs 'followed the rulebook.' This was unlike the older CLOs who saw customer service as a matter of principle, not a question of competencies. They viewed it more a matter of behaving in a decent human way to deserving customers. This could lead some older CLOs to, for example, mending broken taps and pipes for elderly people and doing favours for them. All of this was in strict contravention to the new company rule book but they did it anyway. Matlay (2001) has suggested that in the case of small to medium sized enterprises competency approaches may not be as effective as when applied in large organisations. The present data indicates that, in some circumstances, this can also be the case in a very large company employing thousands of people.

The older workers in particular saw themselves as fighting against the competency framework on two interlinked fronts. Firstly, they felt that 'management speak' had taken over all parts of the company and that the competency programme was a part of that. At the same time they remembered nostalgically a period when they operated using a wide range of skills and exercised a great deal of individual judgement and independence. Managers (and managerialist behaviour) were seen as increasingly impinging on this and the competency programme associated with the restructuring of the job was deemed to be a denigration of their 'craft' role. They often reported that they were becoming mere cogs in a (modernistic) machine.

> They knocked the passion out of me a long time ago. I still love the idea of this job but they keep bl\*\*dy wrecking it. This NVQ is the latest in a string of bullshit we've had thrown our way. They'll end up getting rid of us and employing bl\*\*dy robots!
>
> (CLO 'H', 2008)

## How should you write up stories and narratives?

In recent decades, the use of stories as a way of conducting and writing up research has become increasingly popular. A story can be described as a fictional or factual tale, often recounted chronologically (but not necessarily) that has a plot and characters.

Narrative is a term often used as a synonym for story. In many regards narratives are kindred to the notion of stories. Within the literature and discussion on stories and narratives there are, of course, debates on definitions and differences between the two terms. There is a range of material available on stories and narratives (see, for example, Boje, 2001; Bold, 2011; Czarniawska 1998, 2002, 2003, 2004; Gabriel, 2000). In addition to the advice offered in the above sources on the process of actually producing and writing storied accounts, the work of Josselson and Lieblich (1993) and Kohler-Riessman (2008) offer helpful advice and commentaries. Maitlis (2012) also provides a succinct a contemporary and overview of the issues involved in narrative research.

When you employ a story to identify and relate your data, you are often seeking a particular effect. Stories and narratives afford the possibility of a greater degree of characterisation, scene setting, relaying of events in the research field as a series of interlinked, and perhaps, causal or inter-related events. This can serve to provide a poignant and potent portrayal of the research that has been undertaken. You will find that when you read accounts of research that have been produced in this form you may have a closer sense of empathy and identification with the research partici-pants and the researcher. Many, more conventional or, for example, positivistic-style accounts which value objectivity as a core value may not provide these vivid and colourful accounts. This is not to diminish these approaches but rather to highlight differences in style and intent of relaying and presenting research data and findings.

## UNDERSTANDING THE ROLE OF THE DIFFERENT SECTIONS IN DISSERTATIONS, RESEARCH REPORTS AND THESES

### In broad terms, what do you need to think about in relation to the format of your write-up?

It is not uncommon to become confused and lose your way when you writing up your research. Many people find it relatively straightforward talking about their work and plans for writing up, however, the act of actually doing it is a very real test for what you really know about your research and what you want to accomplish in the final work.

There are two things to keep in mind:

- firstly, the *purpose of the sections and structures* that are part of the normal writ-ing up;
- secondly, the *style and rendering of the text* and writing that you produce to present that data.

Alternatively expressed, we might say that these concern the old and long-standing issues of *form and content*.

The boxed texts below indicate the conventional format for the writing up of a dissertation-style document and a proposal. There are of course other forms and formats in which research write-ups may be presented. These include, for example, research papers, books, film reports, practitioner articles and business reports. Of course, as has already been discussed above, each of these may also employ, for instance, stories, case studies, ethnography and other presentations.  In relation to the types of write-up each of these will have their own particular norms and strictures and you will need to learn and respect these (McMillan and Weyers, 2011). By way of illustration, a report will often need opening sections that, in addition to an 'Introduction' include an 'Executive Summary' and 'Terms of Reference'. Moreover, journal articles need to follow a format not dissimilar to a dissertation or research proposal; however, it is important to look over academic articles to study the formatting requirements of particular journals in detail. Formats can vary from journal to journal and from discipline to discipline and it is important to respect the conventions of the field in which you are writing. Vignette 7.2 below illustrates the structure of a typical dissertation discussed in Chapter 1, and Vignette 7.3 illustrates a structural typical of an action research type project.

---

**A reminder of the discussion in Chapter 1 – typical layout of sections of a dissertation**

Introduction

Literature Review

Methodology

(Case Overview – if you are doing a case study)

Findings

Discussion (Findings and Discussion are often combined)

Conclusion

VIGNETTE 7.2

**Typical layout of sections of an action research dissertation**

Introduction

Review of Situation (or Review of Problem Situation)

Literature Review

Methodology

Action Research Cycle 1 – Discussion/Findings

Action Research Cycle 2 – Discussion/Findings

Action Research Cycle 3 – Discussion/Findings

Overall Findings

Conclusion

There is an extensive range of books available that deal uniquely and expressly with study skills issues. If you make a point of accessing and reading the advice and recommendations of such texts then you will improve your chances of writing an enhanced piece of work. Some of these texts are very well known and are widely used. Good examples of these include the work of:

- Cottrell (2013) – *The Study Skills Handbook;*
- Day (2013) – *Success in Academic Writing;*
- Greetham (2014) – *How to Write Your Undergraduate Dissertation.*

### What are the logical building blocks – 'new information follows old information'?

- This is reflected in the idea of new information follows old information which is discussed at some length in the chapter on literature reviews. It is important to ensure that one idea and comment in your argument and writing flows smoothly on from the previous one (Hickey, 1993).
- One way that this can be achieved is by reading your work in a number of different ways. When you have written a piece of text and you are reasonably happy with it, it is a good idea to plan to 'read it' in a number of ways and directions:
  - First, read the text for sense-making. So, as you are building up your argument and discussion, read back over the work sentence by sentence. Ask

yourself the question, 'does each sentence logically and reasonably add to the next?'.

- Then when you have done that, equally, ask yourself if each paragraph containing those sentences logically and reasonably flow into the next paragraph and so on and so forth.
- In addition, and in conjunction with this, look 'backwards' at your work from the last sentence towards the first sentence of a given paragraph and decide if you ended up where you wanted to arrive when you started writing (Hart, 2001).

### How do you build drama and engagement in the piece – narrative flow?

When you have checked many of the points mentioned above, you begin to look at the overall flow of the piece you are developing. A useful way to think about your text is to employ a metaphor and imagine it is a novel, a film or a piece of classical music (Josselson and Lieblich, 1993; Kohler-Riessman, 2008). Most of these will usually involve creative lyricism with dramatic peaks and troughs. These climaxes and less active, quiet sections in the plot serve to maintain reader engagement and interest. It is a valuable idea for you to think about scope to do the same in your writing. As you write and develop the arguments in your various sections and chapters of your write-up think about how you carry the reader with you by managing the ebb and flow of the drama, thrust and reflection in your argument. Building up the confidence to do this can be quite challenging for people who are not confident writers, however, it is important to remember that writing is a muscle that has to be exercised in order to grow stronger.

### How should you examine your near-finalised draft?

In relation to reading and checking your work a useful technique is to consider *reading and re-reading your work in a number of varying ways*. This can be represented by what will be coined as a term here, *matrix readings*, because we read the text in a number of *different directions*.

### Matrix readings: four ways to review your text

- Word-processing spelling and grammar check.
- Grammar linked to vocabulary.
- Logical Building Blocks – 'new information follows old information'.
- Narrative flow – drama and engagement in the piece.

### Word-Processing Grammar and Spelling Check

This may seem a very obvious and straightforward action to undertake but it is all too often overlooked. Even if it is carried out, it may not be conducted with attention and diligence. Carrying out a software-based set of checks requires you to be systematic and scrutinise each occurrence that is reported. In particular, watch out for:

- Word spellings which are not linguistically authentic to your maternal English. A clear example here is the use of United Kingdom and United States English, for instance *behaviour* (UK) and *behavior* (US).
- Grammar and syntax structure: spelling check will often point to sentence structures that appear to have an error in them or that appear cumbersome.

## Grammar Linked to Vocabulary

The grammar points that are identified by a spellcheck need close attention. Often, the grammar checker is very useful in identifying:

- poorly constructed sentences;
- overly long sentences (often also poorly constructed);
- incorrect person for a verb – that is, use of 'he/she' when it should be 'they';
- incomplete sentences;
- inadvertent and unintended spaces between words;
- When you are approaching the latter stages of a text remember to use a paper-based thesaurus. This can be an excellent device for polishing and honing your prose. Often, an elegant word or term that is just right and captures the mood and tone of the message or idea you are seeking to communicate can be identified. Doing this, sentence by sentence is painstaking but it can enhance your text enormously.

## Referencing

The correct referencing of an academic text be it, for instance, an article, project or dissertation is imperative. Referencing indicates where text has been derived from or writings that are associated with the ideas being presented and discussed in the text. Two key and commonly used systems of referencing are APA and Harvard. While there are similarities between these referencing systems there are also important differences and some of the detailed differences and situational variations can be extensive. There are a wide range of guides available in a range of places including books, university teaching support materials and web-based sites (Pears and Shields, 2010). In addition, there are a number of software packages that can render handling references easier. Examples of these include EndNote, ProCite and RefWorks and texts are available to support their use.

## DISSEMINATION AND PRESENTATION OF YOUR RESEARCH WORK

There may be a number of reasons why people write-up research. Sometimes it is part of a programme of study, such as a dissertation (Greetham, 2009), a research project (Brett-Davies, 2007) or other study. On other occasions it may be a research report commissioned by a third party. On yet further occasions, the write-up may form an attempt to get an article or chapter published in an academic or practitioner publication. All of these forms, and the others that may exist, are aimed at different audiences engaged in varying missions and purpose. When writing up your research it is imperative that you ensure that the manner – form, content and message – will relate to the audience and that they will connect with your work. In order to ensure that this objective is achieved, it is a good idea to try to secure examples of work that have already been produced by third parties. This will provide you with the layout and format of the work and you can pick up lots of useful tips.

There are a range of well-written and insightful works available that deal with this issue in greater detail. From these it is possible to suggest Angela Thody's (2006) work. This text talks very much with the accomplished veteran's voice of experience and has many excellent pieces of advice for aspiring academic writers. In addition, Dunleavy's (2003) work aimed at doctoral write-ups provides a substantive treatment of the subject and is rich in insights and comment. Moreover, Dunleavy and Tinkler (2013) provide a valuable set of guidelines and recommendations for maximising the impacts of the research you undertake.

The actions you wish to take in relation to the dissemination of your research will also depend on the purpose for which you conducted your research in the first instance:

- If you have completed your research in the form of an undergraduate or post-graduate dissertation then you may be content to leave it as a bound volume on your shelf at home.
- If you have completed a doctoral thesis then you will almost certainly be hoping to generate some outputs related to the work including, for example, journal articles, practitioner briefing papers, books etc.
- If you have conducted the research to produce a journal article or a report then these documents are inherently accompanied by an intent to undertake some form of dissemination.

Whatever your intention or ambition there are a number of points and opportunities to consider in relation to wider distribution of your research. It will be for you, and the particular context in which you are working, to decide what may be the most appropriate way forward. The points below are merely suggestive:

- You could send a copy of the article to interested colleagues, friends and associates;
- You may want to post the work, an abridged version or a summary of the work on a social media site, for example, Twitter, LinkedIn, Facebook, mailing list, online forum or blog;
- An issue here is to ensure that you will not be infringing any copyright or ethical code by doing this;
- Alternatively, you might to create a video or podcast related to your work.

In attempting to disseminate your work, remember that you may need to modify it slightly in order to convey the message in a clear and rapid manner, for example:

- You might wish to modify the title to make it concise and to ensure it has a high impact;
- You can identify key search terms based on which people will be able to find, refer to and reference your work rapidly.

## How can you manage your confidence and motivation during the writing up stage?

Researchers describe the experiences of writing up their research as having peaks and troughs, or emotional high and low points. This is not uncommon; most tasks involve learning how to do them well (and feeling proud of our achievements) and doing not so well or struggling. So it is useful to expect such turbulence and to plan for what you will do when you start to experience the lower points. These low points can be less productive for you and your writing up, but can be managed. During these low points you might question:

- whether or not you know what you are actually doing;
- whether or not you have what it takes to complete the write-up;
- whether or not you will pass;
- whether or not others are doing better than you;
- and therefore whether you should continue!

The good news is that you are not alone, and many (if not all) researchers experience some of these emotions or thoughts at least once during their write-up stage. The list below shares some ideas about what you can do when you experience these negative emotions – they may or may not work for you, so you need to find strategies that do work for you.

| Strategy | Why it works |
|---|---|
| **_Stop_ thinking; just do** | The thoughts you may have above are unproductive but still take energy. So it is always useful to become aware of the thought as soon as you have it and stop it. Shift the energy on writing instead. Or if that does not work, focus on a simple task that you know you can achieve quickly. |
| **Do an enjoyable task for 5 minutes** | You may have heard of 'writers' block' which is also described as an unproductive state of mind where ideas are not flowing. It can help the mind get into a more positive and productive state by simply doing something you enjoy for a very short period. The aim is to move the focus from the unproductive thought to one which creates a better mental state and energy for you. Some people do that by playing a game on their phone, washing or ironing some clothes, baking, dancing, and so on. |
| **Connect with others for 5 minutes** | It can become a lonely activity writing up, and connecting with others can make you feel significantly more supported. It might even be spending 5 minutes on social media or having a chat with friends or family. |
| **Kind-eyes-on-_past_** | It can be really useful in managing your motivation and confidence to periodically look at things you have achieved in your past. This might be previous qualifications or writing, but it might simply be the last section you wrote that you are happy or proud of. Appreciate the smallest of things you have written in the immediate research write-up; a diagram, a particular finding, a particular paragraph, a new expression you have written. Your job is to find these small things to appreciate. |
| **Kind-eyes-on-_future_** | Having a plan clearly helps you manage your work, but when you are struggling with confidence or motivation, the plan also reminds you of something in the future to look forward to. This might be finishing a section of your work, finishing the research, or something that will happen as a result of you completing the research (e.g. a grade, a job?). |
| **Shuffling plans** | If you are feeling a sense of anxiety from your plan or other activities in your life, manage it. Space created in your diary is also space created in your mind. Use the red line technique mentioned earlier in this book. |

*(continued)*

| Strategy | Why it works |
|----------|--------------|
| **Seeking feedback** | Should you feel unable to write anymore without knowing whether you are on the 'correct' track, then you might simply seek feedback. Rather than sending everything you have written to your supervisor, however, a more productive and realistic strategy to obtain feedback is to become much more specific about *what* you want feedback on. For example, you might undertake one piece of analysis and present it in a graph before doing all of the 20 graphs you expect to do in your write-up. You could send this one table with the paragraph to your supervisor and ask whether the supervisor feels the paragraph is a valid discussion of the table. Of course, also pay attention to the guidance already offered to you by you supervisor. |

## REVISION QUESTIONS

1. Look at a piece of your writing for a previous assignment.
   Analyse the following in the sentence structure and the vocabulary you use:
   What is good about it?
   • What could be improved?
   • What is the typical length in terms of words of your sentences?
     • Do you vary your sentence length much?
     • Think of ways you might do this and study other people's writing styles.
   • Look over the narrative flow and choreography of your work. Are you engaging and involving the reader in the development of your argument?
     What more could you do to facilitate and enhance this?
2. What opportunities do you take to disseminate the research you have undertaken?
3. What more (based on some of the indications above) could you do to enhance the profile of your outputs?

## GLOSSARY OF TERMS

**Story/narrative** A story is in essence the relaying of a series of events played out by characters and with a plot, or staging points and end points in mind. Narrative is a kindred term often used synonymously; however, usually narrative appears to relate to the flow and lyricism of the recounting of the tale. In recent years, stories have been used increasingly in business management and organisation studies, as well as other disciplines and fields.

**Dissertation** A dissertation is an extended piece of research, writing and argument. It is usually one of the final and larger modules to be completed on an undergraduate or postgraduate Master's programmes.

**Case study** A case study is a piece of research that focuses on a specific and particular organisation, instance and/or moment in time. In terms of writing up it is important to remember that a case study is a specific and particular approach to building and handling data. It is best to conduct the write-up of the case following these conventions which have been laid out in detail in the above text.

**Ethnography** An ethnography is a piece of research that employs inductive and qualitative based strategies so as to be able to get very close to the lived experiences of the research respondents. These approaches will usually use research methods such as participant observation and unstructured interview. The write-up of an ethnography usually requires extensive and in-depth descriptive background.

### Dissertation, report, project and thesis – a reminder of similarities and differences

Dissertation, report, project and thesis are terms that are often used interchangeably by some people however they are all quite distinct. A dissertation is an academic piece of work that usually forms the final stages of an undergraduate or Master's level qualification. As a general guide an undergraduate dissertation might range between 10,000 and 12,000 words in length whereas a Master's dissertation may typically range from 15,000 to 200,000 words in length.

A thesis is also an academic piece of research and is the output from a programme of doctoral level study. This usually ranges between 80,000 and 100,000 words in length. One of the distinctive features of a doctorate is that it is generally considered necessary that it must make a contribution to knowledge (in the case of a Doctor of Philosophy) and knowledge combined with practice for an award such as the Doctor of Business Administration or Doctor of Professional Studies. All of the above word counts are indicative and will depend on the stipulations made in the regulations of the institutions where you are undertaking the study.

'Project Report' and 'Report' tend to be terms used generically. These documents may, or may not, relate to an academic or practitioner style output. Reports will usually adopt a structure which uses numbered sections and points and it will be written in a more direct and succinct style than, for example, a dissertation.

## KEY POINTS

1. When you are writing your dissertation it is often a good idea to get something down on the page (or screen) first rather than thinking about it endlessly. Editing what you have written on the page is often easier than trying to edit it in your head.
2. It is possible to apply a range of metaphors to the process of writing. Remember that writing is about pinpointing and capturing what you are trying to say. This may not be possible in the first draft. Sometimes it takes several drafts to gradually shape and polish up your ideas. In this way, at times, it can feel like a jig-saw puzzle whereby you are gradually discovering, revisiting and fitting the pieces together.

## FURTHER STUDY

1. Copus, J. (2009) *Brilliant Writing Tips for Students*, Series: Pocket Study Skills, Basingstoke, Palgrave-Macmillan.
2. Hart, C. (2001) *Doing a Literature Review*, London, Sage Publications.
   *This text has established itself as an in-depth classic on the subject.*
3. McNiff, J. and Whitehead, J. (2009) *Doing and Writing Action Research*, London, Sage Publications.
4. Murray, N. and Hughes, G. (2008) *Writing Up Your University Assignments and Research Project – A Practical Handbook*, Milton Keyes, Open University Press.
5. Pears, R and Shields, G. (2010) *Cite Them Right: The Essential Referencing Guide*, Basingstoke, Palgrave-Macmillan.
   *Excellent and comprehensive guide to using referencing systems.*
6. Williams, K. (2013) *Planning Your Dissertation*, Series: Pocket Study Skills, Basingstoke, Palgrave-Macmillan.
7. Williams, K. and Carroll, J. (2009) *Referencing and Understanding Plagiarism*, Series: Pocket Study Skills, Basingstoke, Palgrave-Macmillan.
8. Williams, K. and Reid, M. (2011) *Time Management*, Series: Pocket Study Skills, Basingstoke, Palgrave-Macmillan.
9. Woolcott, H. (2009) *Writing Up Qualitative Research*, London, Sage Publications.

## REFERENCES

Alvesson, M and Sköldberg, K. (2000), *Reflexive Methodologies: New Vistas for Qualitative Research*, Sage Publications, London.

Barth, M. Godemann, J, Rieckmann, M and Stoltenberg, U. (2007), 'Developing competencies for sustainable development in higher education', *International Journal of Sustainability in Higher Education*, 8 (4), 416–430.

Bouzdine-Chameeva, T. (2006), 'How wine sector SMEs approach strategic questions: some comparative lessons of causal representation of distinctive competencies', *British Food Journal*, 108 (4): 273–289.

Boyatzis, R. (1982), *The Competent Manager: A Model for Effective Performance*, Wiley, New York.

Boyatzis, R. (2008), 'Competencies in the 21st century', *Journal of Management Development*, 27 (1): 5–12.

Bryman, A. and Bell, E. (2007), *Business Research Methods*, Oxford University Press, Oxford.

Cappellan, T and Janssens, M. (2008), 'Global managers' career competencies', *Career Development International*, 13 (6): 514–537.

CIPD (Chartered Institute of Personnel and Development) (2007), *Learning and Development: Annual Survey Report*, CIPD, London.

Eriksson, P. and Kovalainen, A. (2008), *Qualitative Methods in Business Research*, Sage Publications, London.

Matlay, H. (2001), 'HRD in the small business sector of the British economy: an evaluation of current training initiatives', *Proceedings of 2nd Conference of HRD Research and Practice Across Europe*, University of Twente, Enschede, 26–27 January cited in Garavan, T. and McGuire, D. (2001), 'Competencies and workplace learning: some reflections on the rhetoric and the reality', *Journal of Workplace Learning*, 13 (4): 145.

Maylor, H. and Blackmon, K. (2005), *Researching Business and Management*, Palgrave-Macmillan, Basingstoke (UK).

Gold, R. (1958), 'Roles in Sociological Fieldwork', *Social Forces*, Vol. 36, pp. 217–23.

Thompson, P. and Ackroyd, S. (1999), *Organizational Misbehaviour*, Sage Publications, London.

Tilestone, D. (2011) *Ten Best Teaching Practices*, Thousand Oaks (CA), Sage Publications.

Van Maanen, J. (1978), 'On Watching the Watchers', in Manning, P. and Van Maanen, J. (Eds) *Policing: the View from the Street*, Goodyear, Santa Monica (USA).

# 8
# CONCLUDING THOUGHTS

The ideas, points, examples and materials contained in the chapters of this book have sought to provide concise and accessible overviews and insights into research methods and research methodology. The various chapters have mapped out the key issues and features to be taken into account when preparing a piece of research and these have been illustrated with a range of cases and vignettes.

As was mentioned at the outset in the introduction, a brief text such as those of this series cannot aim to be comprehensive. Rather, its purpose is to be a gateway and an entry point to what is a potentially complex field. There exists a wide span of resources available on research methods/methodologies and this text will hopefully provide a guide on your journey through this array of materials.

The text has worked to render research methods and methodology more accessible and understandable and to make use of these approaches and techniques more achievable. Moreover, one of the key points that the text aims to raise is the conduct of research as one constituting a rich 'lived experience' (Knights and Willmott, 1999). When you employ a particular methodological approach it is, more often than not, because it 'speaks' to you. In other words, its ideological, philosophical, epistemological and ontological characteristics and commitments seem appropriate and valid to you. Yes, you may indeed employ a particular approach because it fits the research field, project, questions and so on and so forth, but from experience, people tend to have a predilection for one particular research approach. The key idea being made here is that of that you can use your journey through research methods and research methodologies to learn about yourself and how you make sense of the world.

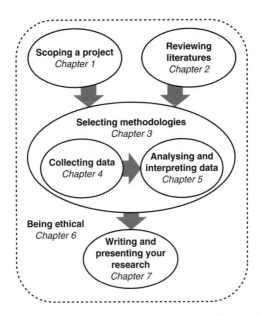

Diagram of the research process and chapters within this book

# BIBLIOGRAPHY

Aarikka-Stenroos, L. and Jaakkola, E. (2012)
'Value co-creation in knowledge intensive
business services: A dyadic perspective
on the joint problem solving process',
*Industrial Marketing Management*, 41(1):
15–26.

Ackerman, F. Eden, C. and Brown, I. (2005)
*The Practice of Making Strategy*, London,
Sage Publications.

Ackerly, B. and True, J. (2010) *Doing Feminist
Research in Political and Social Science*,
Basingstoke, Palgrave Macmillan.

Ackroyd, S. and Fleetwood, S. (2001)
*Realist Perspectives on Organization and
Management*, London, Routledge.

Acton, C., Miller, R., Maltby J. and Fullerton,
D. (2009) *SPSS for Social Scientists*,
Basingstoke, Palgrave Macmillan.

Agrawal, A. (2009) *End Note 1-2-3* Easy,
New York, Springer.

Al-Amoudi, I. (2007) 'Redrawing Foucault's
social ontology', *Organization*, 14(4):
543–563.

Al-Amoudi, I. and Willmott, H. (2011)
'When constructionism and critical realism
converge: interrogating the domain of
epistemological relativism', *Organization
Studies*, 32(1): 27–46.

Alvesson, M. and Sköldberg, K. (2009)
*Reflexive Methodology, New Vistas in
Qualitative Research*, London, Sage
Publications.

Alvesson, M., Bridgeman, T. and Willmott, H.
(2011) *The Oxford Handbook of Critical
Management Studies*, Oxford, Oxford
University Press.

Ambrosini, V., Bowman, C. and Collier, N.
(2010) 'Using teaching case studies
for management research', *Strategic
Organization*, 8(3): 206–229.

American Psychological Association (2014)
Ethical Principles of Psychologists and Code
of Conduct, available at http://www.apa.
org/ethics/code/index.aspx, accessed
9 May 2014.

Armstrong, S.J., Cools, E. and Sadler-Smith,
E. (2012) 'Role of cognitive styles in
business and management: Reviewing 40
years of research', *International Journal of
Management Reviews*, 14 (3): 238–262.

Attride-Stirling, J. (2001) 'Thematic
networks: an analytical tool for qualitative
research, *Qualitative Research*, 1(3):
385–405.

Audi, R. (2011) *Epistemology: A Contemporary Introduction to the Theory of
Knowledge*, London, Routledge.

Baekdal, T. (2004) Technology: Misleading
Statistics (online) USA. 14 May, available
at http://www.baekdal.com/articles/
technology/misleadingstatistics, accessed
03 March 2012.

Baltar, F. and Brunet, I. (2012) 'Social research
2.0: Virtual snowball sampling method
using Facebook', *Internet Research*, 22 (1):
57–74.

Bamel, U., Rangnekar, S., Stokes, P. and
Rastogi. R. (2012) 'Organizational
climate and managerial perspective: an
Indian perspective', *International Journal
of Organizational Analysis*, 21(2):
198–218.

Banerjee, P. and Shastri, V. (2010) *Social
Responsibility and Environmental
Sustainability in Business*, Thousand Oaks,
CA, Sage Publications.

Baron, P. (2013) *Utilitarianism and Situation Ethics: Teleological Ethics*, London, PushMe Press.

Barthe, M., Godemann, J., Rieckmann, M. and Stoltenberg, U. (2007) 'Developing competencies for sustainable development in higher education', *International Journal of Sustainability in Higher Education*, 8(4): 416–430.

Bazeley, P. (2013) *Qualitative Data Analysis*, London. Sage Publications.

Bazeley, P. and Jackson, K. (2013) *Qualitative Data Analysis with NVIVO*, London, Sage Publications.

Bell, S. and Morse, S. (2008) *Sustainability Indicators: Measuring the Immeasurable?*, Earthscan, London.

Berger, P., and Luckmann, T. (1966) *The Social Construction of Reality: A Treatise in the Sociology of Knowledge*, London, Penguin.

Bergström, O. and Knights, D. (2006) 'Organizational discourse and subjectivity: subjectification during processes of recruitment', *Human Relations*, 59(3): 351–377.

Berman Brown, R. (2006) *Doing Your Dissertation in Business and Management: The Reality of Researching and Writing*, London, Sage Publications.

Berners-Lee, M. (2010) How bad are bananas? The carbon footprint of everything, London, Profile Books.

Biggam, J. (2008) *Succeeding with Your Master's Dissertation: A Step-By-Step Handbook*, Milton Keynes, Open University Press.

Black, I. (2010) 'Sustainability and anti-consumption', *Journal of Consumer Behaviour*, 9 (6): 403–411.

Birkinshaw, J. and Caulkin, S. (2012) 'How should managers spend their time: finding more time for real management', *Business Strategy Review*, 23(4): 62–65.

Blumberg, E., Kelly, A., Olmstead, R. and Youmans, R. (2013) 'Usability analysis of a business process management software

platform', *Proceedings of the Human Factors and Ergonomics Society Annual Meeting*, 57(1): 2071–2075.

Böhm, S. and Batta, A. (2010) 'Just doing it: Enjoying commodity fetishism with Lacan', *Organization*, 17 (3): 345–361.

Boje, D. (2001) *Narrative Methods for Organizational and Communication Research*, London, Sage Publications.

Bold, C. (2011) *Using Narrative in Research*, London, Sage Publications.

Bouzdine-Chameeva, T. (2006) 'How wine sector SMEs approach strategic questions: some comparative lessons of causal representation of distinctive competencies', *British Food Journal*, 108(4): 273–289.

Boyatzis, R. (1982) *The Competent Manager: A Model for Effective Performance,* Wiley, New York.

Boyatzis, R. (2008) 'Competencies in the 21st century', *Journal of Management Development*, 27(1): 5–12.

Brace, I. (2013) *Questionnaire Design: How to Plan, Structure and Write Survey Material for Effective Market Research*, London, Kogan Page.

Brett-Davies, M. (2007) *Doing a Successful Research Project: Using Qualitative or Quantitative Research Methods*, Basingstoke, Palgrave Macmillan.

British Academy of Management (2013) available at https://www.bam.ac.uk/sites/bam.ac.uk/files/TheBritishAcademyofManagement's CodeofEthicsandBestPracticeforMembers.pdf, accessed 6 September 2014.

British Sociological Association (2013) available at: www.britsoc.co.uk, accessed 6 September 2014.

Bronner, S. (2011) *Critical Theory: A Very Short Introduction*, Oxford, Oxford University Press.

Brown, P. (2010) 'Qualitative method and compromise in applied social research', *Qualitative Research*, 10(2): 229–248.

Bryman, A. (2007) 'Barriers to integrating quantitative and qualitative research', *Journal of Mixed Methods Research*, January 1 (1): 8–22.

Bryman, A. (2012) *Social Research Methods*, Oxford, Oxford University Press.

Bryman, A. and Bell, E. (2007) *Business Research Methods*, Oxford, Oxford University Press.

Bryman, A. and Burgess R. (1994) *Analyzing Qualitative Data,* London, Routledge.

Bubley, Dean (2009) Misleading Statistics for Mobile Internet and Smartphones: Get Rid of the Hype (online) USA. 11 June, available at http://seekingalpha.com/article/142658-misleading-statistics-for-mobile-internet-and-smartphones-get-rid-of-the-hype, accessed 01 March 12.

Buchanan, E. and Hvizdak, E. (2009) 'Online survey tools: ethical and methodological concerns of human resource ethics committees', *Journal of Empirical Research on Human Research Ethics: An International Journal*, 4(2): 37–48.

Bulmer, M. (2001) 'The ethics of social research', in Gilbert, N. (ed.) *Researching Social Life*, London, Sage Publications, 45–57.

Butterfield, L., Borgen, W., Amundsen, N. and Maglio, A. (2005) 'Fifty years of the critical incident technique: 1954–2004 and beyond', *Qualitative Research,* November 5(4): 475–497.

Buzan, T. (2002) *How to Mind Map: The Ultimate Thinking Tool that Will Change Your Life*, London, Harper Collins.

Buzan, T. and Rustler, F. (2012) *Mind Mapping for Dummies*, Chichester, John Wiley and Sons Ltd.

Cameron, S. and Price, D. (2009) *Business Research Methods: A Practical Approach*, London, CIPD.

Campbell, A. and Groundwater-Smith, S. (2007) *An Ethical Approach to Practitioner Research – Dealing with Issues and Dilemmas in Action Research*, London, Routledge.

Cappellan, T. and Janssens, M. (2008) 'Global managers' career competencies', *Career Development International*, 13(6): 514–537.

Carlzon, J. and Peters, T. (1989) *Moments of Truth: New Strategies for Today's Customer Driven Economy*, London, Harper.

Cassell, C. and Symon, G. (2004) *Essential Guide to Qualitative Methods in Organizational Research*, London, Sage Publications.

Cassell, C., Buehring, A., Symon, G., Johnson, P. and Bishop, V. (2005) *Benchmarking Good Practice in Qualitative Management Research*, London, ESRC, http:/www.shef.ac.uk/bgpinqmr.

Cathcart, T. and Klein, D. (2007) *Plato and a Platypus Walk into a Bar: Understanding Philosophy through Jokes*, New York, Abrams Image.

Chandler, D. and Torbert, B. (2003) 'Transforming Inquiry and Action: Interweaving 27 Flavors of Action Research', *Action Research*, 1(2): 133–152.

Charmaz, K. (2006) *Consulting Grounded Theory: A Practical Guide through Qualitative Analysis*, London, Sage Publications.

Chia, R. (1996) *Organizational Analysis as Deconstructive Practice*, Berlin, Walter de Gruyter and Co.

(CIPD) Chartered Institute of Personnel and Development (2007) *Learning and Development: Annual Survey Report*, London, CIPD.

(CIPD) Chartered Institute of Personnel and Development (2010) *Competency and Competency Frameworks,* London, CIPD June.

Chryssides, G. and Kaler, J. (2006) *An Introduction to Business Ethics*, London, Thomson Business Press.

Clark, P. and Creswell, J. (2008) *The Mixed Methods Reader*, Thousand Oaks, CA, Sage Publications.

Clegg, S., Kornberger, M. and Pitsis, T. (2008) *Managing and Organizations: An Introduction to Theory and Practice*, London, Sage Publications.

Collinson, D. (1994) 'Strategies of resistance: Power, knowledge and subjectivity in the workplace', in Jermier, J., Knights, D. and Nord, W. (eds), *Resistance and Power in Organizations*, Routledge, New York, NY, pp. 25–68.

Collins, D. (2004) 'The machinations of change: BEEPEEARR, debunking and the in-between', *Organization*, 11(5): 671–688.

Collis, J. and Hussey, R. (2009) *Business Research: A Practical Guide for Undergraduate and Postgraduate Studies*, Basingstoke, Palgrave Macmillan.

Collison, D. (2002) 'A Response to Wray-Bliss: Revisiting the Shop Floor', *Organization*, 9(1): 41–50.

Comstock, G. (2013) *Research Ethics: A Philosophical Guide to the Responsible Conduct of Research*, Cambridge, Cambridge University Press.

Corbett, M (1995) Celluloid Projections: Images of Technology and Organizational Futures in Contemporary Science Fiction Film. 2(3/4): 467–488.

Corbin, J. and Strauss, A. (1990) 'Grounded theory research: Procedures, canons and evaluative criteria', *Qualitative Sociology*, 13 (1): 3–21.

Cottrell, S. (2011) *Critical Thinking Skills: Developing Effective Argument and Analysis*, Basingstoke, Palgrave Macmillan.

Cottrell, S. (2013) *The Study Skills Handbook*, Basingstoke, Palgrave Macmillan.

Crane, A. and Matten, D. (2010) *Business Ethics: Managing Corporate Citizenship and Sustainability in the Age of Globalisation*, Oxford, Oxford University Press.

Cresswell, J. (1997) *Qualitative Inquiry and Research Design: Choosing among Five Traditions*, New York, Sage Publications.

Creswell, J. and Clark, P. (2010) *Designing and Conducting Mixed Methods Research*, Thousand Oaks, Sage Publications.

Cryer, P. (2006) *The Research Student's Guide to Success*, Maidenhead, OU/McGraw-Hill Education.

Czarniawska, B. (1998) *A Narrative Approach in Organization Studies*, Thousand Oaks, Sage Publications.

Czarniawska, B. (2002) *A Tale of Three Cities or the Glocalization of City Management*, Oxford, Oxford University Press.

Czarniawska, B. (2003) *Narratives We Organize by*, Amsterdam, John Benjamin.

Czarniawska, B. (2004) *Narratives in Social Science Research*, London, Sage Publications.

Darwell, S. (2002) *Deontology*, Oxford, Blackwell Publishing.

Dass, M. and Shropshire, C. (2012) 'Introducing Functional Data Analysis to Managerial Science', *Organizational Research Methods,* October 15(4): 693–721.

David, M. and Sutton, C. (2011) *Social Research: An Introduction*, London, Sage Publications.

Davis, G. and Pecar, B. (2013) *Business Statistics Using EXCEL*, Oxford, Oxford University Press.

Day, T. (2013) *Success in Academic Writing*, Basingstoke, Palgrave Macmillan.

DeCuir-Gunby, J., Marshall, P. and McCulloch, A. (2012) 'Using Mixed Methods to Analyze Video Data: A Mathematics Teacher Professional Development Example', *Journal of Mixed Methods Research,* July 6(3): 199–216.

Deal, T. and Kennedy, A. (1982) *Corporate Culture: The Rites and Rituals of Organizational Life*, Reading, MA, Addison-Wesley.

Deng, P. (2012) 'The internationalization of Chinese firms: A critical review and future research', *International Journal of Management Reviews*, 10 (4): 367–488.

Denzin, N. (2012) 'Triangulation 2.0', *Journal of Mixed Methods Research*, 6 (2): 80–88.

Denzin, N. and Lincoln, Y. (1998) *Strategies for Qualitative Inquiry*. Thousand Oaks, Sage Publications.

Dereli, C. and Stokes P. (2008) 'Exploring the tension between the scientific and the spiritual in the age of modernism: implications for management theory in the era of postmodernity', *Philosophy of Management*, 6 (3).

DesJardins, J. (2011) *An Introduction of Business Ethics*, New York, McGraw-Hill.

DeWalt K. and DeWalt, B. (2002) *Participant Observation: A Guide for Fieldworkers*, Walnut Creek, Altamira Press.

Dixon, S. and Clifford, A. (2007) 'Ecopreneurship – A new approach to managing the triple bottom line', *Journal of Organizational Change Management*, 20 (3): 326–345.

Donaldson, L. (1996) *For Positivist Organization Theory*, London, Sage Publications.

Donaldson, L. (2005) 'Vita contemplative: Following the scientific method – how I became a committed functionalist and positivist', *Organization Studies*, 26(7): 1071–1088.

Dunleavy, P. (2003) *How to Plan, Draft, Write and Finish a Doctoral Thesis or Dissertation*, Basingstoke, Palgrave Macmiillan.

Dunleavy, P. and Tinkler, J. (2013) *Maximizing the Impacts of Research*, Basingstoke, Palgrave Macmillan.

Easterby-Smith, M. and Lyles, M. (2011) *Handbook of Organizational Learning and Knowledge Management*, London, Wiley.

Easterby-Smith, M., Thorpe, R. and Jackson, P. (2012) *Management Research*, London, Sage Publications.

Edhlund, B. (2007) *Manuscript Writing Using EndNote and WORD*, Form & Kunskap AB, Stallarholmen (Sweden).

EFMD (2010) *The Sustainable Business, European Foundation for Management Development*, Brussels, EFMD.

Eggert, A. and Helm, S. (2003) 'Exploring the impact of relationship transparency on business relationships: a cross-sectional study across purchasing managers in Germany', *Industrial Marketing Management*, 32(2): 101–108.

Elkington, J. (1997) *Cannibals with Forks: The Triple Bottom Line of 21st Century Business*, London, Capstone.

Ellis, N. (2008) 'What the hell is that: the representation of professional service markets in The Simpsons', *Organization*, 15(5): 705–723.

Eriksson, P. and Kovalainen, A. (2008) *Qualitative Methods in Business Research*, London, Sage Publications.

Etzioni, A. (1975) *A Comparative Analysis of Complex Organizations: Of Power, Involvement and Their Correlate*, New York, Free Press.

Fairhurst, G. (2004) 'Textuality and agency in interaction analysis', *Organization*, 11(3): 335–353.

Farrimond, H. (2013) *Doing Ethical Research*, Basingstoke, Palgrave Macmillan.

Feldman, M. (1995) *Strategies for Interpreting Qualitative Data*. Thousand Oaks: Sage Publications.

Fetterman, D. (2010) *Ethnography: Step-by-Step*, London, Sage Publications.

Fisher, C. (2010) *Researching and Writing a Dissertation: A Guidebook for Business Students*, London, FT/Prentice Hall.

Fisher, C. and Lovell, A. (2008) *Business Ethics and Values: Individual, Corporate and International Perspectives*, Harlow, FT/Prentice Hall.

Fleetwood, S. (2005) 'Ontology in organization and management studies:

a critical realist perspective', *Organization*, 12(2): 197–222.

Fowler, F. (2008) *Survey Research Methods*, London, Sage Publications.

Frankl, V. (1959) *Man's Search for Meaning*, London, Beacon Press (originally published in 1946).

Freedman, D., Pisani, R. and Purves, R. (2013) *Statistics*, New York, Norton and Co.

Furseth, I. and Everett, E. (2013) *Doing Your Master's Dissertation: From Start to Finish*, London, Sage Publications.

Gabriel, Y. (2000) *Storytelling in Organizations*, Oxford, Oxford University Press.

Gabriel, Y. (2004) *Myths, Stories and Organizations: Pre-modern Narratives for Our Times*, Oxford, Oxford University Press.

Gee, J. (2011) *How to Do Discourse Analysis: A Toolkit*, London, Routledge.

Geertz (1973) 'Thick Description: Toward an Interpretive Theory of Culture', *The Interpretation of Cultures*, New York, Basic Books.

Ghaye, T. and Lillyman, S. (2008) *Learning Journals and Critical Incidents: Reflective Practice for Healthcare Professionals*, London, Mark Allen Publishing.

Gillham, B. (2007) *Developing a Questionnaire*, London, Continuum International Publishing Group.

Gill, J. and Johnson, P. (2006) *Research Methods for Managers*, London, Sage Publications.

Gold, R. (1958) 'Roles in sociological field observation', *Social Forces*, 36, 217–213.

Gough, D., Oliver, S. and Thomas, J. (2012) *An Introduction to Systematic Reviews*, London, Sage Publications.

Glaser, B. and Strauss, A. (1967) *The Discovery of Grounded Theory: Strategies for Qualitative Research*, Chicago, Aldine Publishing Company.

Goulding, C. (2002) *Grounded Theory: A Practical Guide for Management, Business and Market Researchers*, London, Sage Publications.

Grant, D. and Oswick, C. (1996) *Metaphors and Organizations*, London, Sage Publications.

Grbich, C. (2012) *Qualitative Data Analysis*, London, Sage Publications.

Greenfield, N. (2000) *How I Got My Postgraduate Degree Part-time*, Lancaster/Preston, The Independent Studies Series.

Greetham, B. (2009) *How to Write Your Undergraduate Dissertation*, Basingstoke, Palgrave Macmillan.

Gubrium, J., Holstein, J., Marvasti, J. and McKinney, K. (2012) *The Sage Handbook of Interview Research: The Complexity of the Craft*, London, Sage Publications.

Ha, R. (2011) *Integrative Statistics for the Social and Behavioural Sciences*, London, Sage Publications.

Hair, J., Black, W., Babin. B. and Anderson, R. (2013) *Mutlivariate Data Analysis*, New York, Pearson.

Hammersley, M. (1993) *Social Research: Philosophy, Politics and Practice*, London, Sage Publications.

Hammersley, M. (ed.) (2000) *Social Research: Philosophy, Policy and Practice*, London, Open University Press.

Hammersley, M. and Atkinson, P. (1983) *Ethnography: Principles in Practice*, London, Routledge.

Hammersley, M. and Atkinson, P. (2007) *Ethnography: Principles in Practice*, London, Taylor and Francis.

Hancock, D. and Algozzine, B. (2012) *Doing Case Study Research: A Practical Guide for Beginning Researchers*, New York, Teachers College Press.

Harris, P. (2010) 'Sustainable public affairs – avoiding the double dip', *Journal of Public Affairs*, 10 (4): 233–238.

Harris, P., Lock, A. and Rees, P. (2000) *Machiavelli, Marketing and Management*, London, Routledge.

Hart, C. (2001) *Doing a Literature Search: Releasing the Social Science Research Imagination*, London, Sage Publications.

Hartman, L. and DesJardins, J. (2007) *Business Ethics: Decision Making for Personal Integrity and Social Responsibility*, New York, NY, McGraw-Hill.

Hayat, M. (2013) 'Understanding sample size determination in nursing research', *Western Journal of Nursing Research,* 35(7): 943–956.

Heller, F. (2004) 'Action Research and Research Action: A Family of Methods', in *Essential Guide to Qualitative Methods in Organizational Research*, London, Sage Publications.

Herzberg, F. (1966) *Work and the Nature of Man*, London, Staples Press.

Hickey, L. (1993) 'Stylistics, Pragmatics and Pragmastylistics', *Revue Belge de Philologie and Pragmastylistics*, 71(71–73): 573–586.

Hickey, L. and Stewart, M. (2005) *Politeness in Europe*, Ontario, Multilingual Matters Ltd.

Hill, J. and McGowan, P. (1999) 'Small business and enterprise development: questions about research methodology', *International Journal of Entrepreneurial Behaviour and Research*, 5(1): 5–18.

Hoon, C. (2013) 'Meta-synthesis of qualitative case studies: an approach to theory building, *Organizational Research Methods,* 16(4): 522–556.

Huczynski, A. (2004) *Influencing within Organizations*, Second Edition, London, Routledge.

Hultsch, D., MacDonald, S., Hunter, M., Maitland, S. and Dixon, R. (2002) 'Sampling and *generalisability* in developmental research: comparison of random and convenience sample of older adults', *International Journal of Behavioral Development*, 26(4): 345–359.

Irvine, A., Drew, P. and Sainsbury, R. (2013) '"Am I not answering your questions properly?" Clarification, adequacy and responsiveness in semi-structured telephone and face-to-face interviews', *Qualitative Research*, 13(1):87–106.

Israel, M. and Hay, I. (2006) *Research Ethics for Social Scientists*, London, Sage Publications.

Jakobsen, H. (2012) 'Focus groups and methodological rigour outside the minority world: making the method work to its strengths in Tanzania', *Qualitative Research*, 12(2): 111–130.

Jane, W.-J.(2013) 'Overpayment and reservation salary in the Nippon professional baseball league: a stochastic frontier analysis', *Journal of Sports Economics,* 14(6): 563–583.

Jankowicz, A. (2005) *Business Research Projects*, London, Thompson Learning.

Jobman, D. (1998) *Bar Chart Basics*, New York, McGraw-Hill.

Johnson, P. and Duberley, J. (2011) 'Anomie and culture management: Reappraising Durkheim', *Organization*, 18 (4): 563–584.

Jones, S. (1998) *Doing Internet Research: Critical Issues and Methods for Examining the Net*, California, Sage Publications.

Josselson R. and Lieblich, A. (1993) *The Narrative Study of Lives*, London, Sage Publications.

Junker, B. (1960) *Fieldwork*, Chicago, University of Chicago Press.

Juritzen, T., Grimen, H. and Heggen, K. (2011) 'Protecting vulnerable *research* participants: a Foucault-inspired analysis of ethics committees', *Nursing Ethics,* 18(5): 640–650.

Kessler, E. (2007) 'Human, managerial and strategic implications', *Group and Organizational Management*, 31 (3): 296–299.

King, N. (2004a) 'Using interviews in qualitative research', in Cassell, C. and

Symon, G. (eds) *Essential Guide to Qualitative Methods in Organizational Research*, London, Sage Publications, 11–22.

King, N. (2004b) 'Using templates in the thematic analysis of text', in Cassell, C. and Symon, G. (eds) *Essential Guide to Qualitative Methods in Organizational Research*, London, Sage Publications, 256–270.

King, N. and Horrocks, C. (2010) *Interviews in Qualitative Research*, London, Sage Publications.

Kira, M., Van Eijnatten, F. and Balkin, D. (2010) 'Crafting sustainable work: Development of personal resources', *Journal of Organizational Change Management*, 23 (5): 616–632.

Kleinman, S. (2007) *Feminist Fieldwork Analysis*, London, Sage Publications.

Knights, D. and Willmott, H. (1999) *Management Lives: Power and Identity in Work Organizations*, London, Sage Publications.

Kohler-Riessman, C. (2008) *Narrative Method for the Human Sciences*, London, Sage Publications.

Kraaijenbrink, J. (2012) 'Integrating knowledge and knowledge processes: a critical incident study of product development projects', *The Journal of Product Innovation Management*, 29(6): 1082–1096.

Kremelberg, D. (2011) *Practical Statistics*, Thousand Oaks, Sage Publications.

Kuhn, T. (2009) 'Positioning lawyers: discursive resources, professional ethics and identification', *Organization*, 16 (5): 681–704.

Kvale, S. (2007) *Doing Interviews*, London, Sage Publications.

Labukt, I. (2009) 'Rawls on the practicability of utilitarianism', *Politics, Philosophy & Economics*, 8 (2): 201–221.

Lake, D. (1999) Spotlight: How Big Is the U.S. Net Population? *The Standard*, November 29, available at http://www.thestandard.com/metrics/display/0,2149, 1071,00.html, accessed 14 February 2013.

Larson, M., Schnyder, G., Westerhuis, G. and Wilson, J. (2011) 'Strategic responses to global challenges: the case of European banking 1973–2000', *Business History*, 53(1): 40–62.

Landau, L. and Everitt, B. (2004) *A Handbook of Statistical Analysis Using SPSS*, Boca Raton, Chapman and Hall/ CRC Press.

Lawrence, P. and Barsoux, J.-L. (1997) *French Management: Elitism in Action*, Abingdon, Taylor and Francis.

Lee, B. (2012) 'Using Documents in Organizational Research', in Symons, G. and Cassell, C. (eds) *Qualitative Organizational Research: Core Methods and Current Challenges*, London, Sage Publications, 389–407.

Letherby, G. Scott., J. and Williams, M. (2013) *Objectivity and Subjectivity in Social Research* London, Sage Publications.

Levi, P. (1958/1987) *If This Is a Man*, London, Abacus.

Levi, P. (1986/1988) *The Drowned and the Saved*, London, Abacus.

Linder-Pelz, S. (2010) *NLP Coaching: An Evidence-Based Approach for Coaches, Leaders and Individuals*, London, Kogan.

Linstead, S., Fulop, L. and Lilley, S. (2009) *Management and Organization: A Critical Text*, Basingstoke, Palgrave Macmillan.

Liu, X. (2013) 'Comparing sample size requirements for significance tests and confidence intervals', *Counseling Outcome Research and Evaluation*, 4(1): 3–12.

Lohr, S. (2011) *Sampling: Design and Analysis*, Boston, Cengage Learning.

Luke, B. and Kearins, K. (2012) 'Attribution of words versus attribution of responsibilities: academic plagiarism and university practice', *Organization*, 19(6): 881–889.

Luyt, R. (2012) 'A framework for mixing methods in quantitative measurement development, validation, and revision: a case study', *Journal of Mixed Methods Research,* October 6(4): 294–316.

Machiavelli, N. (2008) *The Prince*, Oxford, Oxford University Press (originally published in 1532).

MacCormack, A., Carliss, B. and Rusnak, J. (2012) 'Exploring the duality between product and organizational: a test of the mirroring hypothesis', *Research Policy*, 41(8): 1309–1324.

MacIntyre, A. (2007) *After Virtue: A Study in Moral Theory*, London, Gerald Duckworth and Co (originally published in 1981).

Maitlis, S. (2012) 'Narrative Analysis', in *Qualitative Organizational Research: Core Methods and Current Challenges*, London, Sage Publications, 492–513.

Marschan-Piekkari, R. and Welch, C. (2004) *Handbook of Qualitative Research Methods for International Business*, Cheltenham, Edward Elgar Publishing Ltd.

Marsh, C. and Elliott, J. (2008) *Exploring Data*, Cambridge, Polity Press.

Maslow, A. (1970) *Motivation and Personality*, New York, Harper and Row.

Matlay, H. (2001) 'HRD in the small business sector of the British economy: an evaluation of current training initiatives', *Proceedings of 2nd Conference of HRD Research and Practice Across Europe*, University of Twente, Enschede, 26–27 January cited in Garavan, T. and McGuire, D. (2001) 'Competencies and workplace learning: some reflections on the rhetoric and the reality', *Journal of Workplace Learning*, 13(4): 144–163.

Maylor, H. and Blackmon, K. (2005) *Researching Business and Management*, Basingstoke, Palgrave Macmillan.

Mayo, E. (1933/1960) *The Human Problems of Industrial Organization*, New York, Viking Press.

McEwan, T. (2001) *Managing Values and Belief in Organizations*, Harlow, FT/Prentice Hall.

McDowall, A. and Saunders, M. (2010) 'UK managers conceptions of training and development', *Journal of European Industrial Training*, 34(7): 609–630.

McMillan, K. and Weyers, J. (2011) *How to Write Dissertations and Project Reports*, Harlow, Pearson Education Ltd.

McMillan, K. and Weyers, J. (2012) *The Study Skills Book*, Pearson Education Ltd.

McMurray, R., Pullen, A., Rhodes, C. (2011) 'Ethical subjectivity and politics in orgabnizations: a case of health care tendering', *Organization*, 18(4): 541–561.

Medlin, C. (2012) 'Peter Drucker's ontology: understanding business relationships and networks', *Journal of Business and Industrial Marketing*, 27(7): 513–520.

Mescher, S., Benschop, Y. and Dooreward, H. (2010) 'Representations of work: life balance support', *Human Relations*, 63(1): 21–39.

Miles, M. and Huberman, M. (1994) *Qualitative Data Analysis: An Expanded Sourcebook,* London, Sage Publications.

Mills, D. and Ratcliffe, R. (2012) 'After method? Ethnography in the knowledge economy', *Qualitative Research,* April 12(2): 147–164.

Milne, M., Kearins, K. and Walton, S. (2006) 'Creating adventure in wonderland: The journey metaphor and environmental sustainability', *Organization*, 13 (6): 801–839.

MINTS (Minnesota Internet Traffic Studies) (2007) Methodology (online) USA, available at http://www.dtc.umn.edu/mints/methodology.html, accessed 14 February 2013.

Monahan, T. and Fisher, J. (2010) 'Benefits of observer effects: Lessons from the field', *Qualitative Research*, 10 (3): 357–376.

Morgan, D. (2007) 'Paradigms lost and pragmatism regained: methodological implications of combining qualitative and quantitative methods, *Journal of Mixed Methods Research*, 1(1): 48–76.

Morris, C. (1993) *Qualitative Approaches in Business Studies*, London, Pitman Publishing.

Murray, R. (2011) *How to Write a Thesis*, London, Open University/McGraw-Hill.

(The) National Student Survey (UK) (2013) available at www.thestudentsurvey.com, accessed 7 November 2013.

O'Brien, M. and DeSisto, M. (2013) 'Every study begins with a query: how to present a clear *Research* Question', *NASN School Nurse,* March 28(2): 83–85.

Oliver, P. (2010) *The Student's Guide to Research Ethics*, Milton Keynes, Open University Press/McGraw-Hill Education.

Pallant, J. (2013) *SPSS Survival Manuel*, Milton Keynes, Open University Press/ McGraw-Hill.

Panayiotou, A. (2010) '"Macho" managers and organizational heroes: competing masculinities in popular films, *Organization*, 17(6): 659–683.

Parkes, J. (2012) *What is Poststructuralism,* Ebook, Academic Bytes.

Payne, G. (2011) *Teaching Quantitative Methods: Getting the Basics Right*, London, Sage Publications.

Pears R., and Shields, G. (2013) *Cite Them Right: The Essential Referencing Guide*, Basingstoke, Palgrave Macmillan.

Phillips, E. and Pugh, D. (2010) *How to Get a PhD: A Handbook for Students and Their Supervisors*, Milton Keynes, Open University Press/McGraw Hill Education.

Pmadvice.co.uk (2013) available at www.pmadvice.co.uk/Userfiles/files/ TermsofReference.

Pollock, A.M. (2005) *NHS Plc*, Verso, London.

Popper, K. (1959) *The Logic of Scientific Discovery*, New York, Basic.

Power, M. (1991) 'Educating accountants: towards a critical ethnography', *Accounting, Organizations and Society*, 16(4): 333–353.

Principles for Responsible Management Education (PRME) (2011), available at: www.unprme.org (accessed 6 March 2012).

Quinlan, C. (2011) *Business Research Methods*, London, Cengage Learning.

Quinton, S. and Smallbone, T. (2006) *Post-graduate Research in Business: A Critical Guide*, London, Sage Publications.

Raub, S. and von Wittich, C. (2004) 'Implementing knowledge management: three strategies for effective CKOs', *European Management Journal*, 20(6): 714–724.

Revans, R. (1980) *Action Learning: New Techniques for Management*, London: Blond & Briggs.

Revans, R. (2011) *The ABC of Action Learning*, London: Ashgate/Gower.

Ridley, D. (2012) *The Literature Review: A Step-by-Step Guide for Students*, London, Sage Publications.

Ritchie, J. and Spencer, L. (1994) 'Qualitative data analysis for applied policy research', in Bryman, A. and Burgess R. (eds) *Analyzing Qualitative Data,* London, Sage Publications, 173–194.

Roan, S. (2009) 'The key to happiness is living in the micro-moment', *Los Angeles Times*, available at: latimesblogs.latimes. com/booster_shots/2009/07/happiness. html (accessed 23 May 2011).

Roethlisberger, F. and Dickson, W. (1939) *Management and the Worker*, Cambridge, Harvard University Press.

Rohlfing, I. (2012) *Case Studies and Causal Inference*, Basingstoke, Palgrave Macmillan.

Rugg, G. and Petre, M. (2004) *The Unwritten Rules of PhD Research*, Maidenhead, Open University Press.

Russell, B. (1995) *An Inquiry into Meaning and Truth*, London, Routledge.

Saldaña, J. (2012) *The Coding Manual for Qualitative Researchers*, London, Sage Publications.

Sales, B. and Folkman, S. (Eds.) (2000) *Ethics in Research with Human Participants*, Washington DC, American Psychological Association.

Sandberg, J. and Alvesson, M. (2011) 'Ways of constructing *research questions*: gap-spotting or problematization?' *Organization,* January, 18 (1): 23–44.

Sartre, J-P. (1943/2003) *Being and Nothingness*, Paris, Gallimard/Routledge.

Saunders, M., Lewis, M. and Thornhill, A. (2012) *Research Methods for Business Students*, Harlow, Pearson Education.

Scott, P., McIntosh-Scott, E. A. and Stokes, P. (2013) 'Sales and strategic marketing practices in the pharmaceutical industry: doctors as customers and their decisions', *Journal of International Business and Entrepreneurship Development*, 7(1): 37–51.

Sharma, S., Starik, M. and Husted, B. (2007) *Organizations and Sustainability Mosaic: Crafting Long-Term Ecological and Societal Solutions*, Cheltenham, Edward Elgar.

Shaw, P. (2010) *Defining Moments: Navigating through Business and Organizational Life*, Basingstoke, Palgrave Macmillan.

Schein, E. (1990) 'Organizational culture', *American Psychologist*, 45: 109–119.

Shinkle, G. and Spencer, J. (2012) 'The social constructionism of global corporate citizenship: Sustainability of Automotive Corporations', *Journal of World Business*, 47 (1): 123–133.

Schön, D. (1987) *Educating the Reflective Practitioner: Towards a New Design for Teaching and Learning in the Professions*, London, Wiley.

Sieber, J. and Tollich, M. (2012) *Planning Ethically Responsible Research*, London, Sage Publications.

Silverman, D. (1993) *Interpreting Qualitative Data*, London, Sage Publications.

Silverman, D. (2006) *Interpreting Qualitative Data: Methods for Analysing Talk, Text and Interaction*, London, Sage Publications.

Silverman, D. (2010a) *Doing Qualitative Research*, London, Sage Publications.

Silverman, D. (2010b) *Qualitative Research*, London, Sage Publications.

Silverman, D. (2011) *Interpreting Qualitative Data*, London, Sage Publications.

Smith, S. (2011) The Relevance of Investors in People, Doctoral Thesis Preston/London, UCLan/British Library.

Spradley, J. (1980) *Participant Observation*, New York, Holt, Rinehart and Winston.

Srivasta, S. and Cooperrider, D. (1998) *Organizational Wisdom and Executive Courage*, San Francisco, CA: New Lexington Press.

Starr, J. (2011) *The Coaching Manual: The Definitive Guide to the Process, Principles and Skills of Personal Coaching*, Third Edition, Harlow, Pearson.

Stebbins, R. (2001) *Exploratory Research in the Social Sciences*, London, Sage Publications.

Stein, R. and Foster, D. (2011) *Statistics for Business: Decision Making and Analysis*, New York, Pearson.

Steinberg, W. (2010) *Statistics Alive!* London, Sage Publications.

Stel, H., Staal, I., Hermanns, M. and Schrijvers, A. (2012) 'Validity and reliability of a structured interview for early detection and risk assessment of parenting and developmental problems in young children: a cross-sectional study', *Arthritis Research and Therapy*, 12: 71.

Stewart, J. and Rigg, C. (2011) *Learning and Talent Development*, London, Chartered Institute of Personnel and Development.

Stibbe, A. (2009) *The Handbook of Sustainability Literacy: Skills for a Changing World*, Dartington, Green Books.

Stokes, P. (2011) *Critical Concepts in Management and Organization Studies*, Basingstoke, Palgrave Macmillan.

Stokes, P. (2012) *Key Concepts in Business and Management Research Methods*, Basingstoke, Palgrave Macmillan.

Stokes, P. and Gabriel, Y. (2010) 'Engaging with genocide – challenges for organization and management studies', *Organization,* 17(4): 461–480.

Stokes, P. and Harris, P. (2012) 'Micro-Moments, choice and responsibility in sustainable organizational change and transformation: the Janus dialectic', *The Journal of Organizational Change Management,* 25(4): 595–611.

Storr, L. (2004) 'Leading with integrity: a qualitative research study', *Journal of Health Organization and Management,* 18(6): 415–434.

Strauss, A. and Corbin, J. (1998) *Basics of Qualitative Research,* Thousand Oaks, Sage Publications.

Streiner, D. (2013) *A Guide for the Statistically Perplexed: Selected Readings for Clinical Researchers,* Toronto, Canadian Psychiatric Association.

Stovall, S. (2010) 'Recreating the Arsenal of Venice: Using experiential activities to teach the history of management', *Journal of Management Education,* 34 (3): 458–473.

Strawbridge, D. and Strawbridge, J. (2010), Practical Self-Sufficiency, Dorling Kindersley, London.

Symons, G. and Cassell, C. (2012) *Qualitative Organizational Research: Core Methods and Current Challenges,* London, Sage Publications.

Tadajewski, M. (2009) 'Editing the history of marketing thought', *Journal of Historical Research in Marketing* 1(2): 318–329.

Tams, S. and Marshall, J. (2010) 'Responsible careers: Systematic reflexivity in shifting landscapes', *Human Relations,* 64 (1): 109–131.

Taylor, F. W. (1911/1967) *Principles of Scientific Management,* New York, Harper.

Teddlie, C. and Fen, Y. (2007) 'Mixed methods sampling: a typology with examples', *Journal of Mixed Methods Research,* 7(4): 77–100.

Tellis, W. (1997) 'Introduction to Case Study', The Qualitative Report, 3 (2) http//www.nova.edu/QR/QR3-2/tellis1.html.

Tengblad, S. and Ohlsson. C. (2010) 'The framing of corporate social responsibility and the globalization of national business systems: a longitudinal case study', *Journal of Business Ethics,* 93: 653–699.

Thody, A. (2006) *Writing and Presenting Research,* London, Sage Publications.

Thomson, B. (2013) *Non-Directive Coaching: Attitudes, Approaches and Applications,* St Albans, Critical Publishing.

Thompson, P. and Ackroyd, S. (1999) *Organizational Misbehaviour,* Sage Publications, London.

Thompson, S. (2012) *Sampling,* New Jersey, Wiley & Sons.

Treiman, D. (2009) *Quantitative Data Analysis: Doing Social Research to Test Ideas,* San Francisco , John Wiley and Sons.

Tripp, D. (1993) *Critical Incidents in Teaching: Developing Professional Judgment,* London. Routledge.

Trönnberg, C-C. and Hemlin, S. (2013) 'Lending decision making in banks: a critical incident study of loan officers', *European Management Journal,* available online April 2013.

Tuuli, M., and Rowlinson, S. (2010) 'What empowers individuals and teams in project settings? A critical incident analysis', *Engineering, Construction and Architectural Management,* 17(1): 9–20.

Van Maanen, J. (1978) 'On watching the watchers', in Manning, P. and Van Maanen, J. (eds) *Policing: The View from the Street,* Santa Monica, Goodyear.

Vilmos, F., Misangyi, V., LePine, J., Algina, J. and Goeddeke, F. (2013) 'The adequacy of repeated-measures regression for multilevel research: comparisons with repeated-measures

ANOVA, multivariate repeated-measures ANOVA, and multilevel modeling across various multilevel research designs', *Organizational Research Methods,* 9(1): 5–28.

Waddington, D. (2004) 'Participant observation', in Cassell, C. and Symon, G. (eds) *Essential Guide to Qualitative Methods in Organizational Research*, London, Sage Publications.

Wall, T. (2011a) Rapid Management Development of Practitioner Research Capacity, 7th European Conference on Leadership, Management and Governance, Nice, 6 and 7 October 2011.

Wall, T. (2011b) Accelerated Practitioner Research Approach (APRA) *Work Based Learning Futures V Conference*, Derby, September 2011.

Wall, T. (2013a) 'Transcending the relevance gap: the accelerated practitioner research approach', *The Macrotheme Review: A Multidisciplinary Journal of Global Macro Trends*, 2(1).

Wall, T. (2013b) Transforming Research-Learning Performance with Professional Lifelong Learners, *5th World Congress on Educational Sciences*, Rome, Italy, 6–8 February.

Wall, T. (2014) 'Transforming the Research-Learning Performance of Professional Lifelong Learners', *Procedia - Social and Behavioral Sciences*, 116, 189–193.

Wall, T. and Leonard, D. (2011) An Accelerated Practitioner Research Approach for Professionals – A Study, *European Association for Practitioner Research on Improving Learning International Conference*, Nijmegen, the Netherlands, 23–25 November.

Walsham, G. (2006) 'Doing interpretive research', *European Journal of Information Systems*, 15: 320–330.

Waring, T. and Wainwright, D. (2008) Issues and challenges in the use of template analysis: Two comparative case studies from the field', *The Electronic Journal of Business Research Methods*, 6(1): 85–94.

Watson, T. and Harris, P. (1999) *The Emergent Manager*, London, Sage Publications.

Watson, T. (2006) *Organising and Managing Work,* Harlow, Pearson Education Ltd.

Weick, K. (1995) *Sensemaking in Organizations*, London, Sage Publications.

Wenger, E. (1999) *Communities of Practice: Learning, Meaning, and Identity*, Cambridge: Cambridge University Press.

White, P. (2009) *Basic Sampling*, London, SMT.

White, P. (2008) *Developing Research Questions: A Guide for Social Scientists*, Basingstoke, Palgrave Macmillan.

Whitmore, J. (2009) *Coaching for Performance: GROWing Human Potential and Purpose – the Principles and Practice of Coaching and Leadership*, Fourth Edition, London, Nicholas Brealey.

Whittle, A. (2008) 'From flexibility to work-life balance: exploring the changing discourses of management consultants', *Organization*, (15)4: 513–534.

Whittle, A. and Spicer, A. (2008) 'Is Actor Network Theory Critique?', *Organization Studies*, 29(4): 611–629.

Wiles, R., Crow, G. and Pain, H. (2011) 'Innovation in qualitative research methods: a narrative review', *Qualitative Research,* October 2011 11(5): 587–604.

Williams, F., Rice, R. and Rogers, E. (1988) *Research methods and the new media*, New York, The Free Press.

Wilson, J. (2010) *Essentials of Business Research: A Guide to Doing Your Research Project*, London, Sage Publications.

Wood, A. (2008) *Kantian Ethics*, Cambridge, Cambridge University Press.

Woods, C. (2007) 'Empirical histograms in item response theory with ordinal data', *Educational and Psychological Measurement*, 67(1):73–87.

Woźniak, A. (2010) 'The dream that caused reality: the place of the Lacanian subject of science in the field of organization', *Organization*, May 17(3): 395–411.

Wray-Bliss, E. (2002) 'Abstract ethics, embodied ethics: the strange marriage of Foucault and positivism in labour process theory', *Organization*, 9(1): 5–39.

www.library.manchester.ac.uk/academic support/howtostructureliteraturesearch (2013) accessed 2 November 2013.

Wright, J. (2003) 'Introducing sustainability into the architecture curriculum in the United States', *International Journal of Sustainability in Higher Education*, 4 (2): 100–105.

Yin, R. K. (2011) *Applications of Case Study Research*, London, Sage Publications.

Yin, R. K. (2003) *Case Study Research: Design and Methods*, London, Sage Publications.

Zhu, Q., Sarkis, J., Geng, Y. (2005) 'Green supply chain management in China: pressures, practices and performance', *International Journal of Operations & Production Management*, 25(5): 449–468.

# INDEX

*Note*: Page numbers followed by "*f*" and "*t*" denote figures and tables, respectively.

action learning, 112
action research, 124–5
aim, 8–10, 21–3
analysis
    archival, 94
    content, 209
    critical, 79–80, 82
    data *see* data analysis
    defined, 209
    statistical, 158–60, 171
    template, 192–3
anonymity, 232
ANOVA, 184
*a priori* codes, 193
archival analysis, 94, 178
argument, 81
Association of Business
        Schools (ABS) Guide,
        68
autonomy, 122–3, 232
axial coding, 191

background literature, 63
bar charts, 184–5, 185*f*
basic theme, coding data, 190
beneficence, 123
bibliography, 8
British Academy of
        Management (BAM)
        Code of Ethics, 222–4
British Psychological Society,
        224
British Sociological
        Association, 225
    Statement of Ethical
        Practice, 224

'bucket'-style technique, 16,
        17*f*, 69

case situation, reflective
        questions on, 13–14
case studies, 92–3, 125
    analyzing, 205–6
    defined, 140–1, 168–70,
        259
    relation to deductive
        methodologies,
        141–2
    relation to inductive
        methodologies,
        142–3
    use in writing up research,
        238–9
cataloguing concepts, 188
categorical data, 176–7
causality, 79, 90, 91, 105, 125
causal research, 89
cautionary note, 11–14
Chambers of Commerce, 167
chronology of literature
        review, 71–2
CIA, 165
closed questions, 146, 153
coaching, 112
Code of Ethics, 222–5
coding
    axial, 191
    cognitive mapping, 194
    data, 189–91
    examples of, 194–205
    mind-mapping, 194
    open, 191

selective, 191–2
    template, 193
cognitive mapping, 194
comparative studies, 94
complete observer, 150
complete participant, 150
comprehensive data
        treatment, 208
conceptual framework, 81–2
conceptualization, 188
confidentiality, 230, 232
consent
    comparative method, 208
    defined, 232
    negative, 233
    positive, 233
    constructivism, 138–9
content analysis, 209
continuous data, 177
convenience sampling, 161,
        163–4
correlation, 178
covert observation, 151–2
critical analysis
    defined, 82
    in literature review, 79–80
critical incident method
        (CIM)
    defined, 144, 170
    relation to inductive
        and deductive
        methodologies,
        144–5
critical management studies
        (CMS), 49, 59
cross-sectional study, 93–4

data
  data *see* data analysis
  coding, 189–91
  collection, 121, 187
  internet sources for,
      164–8
  interpretation, 122
  primary, 45–7
  protection, principles of,
      226
  reading, 188
  re-reading, 188
  secondary, 45–7
data analysis, 97
  coding, 189–205
  defined, 174–5
  generalisability, 209
  qualitative, 186–9
  quantitative, 176–86
  reliability, 206
  research design during, 176
  validity, 206–9
Data Protection Act of 1998,
    225
deductive methodologies
  relation to case studies,
      141–2
  relation to critical incident
      method, 144–5
  relation to ethnography,
      143–4
  relation to interviews, 149
  relation to narrative
      research, 158
  relation to participant
      observation, 152
  relation to questionnaires,
      157
  relation to statistical
      analysis, 159–60
  *see also* deductivism
deductivism, 90, 93, 103–6,
    125
descriptive research, 89
determinism, 90, 105

dilution effect, 113, 119
discourse, 170
discrete data, 177
dissemination of research
    work, 255–8
dissertation, 3–4
  defined, 259
  early views of, 126
  first person, use of, 78–9
  qualitative, 126
  quantitative, 126
double-blind review, 82
drafting literature review,
    69–70

edited volume, 82–3
email questionnaires, 157
empiricism, 138–9
End Note™, 68, 254
epistemology, 12, 94–5, 96,
    125
ethical dilemma, 215–17
ethical transgression, 219–20
ethics, 212–31
  Code of Ethics, 222–5
  committee, 222
  defined, 232
  laws and legal provisions,
      225–6
  relation to conducting
      research, 226–31
  of research, 122–3
  situation, 217–18
  transgression, 219–20
  universalism, 214–17
  utilitarian, 217
ethnography, 80, 99
  defined, 142–3, 170, 259
  relation to inductive
      and deductive
      methodologies,
      143–4
  use in writing up research,
      239–49
executive summary, 5

exploratory research, 89–90
externalization, 101

face-to-face questionnaires,
    156
facts, 95
familiarization, 188
feedback loops, 31–7
feelings, 151
first person in dissertations,
    use of, 78–9
focal literature, 63
focus of research, 117
*Forum des Droits sur
    l'Internet*, 167
frequency, defined, 183
frequency tables, 183, 183t
F-statistic, 184
funnel shape, of literature
    review, 72–4, 73f

Gantt chart, 124
generalisability, 128, 209
global theme, coding data,
    190–1
global village, 164
grammar, 253–4
Grey Zone, 70
grounded theory, 191–2,
    209–10

habitualization, 100
harm
  defined, 232
  emotional, 229
  to research participants,
      avoiding, 228–30
Hawthorne Effect, 106–8,
    221
histogram, 185, 186f
historical narrative, 49–58
hypothesis, 97–8
  defined, 28
  null, 104
  role in research, 28–30

hypothesis – *continued*
  use in deductivism, 103–4
  use in inductive research,
    98

implementation of research,
  123–4
implication, 70, 82
inductive methodologies
  relation to case studies,
    142–3
  relation to critical incident
    method, 144–5
  relation to ethnography,
    143–4
  relation to interviews, 149
  relation to narrative
    research, 158
  relation to questionnaires,
    157
  relation to statistical
    analysis, 159–60
  *see also* inductivism
inductivism, 91, 93, 96–100,
  126
inference, 70, 82
information, 70, 82
informed consent, 227–8, 232
integrity, 230–31
internalization, 101
*International Journal of
    Management Reviews*,
    60
International
    Telecommunications
    Union (ITU), 165
internet sources, for data,
    164–8
interpretivism, 88, 89, 92, 97,
    126–7, 135*t*, 138–9
interviewees, 146
interviewers, 146
interviews, 80, 145–9
  defined, 170
  issues and procedures in
    conducting, 148–9

logistics, 148
personalities, 148
recording, 148–9
relation to inductive
    and deductive
    methodologies, 149
schedule, 146
semi-structured, 147
structured, 147, 178
types of, 146
unstructured, 147
uses of, 145–6

jigsaw concept, 37*f*
justice, 123

laws, 225–6
legal provisions, 225–6
linear regression, 178
linking, 188
lists, making, 38
literature
background, 63
  defined, 44–5
  focal, 63
  review *see* literature
    review
literature review, 43–81
  chronology of, 71–2
  completion of, 80
  critical analysis in, 79–80
  defined, 44
  drafting, 69–70
  evolution of writing,
    49–58
  first person, use of, 78–9
  funnel shape of, 72–4, 73*f*
  historical narrative, 49–58
  key issues and themes,
    59–60
  new information follows
    old information,
    ordering, 74–6
  obtaining, 67–8
  pitfalls, identifying and
    avoiding, 60–1

primary and secondary
    data, 45–7
  primary sources linking
    with, 45
  secondary sources
    linking with, 46
  recording, 68–9
  re-creating, 70–80
  referencing, 80–1
  register, using, 77–8
  re-reading, 70–80
  schools of thought, 58–9
  seminal writings, 47–9
  sources of, 80–1
  starting of, 60–3
  strategies for, 63–70, 64*f*
  thematic flow of, 71–2
  thesaurus, using, 77–8
  word limits, 76–7
log files, 167
longitudinal study, 94

management learning, 25–6,
    27–8
matrix readings, 253
mauvaise foi (bad faith), 220
mean, 181–2
median, 182
mind-mapping, 15, 194
mixed method research, 127
mode, 182
monograph, 83
motivation, 151
multi-stage cluster sampling,
    163
multivariate analysis, 177

narratives, 83
  defined, 158, 170–1,
    258–9
  relation to inductive
    and deductive
    methodologies, 158
  use in writing up research,
    249–50
  *see also* storytelling

National Office of Statistics, 167

National Student Survey, 177

natural science approaches and terminology, 90–1

near-finalised draft, examining, 253

negative consent, 233

NetRatings, 165

'new information follows old information' principle, 74–6

Nielsen, 165

non-probability sampling, 163–4

normal distribution, 180–1, 180*f*

null hypothesis, 104

objectivity/objectification, 8–10, 21–3, 90, 100, 103–4, 127, 207

observer-as-participant, 150

Occam's Razor principle, 113, 119

online questionnaires, 157

ontology, 95–6, 110, 127
realist, 95
relativist, 95–6

open coding, 191

open questions, 146, 153

organizational learning, 25–6, 27–8

organizational performance, 25–6, 27–8

organizing theme, coding data, 190

overt observation, 151

participant-as-observer, 150

participant observation, 80, 178
defined, 150–2, 171
relation to inductive and deductive methodologies, 152

personality, 12

personal learning, 113

persuasion, 113–14, 115

pie chart, 186, 187*f*

pilot study, 148

plagiarism, 231

population, 160

positive consent, 233

positivism, 88, 89, 91, 97, 127, 135*t*, 138–9

positivistic-style study, 29–30

postal questionnaire, 156–7

Post-it™, 15, 77

presentation of research work, 255–8

primary data, 45–7
primary sources linking with, 45
secondary sources linking with, 46

primary sources, linking with primary and secondary data, 45

privacy, 233

probability sampling, 162–3

ProCite, 254

project, 5–6, 259

qualitative, 127
data, 101–3
data analysis, 186–9, 210
dissertation, 126
research, 9

quantifiable data, 177

quantitative, 129
data analysis *see* quantitative data analysis
dissertation, 9, 126
statistical-style study, 9

quantitative data analysis, 176–86, 210
ANOVA, 184
approach of, 178–9
bar charts, 184–5, 185*f*
defined, 176

frequency tables, 183, 183*t*
histogram, 185, 186*f*
pie chart, 186, 187*f*
statistical techniques, 179–80
times/day, 183–4
types of, 176–8

question-driven approach to research methodology, 112–24

questionnaires, 152–7
defined, 152–3, 171
email, 157
example of, 153–6
face-to-face, 156
online, 157
postal, 156–7
relation to inductive and deductive methodologies, 157
structured, 178

quota sampling, 164

realism
linking with methodological considerations, 109–11

realist ontology, 95

re-coding, 188

recording
interviews, 148–9
literature review, 68–9

re-creating literature review, 70–80

reductionism, 79, 90, 105, 129–30

re-evaluation, 189

referencing, 8, 254
literature review, 80–1

reflection, 188

reflective questions
on case situation, 13–14
method of developing, 23–8

reflective questions –
*continued*
reasons for developing,
23–8
reflexivity, 99
refutability principle, 208
RefWorks, 254
register, 71
in literature review, using,
77–8
relativism
linking with
methodological
considerations,
109–11
relativist ontology, 95–6
reliability, 128, 206
representation(alism),
99–100, 130
re-reading literature review,
70–80
research
action, 124–5
approach, 118–20
archive, 178
causal, 89
defined, 1
descriptive, 89
design, 87–94
direction, double
checking, 31–7
early views of, 126
exploratory, 89
field, 151
focus of, 117
methods *see* research
methods
mixed method, 127
participants, avoiding
harm to, 228–30
process, management of,
37–40
purpose, 118
qualitative, 9
quantitative, 9

questions, 8–10
setting, needs to change
or develop, 115–16
timeline, 3*f*
writing *see* writing
research
research area, identification
of, 10–15
issues, 14–15
topic selection, 10–11
cautionary note, 11–14
research design
during data analysis, 176
remember and respect
to, 238
research methodology,
86–132
alternative perspectives or
positions, 114–15
approach for, 108–9,
118–20
coaching, role of, 112
complexities of, 136–7
data collection, 121
data interpretation, 122
deductivism, 103–6
defined, 134
epistemology, 94–5, 96
ethics of research, 122–3
focus of, 117
Hawthorne Effect, 106–8,
221
implementation of
research, 123–4
inductivism, 96–100
ontology, 95–6
patterns of, 136
persuasion, 113–14
purpose of, 118
qualitative data, 101–3
question-driven approach
to, 112–24
realism, 109–11
relativism, 109–11
research design, 87–94

and research methods,
relationship
between, 133–6
research setting, needs to
change or develop,
115–16
sense of the world, 137–8
social constructionism,
100–1
statistics, 120–1
research methods
case studies, 140–2
caution in, 139
complexities of, 136–7
critical incident method,
144–5
defined, 134
ethnography, 143–4
illustrations of, 140
interviews, 145–9
and methodology,
relationship
between, 133–6
narrative research, 158
participant observation,
150–2
patterns of, 136
questionnaires, 152–7
sense of the world, 137–8
statistical analysis, 158–60
research proposal
development of, 6
writing, 6–8
Russian Electronic
Communications
Association, 167
*Russian Internet Forum*,
167

sample
deductivism, 103
defined, 160
establishing, 160–1
inductivism, 97
simple random, 162

stratified random, 162–3
systematic, 162
sampling
    convenience, 163–4
    defined, 171
    frame, 161–2
    multi-stage cluster, 163
    non-probability, 163–4
    probability, 162–3
    quota, 164
    snowball, 164
search terms, 83
secondary data, 45–7
    primary sources linking
        with, 45
    secondary sources linking
        with, 46
secondary sources, linking
    with primary and
    secondary data, 46
selective coding, 191–2
seminal writings, 47–9
semiotics, 171
semi-structured interview, 147
simple random sample, 162
situation ethics, 217–18
SMART mnemonic, 12, 39, 42
snowball sampling, 164
social constructionism,
    100–1, 171
social science approaches
    and terminology, 91–4
sources, literature review,
    80–1
spelling check, 253–4
SPSS, 158
standard deviation, 181
starting with blank sheet,
    avoiding, 16
statistical analysis, 158–60
    defined, 158–9, 171
    relation to inductive
        and deductive
        methodologies,
        159–60

statistical significance, 178
statistics, 120–1
stories
    defined, 258–9
    use in writing up research,
        249–50
storytelling, 158
    see also narrative research
stratified random sample,
    162–3
structured interview, 147
structured interviews, 178
structured questionnaires,
    178
sub-headings, 72
subjectivity, 91, 98–9
supervisor
    -driven quantitative or
        qualitative-based
        research, 13
    reflective questions, on
        case situation,
        13–14
    research title selection,
        difficulties in,
        11–14
Survey Monkey™, 157
surveys, 118, 171, 178
systematic review, 71–2
systematic sample, 162

template analysis, 192–3
terms of reference, 5
thematic flow, of literature
    review, 71–2
thesaurus in literature review,
    using, 77–8
thesis, 4–5, 259
time management, 38
times/day, 183–4
topic of research, 10–11
    engagement with
        methodological
        and philosophical
        issues, 26–8

free choice for, issues
        associated with,
        14–15
    impact on future career, 15
    narrow down, 16–21
    supervisor's difficulties in
        selecting, 11–14
    terms, revaluation of, 25
transparency, 231
triangulation, 128, 168, 207
t-test, 184
typification, 100

universalism, 214–17
unstructured interview, 147
utilitarian ethics, 217

validity, 128, 206–9, 231
variables, 105–6, 177
vocabulary, 254

weltanschauung, 101
Wikipedia™, 66–7
Wil-Harzing, Anna, 68
word limits, 76–77
word selection, 10
writing
    research see writing
        research
    seminal, 47–9
    evolution of, 49–58
writing research
    case study, use of, 238–9
    confidence and
        motivation during,
        managing, 256–8
    ethnography, use of,
        239–49
    format of, 250–2
    grammar and spelling
        check, 253–4
    logical building blocks,
        252–3
    matrix readings, 253
    narrative flow, 253

writing research – *continued*
  narratives, use of, 249–50
  near-finalised draft,
      examining, 253
  proposal, 6–8

qualitative/quantitative
    data, conventions
    and choices in,
    237–8
referencing, 254

research design,
    remember and
    respect to, 238
stories, use of, 249–50
vocabulary, 254